The Acropolis

The Acropolis

R. J. Hopper

PHOTOGRAPHS BY WERNER FORMAN

SPRING BOOKS
LONDON·NEW YORK·SYDNEY·TORONTO

Designed by Gerald Cinnamon
for George Weidenfeld and Nicolson Ltd, London
Maps and plans drawn by Claus Henning
Phototypeset by Keyspools Ltd, Golborne, Lancs

This edition published 1974 by
The Hamlyn Publishing Group Limited
London · New York · Sydney · Toronto
Astronaut House, Feltham, Middlesex, England

ISBN 0 600 30222 9

Printed in the Canary Islands (Spain) by
Litografia A. Romero, S.A.,
Santa Cruz de Tenerife
D. L. TF. 116-74

TO HENRIETTE

Contents

Preface

The Acropolis is such a centre of myth, of art, of archaeology and of history that the problem is most immediate how much of the rich material is to be omitted in a book intended to appeal to a wide public. This is a particular problem in relation to the sculptures of the Parthenon. The sculptures in London are readily available in illustration, and so it seemed sensible to concentrate on the contents of the Acropolis Museum and those fragments of the Parthenon sculptures the existence of which in Athens tends to be forgotten.

The author is grateful for the cooperation of the Greek Archaeological Service in affording facilities for photography, and to museum directors for the provision of photographs.

It is to be regretted that the pediment with Athena and the Giants, ascribed to the Archaic Temple of Athena on the Acropolis, was not available for photography in its new arrangement.

A book such as this, with its many illustrations, presents problems in the organisation of their grouping and succession. It has not always been found possible to adhere strictly to chronological order or categories of illustrative material.

The author would wish to thank most heartily Werner Forman for his splendid photographs; Mrs Sandra Bance and Miss Kathy Henderson for their unfailing interest, cooperation and endurance; and Mr Angus Hulton, of Sheffield University, for translations from the Greek. Among those who have organised the provision of museum material he would particularly wish to thank Dr Reynold Higgins, of the Department of Greek and Roman Antiquities, and Mr G. K. Jenkins, of the Department of Coins and Medals, in the British Museum.

R. J. HOPPER
1970

Introduction

The Acropolis of Athens is the epitome of the long, eventful, and too often melancholy history of Athens and of Greece. Its geological formation – the hill of limited dimensions, rising sheerly and defensibly from the land below – is reproduced again and again in Greece, sometimes in more grandiose dimensions, as at Corinth, but with less distinguished remains of Antiquity. The *acropolis*, the high centre, physically, of the *polis*, the Greek city-state, stood in contrast to the *asty*, the lower town, where the *polites*, the citizen, went to the Market-place for assembly and discussion, and there encountered his fellows on the level, so to speak. To the *polis* he looked up, for defence in time of danger, for the protection of his gods (and this was especially true of the Acropolis of Athens), and sometimes in fear or hatred when the fortress was the residence of a king or a tyrant.

An account of the Athenian Acropolis and its cultural significance falls into various sections. It is possible to deal relatively compactly with the prehistoric period down to the end of the Bronze Age, treating all the different material evidence together (Chapter 1). To most people the name Acropolis chiefly suggests the Parthenon and the other buildings which still stand on it; for many more it suggests the sculptural decoration of the Parthenon, and especially the Elgin Marbles. But both buildings and sculpture were inseparably linked with legend, which the Greeks carried back into the Bronze Age – their Age of the Heroes – and with cult, the very *raison d'être* of the buildings. So the saga-legends and folk-tales and the cults are the subject of Chapter 2.

The use of the Acropolis, the construction of its buildings, and the creation of its sculptural and other art, evolved against a background of history – the history of Athens and in some measure of Greece, of which the Acropolis is the very symbol. This history is outlined in Chapter 3, terminating when, to all intents and purposes, the important structures stood completed, at the end of the fifth century BC or in the early fourth. For the material remains, the rest of history is an epilogue, and there are those who would argue that the end of the fifth century BC was also the end of the creative and dynamic city-state of Athens. There is much to be said for this view, and in consequence the long and absorbing story of Athens and the Acropolis from 400 BC to the deliverance from the Turks in the nineteenth century is treated as an epilogue, perhaps of illogical length, but containing some necessary observations on the recovery of a knowledge of Greece and the Greeks, and on the development of artistic taste (Chapter 6). The classical buildings and their forerunners are dealt with in Chapter 4, and the architectural and free-standing sculpture and other works of art in Chapter 5. Thus, it is hoped, assumptions of background knowledge in the reader will be reduced to a minimum.

Previous page: The Acropolis from the south-west. Taken from the Pnyx.
Opposite: The Acropolis rock as seen from the south south-east over the area of the Theatre of Dionysos.
Overleaf: The Acropolis from the west, showing the Propylaia and the Nike bastion.

ILLYRIA

MACEDONIA

THRACE

Byzantium•

THASOS

CHALCIDICE •Acanthus
Olynthus•
Potidaea•

SAMOTHRACE

IMBROS

LEMNOS

•Troy

EPIRUS

THESSALY

AEOLIS

CORCYRA

Iolkos

LESBOS

•Mitylene

PHTHIOTIS

EUBOEA

SCYROS

LEUCAS

ACARNANIA

LOCRIS

Aegean Sea

ITHACA

AETOLIA

PHOCIS

•Delphi

Gla
BOEOTIA

Chalcis
•Eretria

CHIOS

•Smyrna

CEPHALLENIA

•Thebes

ACHAIA

ATTICA

IONIA

ELIS

Megara

•Eleusis

Marathon

•Ephesos

ZACYNTHOS

ARCADIA

Corinth

•Athens

SALAMIS

ANDROS

SAMOS

Mycenae•

TENOS

•Olympia

Argos•

AEGINA

ICARIA

Miletos•

Ionian Sea

•Tegea

SYROS

MYKONOS

LACONIA

DELOS

CARIA

MESSENIA

•Sparta

PAROS

•Pylos

NAXOS

COS

MELOS

Mediterranean Sea

CYTHERA

THERA

RHODES

CARPATHOS

Knossos
CRETE

•Gortyn

Fig. 1: Map of ancient Greece and the surrounding area.

1. The Prehistoric Acropolis

The earliest indications of occupation on and in the vicinity of the Acropolis are Neolithic. Early Neolithic pottery has been found at surface level (as at the Cave of Pan at Marathon and at Nea Makri in East Attica), and on the south slope, near the Asklepieion, a small Neolithic habitation was found with Middle Neolithic sherds. On the north-west slope some twenty-one wells (near the more recent Klepsydra Fountain) contained pottery of late Neolithic date and some from the period transitional to the Early Bronze Age. There was also a scatter of sherds on the north slope, and a very few on the upper surface of the rock. From this evidence we may deduce the existence of small, scattered communities of Neolithic inhabitants such as existed also in the area of the later *agora*, or Market-place, not far away. As in Attica and elsewhere, these early inhabitants probably first used pit huts, and later, mud-brick houses with stone foundations. They made stone vases with emery from the Aegean and used obsidian from Melos. They were cultivators, kept domesticated animals, made cloth, and produced hand-made pottery. The various changes visible in this pottery over the millennia seem to indicate the arrival of newcomers at intervals – the first wave coming round about 6000 BC – and originating in Anatolia in the Near East, the home of the Great Mother Goddess. They made female figurines, strongly emphasising their sex, which confirms their affinities, as well as their concern with fertility. The figurines are also supremely interesting as indications of the beginning of the long-enduring and complex association of a female power with the Acropolis, which leads from these fertility figures, through the goddess Athena, to the Blessed Virgin Mary.

From these Neolithic beginnings, habitation continued unbroken into the Early Bronze Age, which was marked by the flourishing settlement of Hagios Kosmas on the coast east of Phaleron. A great many sherds of Early Bronze Age pottery have been found on the south slope, on the site of the Neolithic houses and in the small caves in the cliff face. Other sherds

and tools come from the area below the south-east corner of the Acropolis, later the site of the temple and theatre associated with Dionysos, the god of Attic drama. More Early Bronze Age pottery remains have been found to the north-west, around the Neolithic wells already mentioned, and there are confused deposits on the north slope, both in the area of the later sanctuary of Eros and Aphrodite and elsewhere. The presence of sherds and obsidian flakes on the surface of the rock, at its north side and east end, indicate habitation there also.

A major problem in the prehistory of Greece is the relationship of the Early Bronze Age inhabitants with their Neolithic forerunners and their Middle Bronze Age successors. Knowledge is scanty and conjecture abundant, and it is usual to suggest that some of the Neolithic stock was carried over into the later, more developed communities. However, the discovery of an Early Bronze Age metal-working centre on the east coast of Attica at Raphina, close to the Early Bronze Age settlement at Askitario, would seem to suggest that there were fresh incomers with metal-working techniques from Anatolia (or more vaguely the Eastern Mediterranean), and from the same area, therefore, as their Neolithic predecessors. It used to be thought that these people, or their predecessors, spoke a language which later developed into Greek, but the arrival of the speakers of an Indo-European dialect which was the basis of Greek is now placed much later by most scholars.

Some sites indicate destruction by 'invaders' around 2000–1900 BC – the close of the final stage of the Early Bronze Age. Others, such as Lerna in the Argolid, show that destruction occurred at an earlier date, between the middle and final stages of the Early Bronze Age, with attendant changes in house-forms and pottery. Pottery forms are always affected by such 'invasions', and at this juncture we find a very individual grey ware called Minyan from the Minyai, rulers of Orchomenos in Boeotia, where it was first found, and another called Matt-painted from its dull painted decoration. Some scholars have been quick to point out the superficial resemblances of Minyan ware to pottery from Western Anatolia, but it is possible to find other connections. There might, in fact, be evidence for the evolution of Minyan ware in Greece itself. If one theory implies an invasion from the East or North-east, another argues for the North-west from Epirus and Illyricum. To confuse matters further, it has also been suggested that there were no Greek speakers in Greece until the end of the Bronze Age in the twelfth century BC. This uncertainty stems from the vast areas of our ignorance, which are gradually being reduced as excavation and the study of material remains are pursued, but which still allow wide scope for conjecture.

In this, the Acropolis of Athens, with its own particular problems, is involved. After the Early Bronze Age occupation outlined above, there is a gap until the Middle Bronze Age. It must be stressed, however, that the evidence depends largely on pottery dating. For the Middle Bronze Age the material is more diversified. On the south slope the characteristic Minyan

ware was found, and a grave containing six bodies and obsidian arrow heads. Somewhat further south two small graves were excavated, as well as house-walls of the last stage of the Middle Bronze Age. There have been widespread finds of sherds of Minyan and Matt-painted wares – for instance on the south-west slope, around the later buildings, from the theatre of Herodes Atticus to the *temenos* (or sacred enclosure) of Dionysos, by way of the shrine of Asklepios with one of the important springs of water in the vicinity of the Acropolis. Near another spring in use later – the Klepsydra on the north-west slope – are five wells of careful construction which were filled with Middle Bronze Age pottery. The immediate area of the Acropolis would therefore seem to have been a centre of Middle Bronze Age habitation, and there is evidence for continuous habitation of its upper surface. The Middle Bronze Age is conventionally dated from about 1900 to the sixteenth century BC, and apart from the earlier gap, one may say that the site was occupied continuously over several thousands of years. This does not mean that the same people occupied Athens

Right: The stairway descent to the Klepsydra fountain at the north-west corner of the Acropolis.
Opposite: The Klepsydra fountain well-house, of Roman date (later second century AD).

and the Acropolis, any more than it does for other sites in more or less continuous occupation from an early date. It can certainly give no justification for the Athenian claim that the inhabitants of Attica were *autochthonous*, not incomers. Of course there must have been incomers at some time to import the proto-Greek language, and the proud claim of the Athenians may be explained as yet another effort to distinguish themselves from the Spartans, who were part of a later and more barbarous intrusion of Greeks – into the Peloponnese in particular – which had been repulsed from Attica.

On the other hand, we cannot explain everything as an evolution of myth in reaction to the events of the Archaic and Classical periods, when Athens and Sparta represented the polarities of Greek culture, and the Athenians were claiming leadership of the Ionian Greeks, to match the Spartan leadership of the Dorians. A real problem, of special interest for a study of the Acropolis, is that of folk-memory, some of it enshrined in saga – the heroic stories which figured so largely as the material of later literature and art. Of particular relevance to the Acropolis is the conviction of the Athenians, as reflected in literature and learned works from Hekataios and Herodotus in the fifth century BC onwards, that there had once been population elements in Attica alien to themselves. These were the Pelasgians, variously associated in the story by Herodotus with Lemnos, and by later writers with the Tyrrhenians, that mysterious and mobile people who were eventually located in Italian Etruria. Herodotus preserves the legend of the Pelasgians as builders, who at some point in their wanderings constructed the ancient wall of the Acropolis, and as a reward were given land under Mt Hymettos, from which they were expelled through the jealousy or resentment of the Athenians. Later writers associated them with a part or the whole of the Acropolis called the *Pelasgikon*. But it also had an alternative name, the *Pelargikon*, 'the place associated with the storks' (*pelargoi*), and so later writers, hard put to it to explain the divergent names, produced a number of silly stories based on the Pelasgian mode of dress or their migratory habits. Greek legend, especially in the hands of the late and learned writers, tended very often to acquire a peripheral element of manifest nonsense, but one must always be sensitive to the reality of the core. Possibly there were other ethnic elements in prehistoric Attica – survivors of the Early Bronze Age population.

In similar fashion the remote past of the Acropolis, in archaeological terms, may have suggested some of the legendary identifications we have from the Classical and later periods. On the surface of the rock, in its north-western area, five Middle Bronze Age cist graves have been found, which were evidently those of children, though no bones or funerary offerings survive. It has been pointed out that Antiquity may have identified such burials in terms of myth: thus we have the tomb of the mythical King Kekrops adjacent to the Classical Erechtheum, and the tombs of Talos, nephew of Daidalos, and of Hippolytos, on the south slope. How far back did the discovery of such burials, and the genesis of the mythology go? This question of folk-memory and mythological identification is all the more significant because, in the succeeding Late Bronze Age, Athens and its Acropolis were clearly places of some importance. There are two aspects to this importance: that of the remains – which we will consider now – and the other of the saga, which will be dealt with in the next chapter.

In the Late Bronze Age – or even earlier, at the end of the Middle Bronze – the prehistoric civilisation of some areas of Greece seems to have taken a great step forward. It is often pointed out that the earlier Middle Bronze Age in Greece is characterised by simple forms of dwelling and burial, and few objects of art to indicate the existence of wealth. Then at Mycenae, in particular, there suddenly appears the exotic wealth of gold and other objects from the two Shaft Grave Circles, produced or strongly influenced by the Minoans of Crete – as is the associated pottery in the course of its development from Middle Helladic (Middle Bronze) to Late Helladic (Late Bronze) or Mycenaean style. We are not concerned here with how this came about, but there gradually developed a Mycenaean civilisation which rivalled and overtook that of Minoan Crete. It is represented pre-eminently at Mycenae, but also at various other centres which were often the concentration points of later Greek heroic saga.

Mycenaean civilisation is recalled by the palaces, beehive tombs and chamber tombs at these different sites. Because the citadel sites in particular were occupied for several centuries, the earlier structures have been overlaid and modified by those which came later. What is seen today at Mycenae and nearby Tiryns, for instance, represents the latest modification of palace and fortifications. It is by no means certain that there had been fortification walls from the beginning. They may simply have been 'prestige' walls to impress outsiders with the greatness of the ruler, or they may have been defensive walls to provide security from attack. It can tentatively be suggested that they date at the latest from the later fourteenth century BC, which is called Late Helladic IIIA by archaeologists. They may have been earlier, but they were certainly subject to modification and extension in the thirteenth century. At Mycenae and Tiryns provision was made for access from within the walls to a water supply, and the provision of a great refuge enclosure at Tiryns (paralleled by a similar one at Gla on Lake Copais in Boeotia) indicated that attack was expected from an external foe, or certainly that the times were disturbed. In fact such an attack came, bringing destruction to numerous Mycenaean centres, including Mycenae itself.

In the still more disturbed times which followed, centres such as Mycenae only partially recovered, whilst others, such as Ano Englianos in the Western Peloponnese, were completely destroyed. This took place more or less at the end of the archaeologists' Late Helladic IIIB, around 1200 BC. The partial recovery and evidence of further disasters belong to the following stages of Late Helladic IIIC and Submycenaean, of the later twelfth and eleventh centuries, which gradually developed into something new and dynamic. For modern scholars this represents a 'Dark Age' – partly because of our ignorance – and is called the Protogeometric and Geometric period from the pottery styles current from roughly 1000 to 700 BC, the matrix of the Archaic Greek renaissance.

This is the necessary background to a consideration of the Acropolis of Athens in the Late Bronze Age (Late Helladic), in which it ultimately became a fortified stronghold like Mycenae or Tiryns, but was still a place of residence. It is to be expected that the long occupation and manifold changes undergone by the Acropolis would obscure earlier occupation. In fact only one structure, located in the area east of the North Porch of the classical Erechtheum and identified as part of a house, survives from the earliest of the three stages of the Late Helladic culture (Late Helladic I). The date for this house is fixed by pottery sherds, some Middle Helladic, some Late Helladic I. It is difficult to believe that it was the only house in this part of the Acropolis, because it was clearly in an important area, as the extent of later occupation reveals. Then a number of terrace walls have been uncovered on the part of the Acropolis rock which slopes

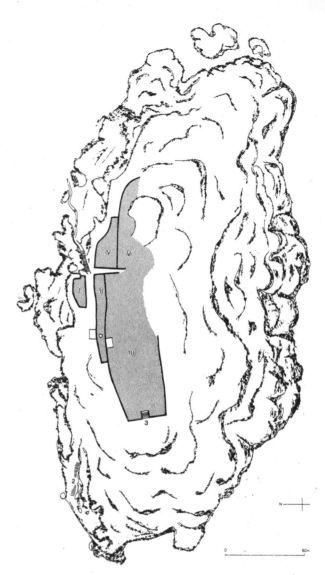

Fig. 2: The Acropolis in the Late Helladic period (stage two): I–V The terraces. 1 The north-eastern ascent. 2 Descent to the north-western caves. 3 Later site of the Bronze Athena.

down westward and northward from its highest point, between the area occupied in Classical times by the base of the so-called Athena Promachos on the west, the Mycenaean postern gate on the east, and the site of the later, Archaic temple of Athena on the south. There are sufficient remains of these walls to permit the plotting of five interrelated terraces at different levels, connected by steps of which some traces remain at the west end of the third and longest [2]. There are traces of two of these terrace walls beneath the later

Erechtheum, and consequently the question arises whether the 'sacred places' or 'signs' – the salt-water well and trident marks – associated with this later temple, were already recognised as sacred at the time of the construction of the terraces. Stratification indicates they are later than the Late Helladic I house mentioned above, and pottery sherds suggest the earlier part of Late Helladic IIIB, that is, the earlier thirteenth century BC, the period of outstanding prosperity at Mycenae, and, in the opinion of some, the era of the expedition against Troy.

If Athens resembled Mycenae, Tiryns, Thebes and Ano Englianos – where palatial establishments seem to indicate the presence of a ruler – then a ruler must be accepted for Athens also. The thirteenth century seems to have been a period of important development for Athens, to judge from the *tholos* 'beehive' tombs on the north-east slope of the Areios Pagos with the remnants of rich contents, and from the chamber tombs and cist graves found in the area of the Market-place. How far Attica was united under Athens, and how far rule was exercised from the Acropolis over other Mycenaean centres such as those indicated by the *tholos* tombs of Menidhi and Thorikos, is uncertain. The ruler's palace – or at any rate his principal residence – can only have been in one place, and that is on the Acropolis of Athens on the terraces described above, but not protected initially by a wall. There must have been a route from the lower town to the palace from the west end of the rock towards the steps at the west end of terrace III [2, 3]. At this time also the access on the north-east, up through the rocks – part path, part staircase – would have been used, from the path around the Acropolis now called the *peripatos* [2, 1]. It is not unreasonable to suppose that there was also in use the north-western descent of similar character, to the caves which later, and probably at this period also, were centres of cult on this side of the rock [2, 2]. Of the palace, which must have stood upon the site of the later Archaic temple of Athena, virtually nothing has survived, save one column-base and some sandstone slabs which may have served as staircase treads. These are small evidence for a structure of more than one storey, and with pillar support. Despite this paucity of evidence, it can sensibly be argued that the Mycenaean palace on the Acropolis would be no different from those of

The north-west slope: the area of the caves, the Klepsydra fountain and the Pythion.

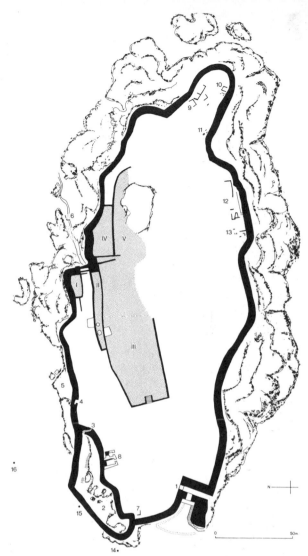

Fig. 3: The Acropolis in the Late Helladic period (third and final stage) – 1 The Mycenaean gateway. 2 Cave terrace, suggested Pelargikon/Pelasgikon. 3 North-west descent to the caves. 4 Descent to the Mycenaean cistern. 5 The cave of Aglauros. 6 Blocked north-east ascent and house remains. 7,8 Unidentified structures. 9 Houses. 10 Guardhouse. 11 Graves. 12 Houses. 13 Graves. 14,15,16 Wells.

Mycenae, Tiryns or Ano Englianos, with court, porch, vestibule, *megaron* (great hall) with central hearth, or multiples of these; but it is well to have in mind also the odd buildings within the great wall circuit at Gla in Boeotia, which are quite different.

It is now agreed that two further *poros* column-bases on the site of the Archaic temple, formerly identified as bases of Mycenaean palace columns, are nothing of the sort. They have parallels in very old Early Iron Age temples elsewhere, as the bases of primitive wooden columns intended to raise the latter above water which might cause them to rot. It is commonly argued that around the ruler's palace lived the closest of his associates, therefore traces of such dwellings have been sought in the maze of walls of varying dimensions between the Classical entrance gate (Propylaia) and the Erechtheum, and south of the latter amid the tangle of walls of the Archaic temple of Athena. Formerly called 'Pelasgian' and thus recog-

nised as prehistoric, they have more recently been down-dated. There is uncertainty about some, but others are Archaic, and yet others post-Classical or even Turkish.

Whatever lack of distinction might be seen in this seemingly modest occupation of the Acropolis in the earlier thirteenth century BC, there can be no doubt of the character of the culminating phase of the Mycenaean occupation. It was converted into a fortress, only less impressive than Mycenaean Mycenae or Tiryns because its walls are only partly preserved or hidden in

Above left: South of the Parthenon platform, showing the terraces elsewhere buried, with the stair descending from upper to lower levels inside the Mycenaean and Kimonian walls.
Above right: The Mycenaean wall surviving south of the Propylaia and east of the temple of Athena Nike.
Opposite: The sheer south face of the Acropolis, forming a natural fortification.

later structures. These fortifications were composed of large, roughly hewn blocks on the two faces, wedged and filled between with smaller stones. Enough of the wall itself survives to give an adequate idea of its nature and dimensions at several points of its circuit [3]. A close and careful study of other surviving groups of similar stones, and of cuttings in the rock, demonstrates that there was a continuous circuit, of which the course can be determined fairly accurately. It largely followed the brow of the rock, but it must be remembered that part of the southern area of the present Acropolis platform is a later construction, related to the platform of the Parthenon and its unfinished predecessor. Pottery has been found at different points in the circuit of the walls (from south-east of the museum, from the south-west corner of the Parthenon, from the west bastion, and from the north wall by the mediaeval bastion). The pottery is remarkably consistent in its dating to Late Helladic IIIB, indicating that the wall was built in one operation in, broadly speaking, the third and fourth quarters of the thirteenth century BC. Its width seems to vary from 3·6 m. to 6 m., being at its thickest where it was pierced by entrances. Its height is calculated as ranging from eight metres to almost ten, and it has been very tentatively suggested that its construction has something in common with that of the walls of Tiryns. Such a structure was not undertaken lightly, and required the resources of a sizeable community, especially if it was built relatively quickly.

There were several notable features about this fortification. As in the previous phase, the obvious principal approach was on the west [3, 1]. An examination of the complicated structures and traces in the

area of the Classical Propylaia and of the bastion south of it, on which the small Ionic temple of Athena Nike was later erected, permits the reconstruction of a simple but strong entrance gate related to the Mycenaean structures under the Nike bastion, the wall traces crossing the Classical Propylaia, and the stretch of Mycenaean wall standing to the south of it. In effect the plan was of an outer and inner gate at right-angles (the inner being also approached with difficulty from the south, where the rock is abrupt), the first facing south-east, the second north-east [3, 1]. The outer gate appears to have been approached from below by a series of shallow steps around the north face of the bastion, or alternatively by a rising track first from south to north across the approach to the gate, then following the outside of the fortification wall to the north of the gate approach. After passing through the first gate the route had to turn at right-angles to approach the second, and the necessary height, over a short distance, was gained by shallow, curving steps. The problems were clearly, first, one of defence, and second, to construct a route which had to gain height from below and yet not be too steep for loaded draught animals. The resulting structure was a simple, massive solution of the problems, very different from the Classical Propylaia.

On the north-eastern side of the Acropolis, amid the rocks of the North Slope, there ascended from the so-called *peripatos* a path so steep at some points that it necessitated artificial or rock-cut steps. It was clearly suitable only for human pedestrian use, not for draught animals. In the second phase of the Late Helladic occupation of the Acropolis – in the early thirteenth century BC – it reached the top of the rock where the later Mycenaean wall turned south and then, after a short distance, east again, not very far east of the east porch of the Classical Erechtheum [2, 1]. It appears to have ended between terraces I and II (mentioned earlier), which possibly supported the Mycenaean palace and its outbuildings. It acted, therefore, as a subsidiary approach and postern gate to the palace. In the final phase of the Mycenaean Acropolis this gate was blocked by the construction of a wall [3, 6]; the date of the blocking therefore being a point in the limited period of the construction of the wall in the late thirteenth century. The abandonment of this north-east approach and entry is further underlined by the subsequent construction of simple houses which clustered, as if for protection, under the North Slope of the rock now surmounted by the great

fortification wall [3, 6]. But these houses were soon abandoned. In archaeological terms the pottery indicates the building of the wall, the blocking of the gate and the construction of the houses in the later Late Helladic IIIB; the use of the houses in the latest Helladic IIIB, and their abandonment at the beginning of Late Helladic IIIC.

In the literary tradition about the Pelasgoi already mentioned, there is repeated reference to a Pelàsgikon or Pelargikon. The former name would suggest some connection with the primitive people previously mentioned, and therefore with the primitive fortifications of the Acropolis. The second name, however, implies the inane connection of Pelasgoi and *pelargoi* (storks) by reason of the garments, it was said, the Pelasgoi wore. A further connection was made between the Pelasgikon or Pelargikon and a primitive monumental feature of Athens, the Enneapylon or Nine Gates. The infrequent mention of the Nine Gates, the ignorance of the location of structures associated with it, have permitted a conjectural association with the Pelasgikon or Pelargikon, to produce either a fortification surrounding the whole Acropolis, or alternatively its western approach or, again, a large area of the lower town of Athens. The most attractive idea is that of a complex of walls on the western approach, with nine gates providing a complex defensive system not unlike that in late Antiquity and under the Turks [6, 13]. Any such identification must be rejected, however, and the Enneapylon down-dated to a later period, particularly in view of the fact that the form of the western entrance of the Mycenacan Acropolis has been reasonably established, and would certainly not be enclosed by an outer defence of the kind postulated. The location of the Pelasgikon/Pelargikon (abandoning the problem of its true name) must be elsewhere. The most reliable authorities – literary and epigraphical – stress the nature of the Pelasgikon or Pelargikon as a rocky, open space from which stones and soil might be taken, and on which both religious and secular structures might be built. Thucydides informs us that it was left unoccupied in response to a Delphic oracle, and a fifth-century decree is directed to the same end. A most important indication is its connection with the Cave of Pan in the western half of the North Slope of the Acropolis. Given this evidence, it has been possible to detect the remains of a wall in this area, north of the Mycenaean wall proper. It starts west of the site of the Arrhephoreion (see page 48), descends the

The area beneath the north wall at the north-west
corner of the Acropolis, showing the stairway descent
to the area of the caves.

northern slope more or less to the terrace above the
peripatos, and rises again to join the fortification proper
just north of the 'North Hall' of the Classical Propylaia
[6, *12*; 3, *2*]. It thus encloses the Caves of Pan, Apollo
and Olympian Zeus, and just excludes the sites of the
Pythion and the later north-western fountain, the
Klepsydra. It was an enclosed rocky space, apparently
inaccessible from the north – hence the need for the
descent: part staircase (through the wall), part stepped
path which left the edge of the rock some 20 ́́117 m.
west of the Classical Arrhephoreion and went down
north-westward to the terrace below the caves [3, *3*;
5, *1*]. It is not easy to see the purpose of the enclosure,
unless the caves in the north face were of paramount
cult importance at this early period. This may well be
so. The rock face, if compared, for instance, with the
area of the north-east ascent, has no apparent need
of extra defences. This area may have been used for
the housing of refugees at the beginning of the Great
Peloponnesian War in 431 BC, but it is far from
suitable, and cannot have been originally devised for
this. Consequently, if the Pelasgikon or Pelargikon
is correctly located here, then the area must have had

a cult importance, and it is therefore probable that
other cults on and around the Acropolis go back to a
remote period.

Another striking feature of the Mycenaean Acropolis in its third phase is in the north-western area of
the rock, beyond the Classical Arrhephoreion, where
a great slab of rock has been separated from the parent
mass in such a way that a cleft is formed [3, *4*; 5, *2*].
The Mycenaean fortification was built on the outside
of this cleft, though later the fortification was replaced
by a wall with the entrance to the cleft built into it.
This cleft was known and used in the Classical period
for cult purposes, and the nine stone steps which
survive date from this and, presumably, an earlier
period. The steps were continued from east to west by
twenty-five wooden steps to a landing from which a
further forty carried the staircase in the opposite
direction down into the cleft, to a point where it was
possible to emerge above the level of the *peripatos* to
the light of day through a cave called the Cave of
Aglauros [3, *5*; 6, *8*]. So far this descent continued in
use for cult purposes, emerging between 13 m. and
14 m. below the upper level of the Acropolis, and as

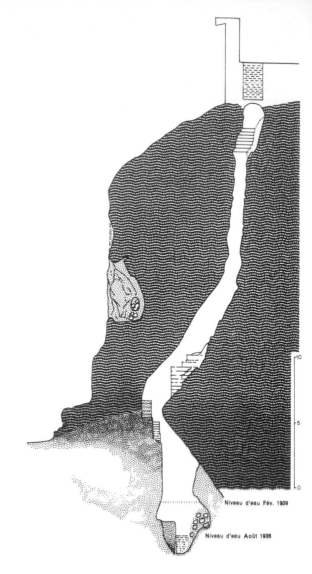

Above: The cleft descending to the Mycenaean well.
Right: Fig. 4: The Mycenaean cistern on the north side
of the Acropolis. Section looking east.

Niveau d'eau Fév. 1939

Niveau d'eau Août 1936

late as the Greek War of Independence it served as a
secret way to and from the fortress. However, the
cleft continued downwards a considerable distance,
forming at its lowest point – some 34·442 m. down –
a natural well in which water accumulated as it
drained down through the rock [4]. The water level
here was some 4 m. above that of the north-western
Klepsydra Fountain, and 5 m. above the Asklepieion
Fountain, and in winter was 3·048 m. deep. Somehow
the Mycenaean occupiers of the Acropolis were aware
of the existence of this water supply, and with great
skill constructed eight alternating staircases inside
the cleft to give access to a point from which the
accumulated water supply might be drawn with
rope and bucket from the well bottom.

A careful study of the remains shows that the two
uppermost staircases were of wood inserted in cuttings in the rock. Below the level of the Cave of
Aglauros, where circulation of air was poor and wood
would rot, it was necessary to use stone treads either
bedded on rubble (held together by wooden lattice
work, again liable to rot) or supported by the walls of
the cleft. It must have been a perilous descent, but
even so a very considerable feat of construction,
clearly undertaken for an emergency. It is also worth
reflecting that it cannot have provided an abundant
water supply for a large number of people. Once
again the finds of pottery permit dating of the staircase
to later Late Helladic IIIB, that is, the later thirteenth
century, when the Mycenaean Acropolis wall was

built. It was in use when the houses on the north-east slope were abandoned, and in all it remained in use for some twenty-five years. It subsequently became the repository of debris which included pottery sherds, indicating when the staircase was abandoned.

The construction and use of this north-west well is less problematic than the evidence of the wall or the abandonment of the houses. The wall could have been intended as a prestige monument and not primarily for defence. The houses might simply have been abandoned for some more convenient situation, and not necessarily for a safer refuge. On the other hand, such a laborious approach to a water supply, and its use for such a limited period, is indicative of an emergency, and it is natural to think of fear of a siege. This fear only seems to have persisted for a limited period, since the supply was fairly soon abandoned. This would imply either that the danger disappeared or the Acropolis was abandonced as a place of habitation.

The evidence for what happened is very slight. The remains of the 'palace' are totally inadequate, yet – given the fortification walls – there must have been a palace. Other traces of occupation are limited. There are, for instance, remains of a Mycenaean structure east of the north wing of the Classical Propylaia, but the site was occupied for so long and so intensively at times, and excavated with such varying degrees of competence, that it is difficult to date the disorderly fragments of structures which survive. It is quite impossible that anything should have survived after the manner of Mycenae or Tiryns, and in this respect the Acropolis resembles Volos in south-eastern Thessaly. Even in Thebes of Boeotia – also in continuous and intensive occupation – more has survived. On the other hand, the Athenian Acropolis definitely shows signs of occupation after the construction of the wall and the use of the well in the cleft. At the south-eastern corner of the rock [3, 9–11] there are houses and graves of advanced Late Helladic IIIC period, as well as a mud-brick wall, bronze and pottery of the Late Helladic IIIC period in the area south-east of the Parthenon, and advanced Late Helladic IIIC graves south of it. The south-east houses, built of mud brick on stone footings, are clearly later than the wall [3, 12–13]. The graves are also later, and indicate occupation in the twelfth century and onwards to the Submycenaean period and the beginnings of the Protogeometric period. The occupation of the Acropolis thus bridges the gap to the first graves on the island of Salamis, and the beginnings of the develop-

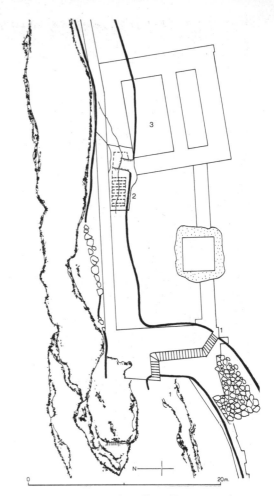

Fig. 5: The Late Helladic north wall – 1 Descent to the caves. 2 Descent to the cistern at the north-west corner of 3, the later Arrhephoreion.

ment of the lower town reflected in the Protogeometric and Geometric graves of the Kerameikos cemetery beside the later wall of Athens, and north-west of the later Market-place. This certainly represents an expansion of the local population, perhaps including also incomers from elsewhere.

As far as the Acropolis habitation at this late date is concerned, little can be said about the status of those who lived there, and nothing about the existence of a ruler. The Athenians themselves imagined or remembered a series of events which might possibly clothe the dry bones of archaeology with some inadequate flesh, and this and the conversion of the Acropolis from a place of habitation to a centre of cult will be the substance of the next chapter.

Herakles and Kerberos
(the Hound of Hell)
in the presence of Athena
his patron. Attic red-
figured vase of the last quarter
of the sixth century BC
by the Andokides Painter.

2. Saga and Cult

A. SAGA

The Greeks, and not least the Athenians of the Classical period, were interested in what in modern times would be called their prehistoric past. From the time of the poet Hesiod on they formalised a series of ages – Golden, Silver, Bronze, Iron – and between the Bronze and Iron Ages (in effect a moral distinction here, and not an archaeological one) they placed the Age of the Heroes, whom they knew by name and who in some cases had links – if distant ones – with Classical times. Herakles, for example, was part culture hero, part heroic baron of Tiryns and warrior of what we would call the Bronze Age, from whom the Classical kings of Sparta were descended. The Greeks of the Classical period were in no doubt as to what event they would place at the centre of their heroic tales or sagas: a great expedition against Troy in north-western Asia Minor. The reason for the expedition was romantic rather than convincing: the recovery of Helen, wife of Menelaos (conceived of as King of Sparta), and sister-in-law of his brother Agamemnon, great King of Mycenae. She had been abducted by Paris, son of King Priam of Troy, and the act was ultimately a contrivance of the Gods, as were all human fortunes. An essential presupposition was an association of local princes under the leadership of Agamemnon as *primus inter pares*. They were 'far-called', from Ithaka in the west to Crete in the south-east, and from all the land in between, from southern Thessaly southward.

The *Iliad*, the earliest preserved literature of Greece, told the tale of an episode of the Siege of Troy, the Wrath of Achilles. The *Odyssey*, the second oldest, narrated the Return Home of Odysseus the cunning and much-enduring, who, after ten years at Troy, had ten more years of adventure before he got back to Ithaka to find his wife beset by suitors for her hand. It is an example of what the Greeks from an early stage of their history believed had really once been: a period of wandering, disturbance and resettlement which they chose to connect with the Siege of Troy, as its sequel. In their belief (and they found it convenient for propaganda purposes continually to elaborate the saga) some of the heroes returned home safely and quickly; thus Odysseus' son Telemachos, in quest of his father, found old man Nestor, doyen of the Greek heroes, back unharmed at Pylos in the western Peloponnese, and Menelaos safe home with a clearly reformed Helen in Laconia. Others did not return home at all, but perished at sea, like the lesser Ajax; others returned safely only to be slain by usurpers (in the earlier tradition) or by wives and their paramours (in the later). So perished Agamemnon himself. Some narrowly escaped this fate and set out again to settle elsewhere; others attempted no homecoming but, tradition said, went west or east to found new settlements. In part this tradition must be based on a memory of the disturbances and movements of peoples of the thirteenth and twelfth centuries BC recorded by the Egyptians, which destroyed the imperial Hittite power and threatened Egypt. In part it must be a backwards projection of later events of the Early Iron Age involving the scattering of Greeks over the Mediterranean and the need to discover founders of Greek settlements overseas.

The Classical Greeks also linked certain later events with the Siege of Troy. On the basis of the Dorian/Ionian polarisation of power and culture mentioned earlier, and by observation of the Greek dialect map of Greece and the Aegean, the Classical Greeks evolved the concept of a primary occupation of 'heroic' Greece (which in modern times we call Mycenaean), to which were added – in varying degrees and in various regions, by a process of invasion and conquest – more and more barbarous Greeks, thought to be the ancestors of the Classical Dorians, and especially of the Spartans. They were led by a displaced clan or

family, the so-called Heraclids or Children of Herakles. Thus a period of disturbance and displacement
was inaugurated in Greece and across the Aegean to
the east, for the Greeks identified as part of this
process the migration of Greeks to Asia Minor, principally to that part later called Ionia, so that the
migration is called in a general way the Ionian migration, and Classical Athens claimed a leading part in it.

Before the position of Athens is considered in this
saga tradition, it is useful to make certain other points
clear. It is well known that the Greeks, in their efforts
to establish a chronology, made considerable use of
generations (of two rather arbitrary lengths, one of
forty years and another of three to a century), and
calculated these in particular from Herakles as a
person, and the Siege of Troy as an event. Thus
ultimately the Trojan War came to be dated, through
conversion to the BC/AD system, to 1193–1183,
though other earlier dates were not unknown. The
'Dorian Invasion' was dated to eighty years later, that
is, to 1103, clearly two forty-year generations. The
Greeks also went back from the Trojan War to the
generation before, or two generations before, which
was in some saga traditions the age of Herakles. Up
to a certain fairly clear point in the saga we have an
ordered, systematic and reasonably logical structure of
generations and events. Some are narrated or hinted
at in the *Iliad* and the *Odyssey*, as, for example, events
of old Nestor's youth, the times of his father Neleus
(an incomer from Thessaly), including the warring of
Herakles against him. Or they are known from other
sources: events such as the expedition of the Seven
against Thebes in the generation before the Trojan
War; the adventures of Jason and the Argonauts in
quest of the Golden Fleece, and the saga of the Calydonian Boar. There is always a clear admixture of
myth and folk-tale, and the frequent attribution of a
heroic ancestor to commerce between god and mortal
woman has been explained as a substitute for some
surer knowledge of more distant human ancestors.

Very rapidly, as Greek story-telling moved backwards, the human, potentially historical, saga element
was outweighed by myth and folk-tale. Some of the
myth is plainly artificial and made up at a relatively
late date. There are dragon's teeth in the story of
Kadmos at Thebes; Danaos and his fifty daughters at
Argos; the Flood, Deukalion and Pyrrha, and the like,
in which the most confident scholars would be chary

Athena (*aigis*-wearing but unhelmeted) receiving
Erichthonios from Ge (Earth) in
the presence of snake-bodied Kekrops.

of attempting to identify elements of early history. It is possible to believe, with discretion, in Nestor or Agamemnon as persons. There is no such possibility in the case of serpent-bodied Kekrops, the earliest King of Athens, even if his grave, the Kekropion, was supposed to exist on the Acropolis. Even Greek myth could not think of a father for him, so it made him *gegenes*, 'Earth-born', and serpent-bodied, though it provided him, by a normal sort of marriage, with a son, Erysichthon ('he who saves the land') and three daughters, Aglauros, Herse and Pandrosos, who were closely connected with the Acropolis and Athena.

In this body of saga stretching backwards and forwards from the Siege of Troy it is interesting to observe the position of Athens and Athena in the scheme of things. In the *Iliad* and the *Odyssey* Athena is a great goddess, the equal of Zeus, Hera, Poseidon, and Apollo, and infinitely greater than the minor and unrespected female deities Artemis and Aphrodite. It is important to stress that there were few more active city protectors than Athena, and she was connected with many more city crags than just that of Athens. In classical times she was associated with the citadel of Mycenae, in the *Iliad* the city of Agamemnon, who led

the expedition to Troy, a city which she also protected. At Troy she was represented by a seated statue – so the *Iliad* states – on the lap of which the Trojan women laid an offering of an embroidered garment. This might have been the Palladion of Troy carried off (as variously related) by the Greeks or by Aeneas. On the other hand, some Attic vase painters thought this was a standing figure of the goddess armed with shield and spear, as befitted a city-protector. There is no better example of the diversity of myth-making than the adventures of the Palladion, and the modifications the story underwent to satisfy local pride.

The great part played by Athena in the Homeric poems cannot but draw attention to the small share Athens has in the story of the *Iliad* and the wider tale of Troy, and the small account taken of Athens in the *Odyssey*, in which so many cities and men find mention: a striking contrast to the prominence of Classical Athens. The Athenians, it was felt in Antiquity, would take this hardly, and remedy it if they could (not so easy to do), for general reasons of prestige or for specific purposes such as their claim, against their neighbour Megara, to the island of Salamis. So those scant passages where Athens is mentioned were suspect

Ajax tearing Cassandra from her refuge at the ancient statue (Palladion?) of Athena in Troy.

in Antiquity, and in modern scholarships they are castigated as 'late', though late, in this context, could still mean 6th century BC. So it happens that the historian of Greek Antiquity, always involved with the problem of how the Greeks could have known what they thought they knew of their early history, is worse off here – in the crown and centre of Classical Greece – than elsewhere. For all that, the passages in question are worth considering.

First it must be admitted that the Athenians, by fair means or foul, had to appear in the Catalogue of the Greeks who went to Troy in Book II of the *Iliad*[1]. This book is a much discussed portion of the poem, which some scholars have argued as being of considerable antiquity, perhaps preserved from Mycenaean times by some form of oral tradition, and perhaps influenced by Boeotian sources. It presents a picture of Greece very different from the Classical one, and in it the details relating to Athens are, in some cases, suspiciously unsuitable. The description of their leader at Troy, Menestheus (whom it will be necessary to look at again), is what might be expected, though it recalls suspiciously the importance accorded to him in late colonising legends. A reference to Nestor comes in appropriately enough to recall (for Athenians) the connection of his family – the descendants of Neleus – with Athens and Ionia, which might possibly be a relatively late confection.

On the other hand, the mention of Erechtheus seems largely irrelevant, though highly important to the present theme. This ancient figure is closely associated with the Acropolis. Like Kekrops hê was Earth-born, an ancient ruler of Athens. Like Kekrops he might be thought to be serpent-bodied or, in his extreme childhood, associated with serpents. Like Kekrops he is an element of timeless Attic mythology rather than belonging to the more substantial saga. He may be a double of Kekrops, one of the 'venerable ancestors' as they have been called, or more sceptically he might be identified as the eponymous ancestor of the clan of the Erechtheidai, for they, as Euripides suggests[2], set upon their infants amulets or bracelets in the form of golden serpents. Be that as it may, in the Catalogue of the Ships Erechtheus appears as the nursling of Athena, born of the Earth, and a lodger in Athena's temple, which is a point to be noted.

Erechtheus and Athena appear again in the *Odyssey*[3], where Athena, about her business of benefitting another protégé, Odysseus, 'came to Marathon and Athens of the wide ways, and entered the strong house

of Erechtheus'. So here we have the interesting association of an ancient king and Athena, with the difference that in the *Iliad* Erechtheus is a lodger in Athena's temple, and in the *Odyssey* Athena is a visitor, if not lodger, in Erechtheus' palace. It is not fanciful to see in the *Iliad* the accommodation of a 'venerable ancestor' in what undoubtedly existed – a temple of Athena of indeterminate, but probably early, date. In the *Odyssey* there seems to be the primary idea of the 'king' and his 'palace', and the association of a goddess with it. With the additional example of Mycenae, where a temple of Athena succeeded a Mycenaean palace, it requires no excessive leap of the imagination to think of Minoan (i.e. Cretan) goddesses and shrines in palaces, and to transfer this association to Mycenaean Greece, including Athens. Thus, it can be suggested, the belief survived that there were kings in Athens, that they lived in a palace on the Acropolis, and they had a goddess as a 'lodger'. If it seems the *Odyssey* preserved a more ancient tradition, this could be supported by the references, in the *Odyssey* again[1], to Theseus and his Cretan adventure (see below), and to Daidalos, 'who made the dancing-floor for Ariadne', the Daidalos of the far-off and intriguing myth involving Ikaros and Minos, not the putative eponym of later artistic achievement.

The problem in all this is that Athena, in her activities after the Trojan War on behalf of Odysseus, is associated with the timeless mythological ruler of Athens, Erechtheus, whom no one in Antiquity pretended to date. Here is the bridge from distant mythology and folk-tale to more substantial saga, and, with discretion, to the makings of history, but with a warning against any attempt at exact chronology.

After the shadowy 'venerable ancestors' there is a gap until the generation before the Trojan War. This was the period of Theseus, firmly rooted in Attic tradition as a personification of all manner of cultural and political development. In him the idea of a culture hero is united with a possible figure of history. His father was Aigeus, his mother Aithra: in effect if Aigeus himself was not a by-form of Poseidon, then Poseidon was his father. From Troezen in the eastern Peloponnese, near Kalaureia where there was a famous shrine of Poseidon, he came to Attica to be united with Aigeus, and both during and after the journey he carried out, like another culture hero, Herakles, a series of exploits to rid the region of monsters – a

Red-figured Attic cup showing the exploits of Theseus
in the presence of Athena.

favourite subject of Attic vase painters. Arriving in Attica he delivered Athens from a hateful thraldom. This is one of the most intriguing episodes of Greek heroic myth.

Androgeos, son of Minos, ruler of Crete, had been killed in Attica in an encounter with a portentous bull. This suggestion of a connection, in a remote period, between Crete and Greece was not confined to Attica. For example, a rather late legend represented Minos, in Greek tradition son or associate of Zeus, as ruler of Crete and the southern Aegean (thence Sir Arthur Evans' name 'Minoan' for the Bronze Age civilisation of Crete) and at the same time besieger of Megara. This, and the occurrence of the name Minoa on the mainland of Greece, makes it difficult to discount some kind of association between Bronze Age Crete and contemporary Greece. In Athens Theseus found his father's city committed to paying in compensation for the death of Androgeos, a tribute of youths and maidens, to be sent to Knossos, and to be slain in the labyrinth by the Minotaur. Neither this monster, nor the labyrinth in which it lurked, is strictly relevant to the present narrative, except in so far as it forms part of the Attic saga. The story is well known, in literature and vase painting, how Theseus went with the youths and maidens to Crete, proved his kinship with Poseidon when this was challenged by Minos, won the heart of Ariadne, and by her aid slew the Minotaur, and escaped from the labyrinth and from Crete with her, only to desert her on Naxos. Ariadne finds her place in the *Odyssey* among the fair women whom Odysseus saw in the realm of the dead, and so Theseus and his Cretan adventure find a mention. Punishment followed, for on his homecoming to Athens, Theseus forgot the agreement with his father that if he returned safely his ship would have white sails, and not the black of the outward journey. So the old man, concluding that Theseus had perished, cast himself down from the Acropolis.

Thus, in the saga, Theseus came to rule Athens and Attica too, since he was credited with a primitive union of a divided Attica in a synoecism, celebrated by Athenians in a state festival. It worried no one that if Attica had been united in the distant past, it was to experience this again, and was not in fact one state until the seventh century. Nor did it trouble the Athenians that the story of their ancient king and culture hero showed strong folk-tale elements of a timeless hero, as well as elements of saga which were important for the Acropolis. It must be firmly borne in mind that such saga was embellished and modified by accretions of very different dates, but possessed a core of respectable antiquity. The saga tradition of Attica claimed to record much strife for the kingship: the ejection of Pandion, descendant of Kekrops, to Megara, by the sons of Metion; the return of his sons, one of whom was Aigeus; another was called Pallas (a title of Athena and the name of one of the Titans); yet a third was Nisos who retained the kingship of Megara and had a fatal encounter with Cretan Minos. The tradition postulates a divided Attica, until the sons of Pallas were defeated by Theseus.

In the story of his career from the time of his coming to Attica from Troezen, the folk-hero element is strong, and so is the determination to work Theseus' presence into every great mythological exploit: the Battle of the Centaurs and Lapiths in Thessaly in aid of his friend Peirithöos, the expedition of Jason in quest of the Golden Fleece, and the Calydonian Boar Hunt. He was also made to conduct an expedition against the Amazons, who in turn invaded Attica. Aided by Peirithöos he carried off Helen, while she was still a young girl, from Sparta, and in turn aided Peirithöos in an attempt to do the same to Persephone, which meant imprisonment for a time in the Underworld until his rescue by Herakles. The abduction of Helen entailed the invasion of Attica by her brothers Kastor and Polydeukes who took Helen back, and with her Theseus' mother Aithra, who eventually reappeared at Troy to be rescued by her grandsons. It was somehow felt that all these activities weakened Theseus' hold on Attica, and permitted a rival, Menestheus, to displace him and drive him out to exile in Skyros, where he was treacherously killed. So it came about that in the Catalogue of the Ships in the *Iliad* Menestheus leads the Athenian contingent, and while Theseus' sons Demophon and Akamas were later taken to be present at Troy, the Homeric poems do not mention them.

It is easy to see in Theseus the Attic parallel to Herakles: to deny his historicity, and to identify elements of his story with later propaganda efforts of the Athenians in their sixth- and fifth-century rise to greatness among the Greek states, especially when, in the early sixties of the fifth century, the Athenian soldier and statesman Kimon brought back the 'bones of Theseus' with great éclat from Skyros – a suitable counterblast to Spartan Herakles. On the other hand there are details of the story which are truly odd, especially the ejection of the great hero; the unsatisfactory history of his sons, who do little or nothing to restore his line, and the obscurity of Menestheus the leader at Troy. In the matter of the Catalogue of the Ships, whatever may be thought of the story which associated Ajax and Salamis with the Athenians, and clearly helped to bolster Athenian claims to that island, one is in fact surprised that if the Athenians did forge the entry, they did not do so more competently. Their ships represent a respectable total of forty or fifty, about half of the one hundred led by Agamemnon, and the ninety commanded by Nestor. Their leader, on the other hand, is obscure and inglorious, and the claim that Nestor was his only rival as marshaller of horse and foot sounds forced and artificial. Later writers felt it wrong that the House of Theseus was displaced, and Euripides, for instance, did better in both ships and leader[5].

The conviction, whether very ancient tradition or more recent confection, that Athena shared the Acropolis with the incumbents of an unstable kingship is clear also in the stories of the sequel to the Trojan War. The Theseids, despite their descent from Poseidon, continued to be unsatisfactory. A tradition which the Athenians later found to be most useful was that of the coming of a Neleid stock (descended from Neleus, son of Poseidon, and so in this sense no propaganda counterblast to the children of Theseus) from Messenia to Athens, as part of the disturbance caused by the so-called 'Return of the Herakleidai' or the 'Dorian Invasion'. Two generations after the expedition to Troy, according to the saga, Melanthos the Neleid, displaced from Peloponnesian Messenia like so many other refugees, came to Athens and there found his opportunity. These events in Greece, it is useful to recall, are summarised by Thucydides in his outline of early Greek history:

'Sixty years after the capture of Ilium the modern Boeotians were driven out of Arne by the Thessalians and settled in the present Boeotia, the former Cadmeis ... Twenty years later the Dorians and the Heraclids became masters of the Peloponnese.'[6]

In the context from which this passage is taken, Thucydides is commenting on the disturbed state of Greece in the period subsequent to the Trojan expedition and culminating in the so-called Dorian Invasion. It has been said earlier that some of this story may have evolved much later to explain the Ionian/Dorian division of Greece, and the map of its dialects. It is hard to pin down these earliest

Dorians, and their penetration may have been gradual and later. But there is the evidence of a threat: in the case of Attica, a threat seemingly from the north, from Boeotia. Thymoites, the great grandson of Theseus, failed in his kingly duty to protect the state, and Melanthos took his place and effected a change of dynasty, and repelled the enemy. Melanthos, according to the genealogists, lived in the second generation after Troy, and was contemporary with the Heraclid leaders of the Dorians, Kresphontes, Temenos and Aristodemos. Kodros, his son, lived in the next generation, and was the contemporary of Prokles and Eurysthenes, the founders of Dorian Sparta. Kodros occupied a very special position. During his rule Attica was again threatened by Dorian invasion, this time from the south, a movement which, in the tradition, made Megara Dorian. By the willing sacrifice of his own life Kodros saved Athens, and the grateful Athenians commemorated him by abolishing the kingship, or so it was said afterwards, though it was also claimed that subsequently Attica was governed by Medon and twelve successors (the Medontidai), in the function of life magistrate (little different from kingship), followed by a series of ten-year magistrates, until in 683 BC the archonship was reduced to a tenure of one year and put into commission. The official abolition of the kingship has the support of a late authority only, and it is more likely that the process was one of transition, under the pressure of rivalry, from hereditary kingly rule to aristocracy. But whenever and however it took place, it must have marked the end of the use of the Acropolis as a royal residence. No aristocracy would permit one of its number to hold, even temporarily, such an important centre and fortress. Finally Kodros was put forward by the later Athenians, when they claimed Athens as the mother city of the Ionians, as father of the Kodridai (including another Neleus), who were taken to be the leaders of a migration from Attica to Ionia, of those displaced inhabitants of Greece who had been affected by the Dorian Invasion. Like the 'Invasion' itself there is telescoping in this narrative of events: the generations may well be simplified, and the chronological problems are considerable. Yet if the basic ideas are extracted and compared with the archaeological record – without any precise attempt to reconcile absolute dates – then the saga can be said to throw light on the archaeological evidence.

It is worth recalling what Thucydides has to say on the rise of Mycenae:

'What enabled Agamemnon to raise the armament was more, in my opinion, his superiority in strength, than the oaths of Tyndareus, which bound the Suitors to follow him. Indeed, the account given by those Peloponnesians who have been the recipients of the most credible tradition is this. First of all Pelops, arriving among a needy population from Asia with vast wealth, acquired such power that, stranger though he was, the country was called after him: and this power fortune saw fit materially to increase in the hands of his descendants. Eurystheus had been killed in Attica by the Heraclids. Atreus was his mother's brother; and to the hands of his relation, who had left his father on account of the death of Chrysippos, Eurystheus, when he set out on his expedition, had committed Mycenae and the government. As time went on and Eurystheus did not return, Atreus complied with the wishes of the Mycenaeans, who were influenced by fear of the Heraclids – besides, his power seemed considerable, and he had not neglected to court the favour of the populace – and assumed the sceptre of Mycenae and the rest of the dominions of Eurystheus. And so the power of the descendants of Pelops came to be greater than that of the descendants of Perseus. To all this Agamemnon succeeded.'[7]

Thucydides thus expressed the idea that at a certain point in the chequered history of Mycenae, with the replacement of the Perseid dynasty by the Pelopid, an incomer worked a radical change in the fortunes of the state, inaugurating the great period of the history of Mycenae in what archaeologically was probably the late fourteenth century BC, but in the traditional Greek historic dating the late thirteenth century, before the Trojan War.

In the case of Athens, it may be suggested, a similar process took place rather later after the war. Here an undistinguished and minor state, inferior to Mycenae, in an extended period of crisis, experienced a change of dynasty. It would be unwise to try to coordinate this with the 'Dorian Invasion', but it is possible that the time of troubles in the later thirteenth century and in the early twelfth, and a crisis in the affairs of Athens (paralleled ultimately by disaster and destruction elsewhere), led not only to a change of dynasty, but also to the fortification of the Acropolis under a new dynamic ruler. The justification for this was a threat from the north, if one interprets reasonably the narrative of Thucydides. Events in the Peloponnese,

marked by the improvements in the fortifications of Mycenae and Tiryns and the construction on the Isthmus of Corinth of what appears to be a defensive wall, coupled with the preparations at the Mycenaean palace of Ano Englianos in Messenia, supplement the evidence for the Acropolis of Athens.

Somehow, thanks to the resolution of an ancient king, whether his name was Melanthos or not, the attack was averted or repulsed, and the preparations for siege were no longer needed. It may be added that all this – the building of the wall on the Acropolis and the preparation of access to the water supply – may have taken a generation or, under pressure of extreme necessity, much less time.

In the next generation there was another attack, this time from the south, which was again repelled. Once again the archaeological and traditional dates are different, but a period of danger seems to have been followed by a period of consolidation: the establishment of the lower town of Athens, and the beginning of an emigration to Asia Minor. For Athens and the Acropolis the crucial matter is the end of the kingship and of its association with the Acropolis.

B. THE ACROPOLIS CULTS

For the Athenian Acropolis, as for other Mycenaean centres, questions of religion are matters for conjecture. Possibly some female principle, concerned with fertility, was an object of concern to the Neolithic and later inhabitants of Athens and the Acropolis, though in Greece as a whole there is little or no specific evidence. What is conjectured is vaguely derived from the impressions we have of Minoan-Mycenaean religion, for which there is a mass of archaeological material. But the interpretation – if it is to be interpreted at all – is ambiguous, and there is almost nothing in the way of written evidence. The bulk of the material evidence comes from Minoan Crete, though the style is the same for the same category of object when found in Bronze Age (Mycenaean) Greece, and there is little distinction of period or place to be made. Despite the lack of written texts it is broadly agreed, on the basis of the material available, that the Minoan culture, apart from a tree

Opposite: Athena in gilded bronze (attachment to a bronze vessel).
Overleaf: Erechtheum, Parthenon and the rock surface seen from the Propylaia.

Above: Athena, olive tree and owl, on an Athenian bronze coin of Imperial Roman date; possibly suggested by the Athena of the western pediment of the Parthenon.
Opposite: The eastern façade of the Parthenon.

and pillar cult, centred on a female deity (with a subsidiary male associate) connected with animals, birds (as Athena was with the owl), and snakes. Other features of Cretan culture (though possibly not of Mycenaean) are bulls and bull-leaping, the 'horns of consecration' which might be a symbol of the bull's horns, and the double axe, the *labrys*, which slew the bull and was often set between the horns of consecration. It is natural to think of a bull god, and there is a temptation to equate him with Poseidon, also worshipped with bull-sacrifice as at Nestor's Pylos. Crete is liable to earthquakes, and it may be that the god was worshipped as 'Earth-shaker'. Thus the double-axe came to be placed on pillars supporting Minoan buildings, as in the Pillar Crypt at Knossos.

In addition to the 'goddess' and the bull god (if there was such a distinct recipient of cult), a youthful male 'deity' has also been recognised, sometimes represented as descending from the sky. But all this is conjecture based on the abundant cult objects found everywhere, in cave and hilltop shrines, and in domestic shrines such as that in the palace at Knossos. It must also be borne in mind that the archaeologist, when puzzled for an explanation of an object, tends to call it a 'cult object'. Similarly, a figure scene which does not clearly represent some mundane activity may be accorded a religious significance. Minoan religion

has always been subject to interpretation by parallel. In later and well-documented times and in Anatolia and the East Mediterranean, which in some respects seem to have a connection with Crete, the 'Great Mother Goddess' – often associated with a junior male consort – is a feature of religious belief clearly concerned with fertility. The death and resurrection of the consort is a symbol of the death of nature in winter and its renewal in spring. This female principle of oriental origin, concerned with the fertility of the cultivated earth in a society sometimes matriarchal and matrilinear, has been contrasted with the 'sky gods', who are supposedly typical of the Hellenic Greeks, and in general of Indo-European language-speakers and patriarchal, pastoral societies. There is something in this, if it is not pushed too far for the sake of cultural distinction or racialist propaganda. It has all helped in the interpretation of Minoan religion. It is not, on the whole, invalidated by the generally (though not universally) accepted decipherment of the Linear B tablets, found only at Knossos in Crete, and at several sites in Mycenaean Greece, but not as yet in Athens. The reasonably sceptical believer in the decipherment may accept Zeus (di-we), Hera, Artemis and Poseidon (po-se-da-o-ne) in the abundant archives of Pylos (Ano Englianos). Poseidon appears also at Knossos. Most important for the present study is A-ta-na po-ti-ni-ja at Knossos, and the appearance of Po-ti-ni-ja at Pylos in the western Peloponnese. Potnia is 'the Mistress', a title given to Athena in the Homeric poems. All this tends to complicate a neat categorisation of 'earth goddess' and 'sky gods', since here already, in a seemingly alien context, are the gods of the Hellenic Greeks. It is not difficult to see indicated in the Linear B tablets at Knossos the presence, during a limited period (*c.* 1450–1375/50 BC), of aliens using elements of proto-Greek; imposing their own language; having it written in an adapted script; using the bureaucracy which had been evolved in palace-centres before their coming, but retaining their own religion. Since the religious preoccupations of all peoples are ultimately the same, their religion consequently had some point of contact with what went before. It is unwise to go further than this. One could say that they were able to see a parallel to their own Poseidon with his bulls and horses in the religion of Crete. If they found a 'mistress' goddess they might identify her with their own Athena. The difficulty is that there is no way of explaining these names.

This, then, is the position in Crete, with ample material remains for conjecture on questions of religion. It is different in mainland Greece. It is not difficult to see a possible line of continuity from the palace shrines at Knossos with a female deity who was, for a brief period, Potnia Athena, to the Mycenaean strongholds on the mainland of Greece on sites where, in the Classical period, there were temples of Athena – as at Mycenae and Athens. In mainland Greece, however, there is no direct evidence for such Cretan-type shrines.

In this connection it is useful to quote a recent observation by a distinguished Mycenaean archaeologist:

'The Greek situation is in stark contrast to Crete, where every major palace, villa, farmhouse, mountain top and cave bears testimony to public cult. In Greece there are no proven centres of cave or mountain worship, no independent rustic shrines have been found, and even within the palaces there are no rooms particularly constructed as sanctuaries. Cult was an integral part of palace life, handled in palace halls which had other domestic functions as well. The focus of the palace was always the megaron with its huge fixed hearth. At Pylos a portable altar stood by the hearth: at Mycenae traces of an altar and offering tables were discovered in the porch of the megaron. Everything suggests that throne, hearth and moveable altar formed a traditional complex, and that the hearth itself was the centre of sacrificial ritual carried out or supervised by the prince or his palace priest.'[8]

This is an honest statement of conjecture to fill the gaps in properly based knowledge. From archaeological material such as seal-rings and frescoes the conclusion might be drawn that there was a close cultural, and therefore religious, link between Minoan Crete and Mycenaean Greece. The seal-rings, however, may be gifts or booty; the frescoes and other works of art showing Minoan motifs may have been produced purely as attractive artistic decoration borrowed from another more 'refined' civilisation. To quote parallels from other places and times: the use of Pompeian-style wall decoration, of Classical-style architecture, or of *chinoiserie*, is no indication of cultural unity. The same may be true of Mycenaean Greece in relation to Minoan objects and motifs.

The most that can be said is that during the Bronze Age occupation of the Acropolis there was a female deity of importance in Crete, and that deities with names resembling Athena and Poseidon may have been recipients of cult in the period 1450–1375 BC. For the rest, even taking account of what is found in the Homeric poems, it is necessary to start from the other end, from the cults of the Classical period.

These were in part located in buildings and *temene* (sacred enclosures) on the Acropolis, in part linked with buildings in the town below, and in certain cases connected with cults located elsewhere. Most significant in this connection is the Archaic temple of Athena, of which only the foundations are preserved, on the north side of the rock. The fact that Athena Polias (Protector of the City) was worshipped here is undisputed, and the ancient statue – to be discussed later – was housed in this building. This ancient temple existed in the sixth century, but was destroyed when the Persians sacked Athens in 480 BC. What happened to it subsequently will be mentioned later. A curious and complex building was constructed to the north of it, in close proximity, in the later fifth century BC. The Greek traveller and guide-book writer Pausanias called it the Erechtheion (Latin, Erechtheum), though this does not seem to have been its official name. It is such a complicated building that it was clearly constructed to suit a number of cults. The ancient statue of Athena was housed in its eastern portion, and it is reasonable to suppose that her cult was celebrated there. Pausanias, whose description leaves a good deal to be desired, entered the temple through a North Porch past an altar of Zeus Hypatos ('All-Highest'), and in his comment on the western interior, says:

'As you go in, there are three altars, one sacred to Poseidon, on which sacrifices are offered to Erechtheus, in accordance with the command of an oracle; one to the hero Boutes, and one to Hephaistos. The paintings on the walls represent the race of the Boutadai. And the building being divided into two compartments, within there is a well containing seawater. This in itself is not wonderful, for there are salt wells even far inland. ... But the remarkable point about this well is that when the south wind blows it gives forth a sound like that of breakers. There is also the imprint of a trident on the rock. These things are said to have been produced by Poseidon in support of his claim to the country.'[9]

It may be said here, in anticipation of the description of this odd building, that while it is divided by two

The Erechtheum and the Doerpfeld Foundation
(Ancient temple of Athena Polias) seen from the top
of the Parthenon.

north-south cross walls, and the eastern section is isolated from the other two, Pausanias is undoubtedly referring to the fact that the western section, entered principally from the North Porch has a basement-like understructure necessary to give access to the 'trident' marks, which were also exposed to the light of day through an aperture in the paving of the North Porch, and another in its roof. This building was therefore the setting of four cults; of Athena, of Poseidon, of Boutes the Ploughman, and of Hephaistos the smith god.

West of the Erechtheum was an extension of this area of sanctity. In the angle between the west front of the Erechtheum and the rough northern retaining wall of the platform on which the Archaic temple of Athena partly stood, there is a gap in the western face of the Erechtheum, bridged by a single large horizontal block. The gap gives access to the western section of the temple. Above it there is the Maiden or Caryatid Porch with a stair to the interior. Here again there seems to be a careful contrivance for a special purpose. In antiquity the Kekropion was located

here, named after Kekrops, the ancient king of Athens, and thought of as his burial place. An ancient burial may in reality have given rise to the belief, and in ancient times it was surmounted by a mound which has now disappeared.

In the same vicinity was the home of the sacred snake, which became associated with Athena as protector of the city, being thought of as house-protector of the palace of the ancient kings. However, snakes – as dwellers in the ground – were also thought of as symbols of the heroic dead, and in effect Athena took over what originally belonged to (or was) the snake-bodied Kekrops. Also close at hand was the sacred olive tree, Athena's gift to the land and her contribution to the famous contest which took place here between herself and Poseidon, for judgement and decision either by the Twelve Gods or by Kekrops and the elders of Athens. It seems altogether fitting that the olive (mother of numerous other sacred olives in Attica) should carry the day. Poseidon, apart from his connection with the sea, bulls and earthquakes (from which Attica does not greatly suffer), had also an association with horses. He was worshipped as Poseidon Hippios, and, as such, Aristophanes, in his comedy *The Knights*, makes the gallant horsemen of Athens hail him as their leader, but Athena is not forgotten. Only very late versions of the 'Contest for the Land' make Poseidon produce the horse as his gift. Early versions name the salt well, a less than useful creation. In effect both trident mark and well are demonstrations of might, not beneficence, and may well go far back beyond the period of elaboration of the story of the Contest. It should be noted that the well was actually called the 'Sea of Erechtheus', the ancient king either inhabiting the palace to which Athena came, as in the *Odyssey*, or lodged in her temple, as in the *Iliad*, but in Classical times sharing the altar of Poseidon in the Erechtheum 'according to an oracle'.

In the 'Contest for the Land' Athena is, in one tradition, made to vow an ox to her father Zeus Polieus, another city protector. Pausanias, before getting to the ancient temple of Athena and the Erechtheum, mentions in an obscure passage[9] a statue of Zeus Polieus as standing somewhere between the Parthenon and the ancient temple. It was possibly a primitive statue, and he goes on to say:

> 'I will describe the customary mode of sacrificing to the latter, but without giving the reason assigned for it. They set barley mixed with wheat on the altar of Zeus Polieus and keep no watch; and the ox which they keep in readiness for the sacrifice goes up to the altar and eats of the grain. They call one of the priests the Ox-slayer, and here he throws away the axe (for such is the custom) and flees away; and they, as if they did not know the man who did the deed, bring the axe to trial.'[10]

Pausanias' account is incomplete, and his references to what is in effect the Bouphonia or Diipolia (celebrated on the 14th day of the month Skirophorion i.e. end of June), supplemented by his statement in another place that the axe was brought to trial at the court of the Prytaneion (the building housing the public hearth of the city), is more fully explained by a writer of the third century AD quoting another of the late fourth century BC. Added detail is given thus on the ceremony.

> 'They choose out maidens as water-carriers; these bring water that the axe and the knife may be sharpened. And when it has been sharpened one person

hands it and strikes the bull, and another slays the animal, and those who skin it afterwards all partake of it. When this has been done, they sew up the skin of the ox, and they stuff it with hay and set it up, looking just as it did when it was alive, and yoke it to the plough as if it were going to draw it. And when judgement is held about the slaying, they all cry off on to the others who shared the deed. Those who brought the water accuse those who sharpened the knife, rather than themselves; those who sharpened the knife, him who handed it; he who handed it, him who struck; he who struck, him who slew; he who slew, the knife itself; and the knife, as it cannot speak, they condemn.'[11]

The ritual, as described, sounds primitive, and it was felt to be old-fashioned in the late fifth century BC. The explanation – that this was in expiation of the unlawful slaughter of the ox, 'sharer in the labours of men' as pulling the plough and the wagon, an attempt to secure blood sacrifice and yet avoid 'the ploughman's curse' – sounds late and intellectual, though there is repeated preoccupation, as will be seen, with oxen and ploughing.

Pausanias does not say where this ritual took place. There might have been an altar of Zeus Polieus on the Acropolis near his statue, and it has been suggested that the ox devoted to the ritual was housed near it. On the other hand, down in the lower town was a structure called the Boukoleion, 'the ox-steading', near the Prytaneion and perhaps in the area north of the Acropolis. It was, significantly enough, the residence in early times of the *archon basileus*, the magistrate responsible for affairs of religion, and in it other primitive ceremonial took place, the 'sacred marriage' of his wife to Dionysos. And yet it is difficult to believe that the ruler of gods and men in his capacity as 'city god' was not represented in the Acropolis cults, at any rate before the tyrant Peisistratos deemed him worthy of a temple in the area south-east of the Acropolis, in what was later to be the Emperor Hadrian's new town.

No great distance west of the Erechtheum, close to the edge of the rock, there stood in Classical times a square building with a frontal colonnade, of which only the foundations now remain. At its north-western corner was the beginning of the staircase which led down to a cave on the north slope (in antiquity the 'Long Rocks') and ultimately to the Late Mycenaean well. In it for a time each year resided two

The north wall, showing built-in architectural fragments.
It also shows the lower entrance to the
underground passage at the Aglaurion used by the Arrhephoroi.

small girls chosen of four from the noblest families of Athens by the *archon basileus*, the 'King Archon'. Their office was one of those which marked the youth of the high-born maidens of Athens, as Aristophanes makes his chorus of women narrate in *Lysistrata*:

'I, who to her thoughtful tender
    care my happiest memories owe;
Bore, at seven, the mystic casket;
Was, at ten, our Lady's miller;
    then the yellow Brauron bear;
Next (a maiden tall and stately
    with a string of figs to wear)
Bore in pomp the holy Basket.'[12]

These little girls served Athena for a year, helping in the weaving of the robe for the Archaic statue of Athena, but in particular serving as Arrhephoroi or Errhephoroi, and so giving the name to the building. In the month of Skirophorion they carried out a

curious ritual described by Pausanias in his account of the Acropolis:

'Two maidens dwell not far from the temple of Athena Polias, called by the Athenians Arrhephoroi. For a time they live with the goddess, but when the festival comes round they perform at night the following rites. Having placed on their heads what the priestess of Athena gives them to carry – neither she who gives, nor they who carry have any knowledge what it is – the maidens descend by the natural underground passage that goes across to the adjacent precinct within the city of Aphrodite in the Gardens. They leave down below what they carry and receive something else which they bring back covered up.'[13]

They thus used the first two flights of the descent to the Mycenaean cistern, and emerged from the cave at the bottom of the second, to make their way eastwards

The north face of the Acropolis: the area of the Sanctuary of Aphrodite and Eros, with niches for votive offerings or for lamps.

along to the vicinity of the north-eastern upward path to the Mycenaean postern, where the precinct of Aphrodite and Eros appears to have been located. As Arrhephoroi, their name suggested the similar-sounding Arrhetophoroi ('bearers of secret objects'), or as Errhephoroi that they were dew-bearers. Their bearing of secret objects, and the location of their residence on the Acropolis, must surely connect them with the story of the daughters of the ancient King Kekrops, who were perhaps originally two in number – Aglauros and Pandrosos – to whom Herse was later added as a third, since the women of Athens swore only by Aglauros and Pandrosos. The story is bound up with that of Erichthonios, touched on by Euripides in his *Ion*, which deals principally with the theme of the eponymous ancestor of the Ionians, 'the founder of an Asian realm', namely Ion, the son of Kreousa ('the queen') and Apollo, who forced her in one of the caves near the north-west corner of the Acropolis, close to the Pythion and the Klepsydra Fountain:

'There is a city, famous 'mongst the Greeks
(From Pallas, mighty with her golden spear
Its name it holds); there on the northern rocks,
By Pallas' hill, which men of Attica
Call the Long Cliffs, Apollo took by force
Erechtheus' child Kreousa.'[14]

The play, one of Euripides' best, makes frequent mention of the Acropolis, as does also Aristophanes' *Lysistrata*. The *Ion* illustrates in its detail the way mythology might be bent to literary purposes while contradictions and anachronisms were ignored. It also illustrates the use of pseudo-mythology to produce eponyms for the divisions of the Greek race, and to urge points of contemporary moment in the Greek political scene. It might be added that this sort of thing and many less obvious elements, were used to give antiquity to the noble families of Athens and the cults in which they officiated. Thus Kreousa is not only an ancient Erechtheid, but also personifies the Athenians' claim to autochthony, and their dislike of strangers and incomers. Xouthos, son of Aiolos in the play, and husband of Kreousa, is one of these, receiving her in marriage as reward for military service to her father. In the *Ion* Aiolos and Doros, named as sons of Helen, represent two of the leading branches of the Greek race. In fact a schematic organisation of eponyms, known from other sources, is adapted to Attic political and pacific propaganda with the intention of reconciling Ionians and Dorians,

Athenians and Spartans, in the hostilities of the fifth century BC. Ion himself, ancestor of the Ionians – Athens' nearest kin – cannot be the son of an alien Xouthos, so Apollo is made to intervene. But Kreousa and Xouthos can (in a version modified from that just mentioned) produce Doros, eponym of the mother-state of the Dorians, and Achaios, as ancestor of the Achaians of the Peloponnese, without offending Athenian sentiments. They are all, therefore, of the same kin. All is neat, formal and manifestly artificial: which should give a warning not to rest too many arguments on other more primitive-seeming, less obviously artificial, material.

The *Ion* also glances at other aspects of the Acropolis and the Erechtheid house. Thus there is an indirect reference[15] to the practice of watching for the lightning flashes on Mount Parnes – a signal for the despatch of a sacred embassy to Delphi – which took place at the Pythion below the north-west corner of the Acropolis. There is reference also to Erechtheus' sacrifice of one of his daughters, Chthonia ('the Earth girl') to gain victory in his war with Eleusis, and his slaying, in the same war, of Eumolpos thé Thracian (or his son), with the reaction of Poseidon as father of Eumolpos, who with a blow of his trident caused the earth to open and swallow up Erechtheus. This is possibly bound up with the trident-marks on the Acropolis. Were they connected with the 'Contest for the Land', and the salt well, or with the death of Erechtheus; and did Poseidon do the deed with his trident, or Zeus with his thunderbolt? To disentangle the permutations of myth is almost impossible, or to detect genuine early elements. For Euripides and other artists, not yet touched by the scholarly and antiquarian urge of a later day, all this is the stuff of literature, not a canon of belief. The same is true of the graphic artists who used these themes in sculpture and painting.

Learned commentators can enjoy a field day with these legends. They have not failed to notice that Eumolpos, as son of Poseidon, is the enemy of a king who might originally have been a cult-title or fore-runner of that god (we may cite Poseidon-Erechtheus in an inscription of the Erechtheum), and that in strict genealogy Eumolpos was the great-grandson of Erechtheus, being son of Chione 'the snowmaiden', child of Oreithyia daughter of Erechtheus, and of Boreas, the North Wind – a suitable enough father of a snow maiden in wintry Thrace. It is easy enough to see the myth-making literary tendencies at work

here, and to suspect that some elements of this legend relate to the Athenian interest in northern Greece. But how is the manifest preoccupation with *chthōn* (the Earth or the Land) to be evaluated? Chthonia is daughter of Erechtheus, himself Earth-born. Kekrops is the same. There is also the question of begetting. Kekrops conventionally enough married Aglauros, daughter of Aktaios ('shore man' or 'grain man') and begot Pandrosos, Aglauros and Herse, and a son Erysichthon ('land deliverer'). An alternative for Aglauros is Agraulos (not attested in inscriptions). It is difficult to avoid the temptation to point out that this word, as an epithet, means 'piping in the fields'

or 'dwelling in the fields', and is a description of the *kerkope* or cicada, not so far from Kekrops in form. The cicada, it was said in Antiquity, lived on dew – a substance with which Herse and Pandrosos are obviously associated. And it must be recalled that old-fashioned Athenians wore hair-pins decorated with golden grasshoppers or cicadas. Is all this artificial, late and far-fetched?

If these children of Kekrops, with their interesting associations, came into the world in the ordinary way another figure of Athenian mythology, Erichthonios, did not. Like Erechtheus, he may be a cult-epithet of Poseidon. Pindar, in the earlier fifth century BC, is the earliest writer to distinguish the two. Erichthonios was a protégé of Athena. A story, possibly early, suggested that he was the son of Athena and the god Hephaistos, in so many ways closely connected with the goddess. If this story was true, she was no virgin. So to save her virginity an alternative story was elaborated. It may be noted in passing how fertility and virginity are closely linked. Even Hera, the wedded goddess par excellence and patron goddess of marriage, still renewed her virginity yearly at a spring in Argos. This ambivalent attitude must have arisen from the conviction that virgins exercised great power (after all, in later times they could subdue unicorns), and yet unless they lost their quality, life could not continue. In the case of Athena the alternative story was that she suffered the lustful onslaught of Hephaistos, and as she fled his advances his seed was shed upon the ground and Erichthonios was begotten and brought forth from the Earth, from which source Athena received him (a sort of virgin birth in reverse) and placed him in a chest with a protecting serpent or serpents. He was the ancestor of the Erechtheid line of Erechtheus, Kreousa and Ion; the snakes were later replaced by gold snake amulets (a widely used form of bracelet). In the *Ion* of Euripides Kreousa exposes her son decked with them:

'Upholding this the custom handed down
From earthborn Erichthonios to her race
Whom once Zeus' child gave to the Aglaurid maids
Safely to keep, and fastened to his side
Two guardian serpents; whence the custom is
To deck their nursling babes with snakes of gold.'[16]

The begetting of Erichthonios in this way was better than spontaneous generation. We may compare how Athena sprang from the head of Zeus because he had swallowed Metis, lest she bear a greater than himself. Erichthonios in his chest was committed by Athena to Herse, Pandrosos and Aglauros, with the injunction not to open it – an age-old folk-tale element. But Herse and Aglauros did, while Pandrosos obeyed the command. So the pair, or perhaps in the original story only Aglauros, alarmed by the snakes, cast themselves from the Acropolis, where beneath the Long Rocks of the North Face, Aglauros in Classical times had a cave and an important precinct. Pandrosos had her reward – a precinct on the Acropolis to the west of the Erechtheum, and enclosing the Kekropion. In a charming passage of the *Ion* Euripides makes the chorus address the Cave of Pan:

'Oh Athens, what thy cliff has seen!
The northward scar, Pan's cavern-seat
With rocks before and grassy floor,
Where dancing tread the Aglaurids' feet
Their triple measure on the green
'Neath Pallas' fane,
Whene'er the god in his retreat
Plays on the reed a quavering strain.'[17]

The cave, Pan-haunted, with dancing nymphs, is represented on a late relief.

Even if Erechtheus and Erichthonios were cult-epithets of Poseidon or ancient gods reduced by him

Above: Red-figured Attic vase showing Athena with Erichthonios, his chest and guardian serpent, on the rock of the Acropolis.
Opposite: Ge (Earth) produces Erichthonios and hands him to Athena in the presence of Zeus.

Pan in his cave with nymphs and votary. From a relief
now in the National Museum, Athens.

to the status of heroes and ancient kings, it is hard to believe that Aglauros and Pandrosos were cult-titles of Athena. They had in common their virginity. Indeed the Acropolis rock seems quite a place for virgins even if Kreousa lost her virginity there. To the south-west of the Parthenon itself was the enclosure of the sanctuary of Artemis Brauronia, of which Pausanias has remarkably little to say:

'There is also a sanctuary of Artemis Brauronia, the image in which is by Praxiteles. The title of the goddess is derived from the deme of Brauron, and the ancient wooden image, the Tauric Artemis as they describe it, was at Brauron.'[18]

Whether the celebrated image of Artemis brought by Iphigeneia (herself bearing a cult name of Artemis) from the Tauri (to whose land she had been conveyed by Artemis when her father Agamemnon was about to sacrifice her at Aulis to secure a favourable wind to Troy) was left at Brauron (modern Vraona/Vravron) in East Attica or preserved in Sparta, as far as Attica is concerned the sanctuary seems to have been in Brauron. Artemis Brauronia was the recipient of dedicated female clothing; such dedications, carefully recorded, certainly took place on the Acropolis. In Arcadia she was associated with bears, and it may be that in the Attic ceremonial the high-born children were originally wrapped in bear-skins. Later these were replaced by saffron-coloured robes: so in Aristophanes' play *Lysistrata* the heroine is made to say: 'Wearing the saffron robe, I was a bear in the Brauronian festival.'[19]

How far this ceremonial took place in the Acropolis precinct of Artemis Brauronia is unclear. The charming child portraits in sculpture from Brauron itself might indicate that it did not. One can only say that there may have been an archaic statue on the Acropolis in addition to the one by Praxiteles, and possibly only a precinct and a colonnade. There is no clear indication of a temple.

There were, then, closely connected with the Acropolis the virgin daughters of Kekrops and Aglauros, and the virgin Artemis. There were others: the *parthenoi Erechtheides*, Protogoneia and Pandora – associated with Pandrosos. Aglauros (her sister) was also connected with Athena, and there were other virgins: the Arrhephoroi, the weavers of Athena's *peplos*, and those noble maidens of Athens who participated in the Panathenaic festival procession as *Kanephoroi* (basket-bearers).

There were a great many maidenly activities connected with the Acropolis, which might be the source of the name Parthenon applied specifically to the western portion of the great Periclean temple, and justify the suggestion that from it Athena derived the epithet Parthenos, which was not a cult title, even if she came to be thought of as the Virgin par excellence. But in the Erechtheum, in the ancient temple its forerunner, at the altar south-east of it and north-east of the Parthenon – her chief altar – and in the great gold and ivory statue of Pheidias, Athena is Athena Polias,

Fragment of a relief, probably from the Cave of Pan and now in the Acropolis Museum, showing Pan seated on a rock with nymphs approaching.

Athena defender of the citadel, more fitted to this function standing and armed than seated. Yet a multitude of terracotta figures show a seated female figure which might be interpreted as the goddess. At Troy, in the *Iliad*, the Trojan women placed offerings on the lap of the goddess's statue. Strabo points out that in his own day the *xoanon* or archaic statue of Athena there was a standing one, while Homer makes it seated; he goes on to say that many such ancient statues are seated ones. It is to be wondered if this is in effect the same statue as the Palladion from which Ajax the Less tore Cassandra, and which was carried away by Diomedes. The story goes that on his return from Troy he unwittingly landed in Attica and was repulsed by Demophon, who was then purged of involuntary blood-guilt at the court 'at the Palladion'. Was the statue thought of as remaining in Attica? And if so, where? The Argives, on the other hand, put themselves forward as the ultimate posessors of it, and the Argive women bathed it (and the shield of Diomedes) in the river Inachos.

It was all terribly confused, like the question of the statue of Artemis Tauropolos brought by Iphigeneia from the Tauri. Artists in pottery and bronze certainly thought of the Palladion as a standing, rather plank-like figure, very similar to the figure of Athena issuing from the head of Zeus on the early sixth-century

The birth of Athena, with Eileithyia and Hephaistos in attendance. Drawing of an early sixth-century bronze relief found at Olympia.

bronze reliefs found at Olympia, and that on an Attic red-figured vase. Indeed, what looks like a crude picture of a warrior-goddess appears on an early seventh-century Protocorinthian perfume pot in Oxford, whether or not the picture is correctly interpreted as the recovery of Helen (from Attica) by her brothers Kastor and Polydeukes. Yet Pausanias mentions a statue of a *seated* Athena in the temple of Athena *Polias* at Erythrai in Ionia, but he describes this figure as wearing a tall crown and holding a distaff. It was a wooden statue and Pausanias adjudged it to be by the early sculptor Endoios, whom he also named as the artist of a seated Athena on the Acropolis. It is possible that this latter, in a headless and battered state, has survived, but neither is likely to represent the Polias. The form of the ancient statue, therefore, remains something of a mystery.

The Birth of Athena was celebrated in the eastern pediment of the Parthenon. Whatever intellectual overtones the story later acquired, it must be primitive enough in its origins. In Homer Athena sometimes bears the title Tritogeneia. Suggestions in Antiquity that this referred to the day of the month when she was born, or again that it means 'head born' (from a supposed word for the head), or that it has something to do with Lake Tritonis in Libya, all seem equally artificial. Its use in Homer, and again somewhat later in Hesiod, might indicate that it is an ancient survival. The poet Hesiod in his *Theogony* explains how Athena was begotten, if that is the word:

'Now Zeus, King of the Gods, made Metis his wife first, and she was wisest among gods and men. But when she was about to bring forth the goddess bright-eyed Athene, Zeus craftily deceived her with cunning words and put her in his own belly, as Earth and Starry Heaven advised. For they advised him so, to the end that no other should hold royal sway other than eternal Zeus among the eternal Gods; for very wise children were destined to be born of her, first the maiden, bright-eyed Tritogeneia, equal to her father in strength and in wise understanding; but afterwards she was to bear a son of overbearing spirit, King of gods and men. But Zeus put her into his belly first, that the goddess might devise for him good and evil.'[20]

Further on Hesiod narrates the birth:

'But Zeus himself gave birth from his own head to bright-eyed Tritogeneia, the awful, the

Athena being born from the head of Zeus,
attended by Hephaistos with an axe. A lip cup by Phrynos
now in the British Museum.

strife-stirring, the host-leader, the unwearying, the
queen, who delights in tumults and wars and battles.
But Hera without union with Zeus – for she was very
angry and quarrelled with her mate – bare famous
Hephaistos, who is skilled in crafts more than all the
sons of Heaven.'[21]

There is here no direct reference to an armed Athena,
but there is one in an alternative version which was
quoted by the Stoic Chrysippos and the physician
Galen, and which also makes reference to the aegis
borne by the goddess:

'The father of the gods and men gave her birth by
way of his head on the banks of the river Trito.
And she, even Metis, remained hidden beneath the
inward parts of Zeus, Athena's mother, worker of
righteousness, who was wiser than gods or mortal
men. There the goddess [Athena] received that [i.e.
the aegis] whereby she excelled in strength all the

deathless ones who dwell in Olympos. And with it
[Zeus] gave her birth, arrayed in arms of war.'[22]

Such a birth of Athena may well be represented on a
jar decorated with reliefs from Tenos, of the first half
of the seventh century (see overleaf). A late and
learned commentator speaks of Stesichoros (in the
early sixth century) as the first exponent of the birth
of an armed Athena. Possibly earlier than this (but of
uncertain date) is a charming *Hymn to Athena*:

'I begin to sing of Pallas Athene, the glorious goddess, bright-eyed, inventive, unbending of heart,
pure virgin, saviour of cities, courageous, Tritogeneia. From his awful head wise Zeus himself bare
her arrayed in warlike arms of flashing gold, and
awe seized the gods as they gazed. But Athena
sprang quickly from the immortal head and stood
before Zeus who holds the aegis, shaking a sharp
spear; great Olympos began to reel fearfully at the

Above: Detail of an amphora from Tenos showing the birth of Athena from a four-armed Zeus (influenced by the Orient). This probably dates from the seventh century BC, although Athena wears an eighth-century helmet.
Opposite: The birth of Athena from the head of Zeus, attended by Hephaistos (left) and Eileithyia (?) (right). Attic red-figured *pelike*.

might of the bright-eyed goddess, and earth round about cried dreadfully, and the sea was moved and tossed with dark waves, while foam burst forth suddenly: the bright son of Hyperion stopped his swift-footed horses a long while, until the maiden Pallas Athene had stripped her heavenly armour from her immortal shoulders. And wise Zeus was glad.'[23]

The type was thus set for the representation of the Birth on early sixth-century bronze reliefs from Olympia, and on Attic black-figure vases of the mid-century. In earlier literature no mention was made of the good offices of Hephaistos (or Prometheus) whose axe split the skull of Zeus, though he is present on the Olympic bronzes and on the Attic Phrynos cup. He is mentioned by Pindar:

'When through Hephaistos' arts and his bronze-bound axe, Athena sprang down the crest of her father's head, and shouted with an exceeding great cry, and heaven and mother-earth shuddered before her.'[24]

The begetting of Athena and the happenings described as attendant on her birth, coupled with the thunderbolt-hurling and cloud-gathering propensities of her father, have in both ancient and modern times contributed to interpretations in terms of intellectual ideas and natural phenomena, and it cannot be denied that there is this element in the developed myths. On the other hand, the swallowing of Metis at any rate seems an early idea, together with the reasons given for it, to match the stories of the overthrow of Ge (Earth) and Ouranos (Heaven), to be replaced by Kronos and Rhea, and the displacement of Kronos by Zeus. The stories are clearly primitive, as with the castration by Kronos of his father, and the swallowing of his children, and Rhea's deception by substituting the swaddled stone for Zeus. Something of the same primitive quality attends what became the prime symbol of Athena: the aegis or goat-skin on which was set the snake-locked head of the Gorgon Medusa slain by Perseus. The episode of the slaying came in in the seventh century; it clearly contains elements of folk-tale and oriental imagery suitable to that period. Exactly when Athena was established in legend as the protector of Perseus is not clear, but she certainly did become his ally and acquired from him the Gorgon's head, which in origin was an apotropaic grimace combined with

The Gorgon Medusa
decapitated, Hermes, Athena
and Perseus. From an Attic
black-figured amphora now in
Munich.

what modern psychologists would call a 'threat stare', ultimately a protective device, and so suitable for a city-protecting goddess (she gave one of its snakes to Tegea to make it impregnable). The goat-skin was originally the storm-raising, terror-inspiring attribute of Zeus, and primitive enough.

Athena, Polias, Poliouchos (as she is called in an archaic dedication), and Archegetis (as she appears in several inscriptions) was protector and leader. A closely associated idea was Bringer of Victory. In a passage of the *Ion* which can only be described as tortuous and turgid, the Chorus summons Athena, referring to her birth from the head of Zeus (and incidentally replacing the intervention of Hephaistos by that of Prometheus), and calling her 'Lady Victory'. In another she is referred to as:

... 'Athena, Queen of victory,
Who by Zeus' chariot once, with spear well armed,
Against the earth-born brood of Giants went, ...'[25]

The participation of Athena in the Battle of the Gods and Giants was an outstanding example of victory-bringing. On the Acropolis the struggle was represented on the metopes of the eastern front of the Parthenon and on the shield of the Parthenos, and Athena's participation – deploying the aegis – in the Peisistratid pediment of the Archaic temple. Similarly Aristophanes, in *The Knights*, calls on Pallas Poliouchos to come bringing Nike (victory). At the great festival of the Panathenaia, all except one of the sacrificial heifers (so splendidly portrayed in the Parthenon frieze) were offered on the great altar of Athena. The one, 'the finest of the best', was sacrificed on the altar of Nike, to Athena Polias and Athena Nike. Pausanias dealing with the Propylaia or entrance gate of the Acropolis mentions very briefly 'on the right of the Propylaia the temple of Nike Apteros'[26]. He goes on to associate this area of the rock with the tale of Aigeus sighting the black-sailed ship of Theseus and casting himself down in despair. Pausanias here calls the tiny temple of the Ionic order, which stands on the south-west bastion of the Acropolis, a temple of Wingless Victory.

Victory was conventionally rendered with wings deployed, as for example the one held by the gold and ivory statue of Athena in the Parthenon, the work of

Detail of an Attic black-figured jug showing the combat of Athena against the Giant Enkelados.

The 'best of the best'. A probable representation of the sacrifice to Athena Nike at the open-air altar on the site of the temple of Athena Nike. Attic black-figured vase.

Pheidias: presumably also the gold-covered Victories dedicated on the Acropolis as a reserve of wealth were similar. The Victories are winged on the Nike Balustrade, and airborne, too, in the case of the Nike of Paionios at Olympia. But these were detached personifications, and it is clear from other evidence that Victory on the Acropolis was an attribute of Athena, and the temple was that of Athena Nike. The bastion, which was certainly of great importance already in Late Mycenaean times, is a very suitable place for the cult of a protecting and victorious goddess – Polias united with Nike, as at the sacrifice in the Panathenaia, which must have taken place here. A standing, or better, a striding figure of Athena as on the prize amphorae of the Panathenaia (and Nike could relate to victory in festival contests too) must have stood upon the bastion. It seems there was an altar here from the second quarter of the sixth century. In the later Ionic temple a late lexicographer claims there was an ancient statue, but that it held a helmet in its left hand, and a pomegranate in its right: the latter attribute as unsuited to Victory as the distaff (of female pursuits) at Erythrai to Athena Polias. The best way out is to say it may not originally have stood in this location.

An important inscription of the fifth century (unhappily of disputed date) provides for a priestess of Athena Nike, and her office (unlike so many connected with the Acropolis) was democratically (or seemingly so) open to all the women of Athens. There was also to be constructed a stone altar and a temple. The inscription makes clear that there was already in existence a *hieron* (sanctuary) for which a gate was to be provided. This was either the ancient precinct or an earlier fifth-century shrine.

Under the southern wall of the Acropolis, Asklepios the God of Healing had his shrine. His daughter was Hygieia, and it appears that on the Acropolis – one virgin to another – Athena assimilated her to herself in a cult of some importance, since a number of dedications survive to Athena Hygieia, including one by the potter Euphronios. It is difficult to say how old the cult was. It has been suggested that Hygieia was concerned not only with physical but also with mental health, and was thus suitably assimilated to the goddess of wisdom. On his visit to the Acropolis Pausanias saw, inside the Propylaia at the inside south corner (or at any rate between the Propylaia and the precinct of Artemis Brauronia), a statue of Athena Hygieia, the work of Pyrrhos. Like several other dedications on the Acropolis, it illustrates the way archaeology and material remains can frequently augment or even correct the vague or sometimes slipshod narratives of ancient writers. With this dedication it seems possible to connect a story of Plutarch in his *Life of Pericles*, telling of the workman who fell from the Propylaia and seemed injured beyond recovery. Athena (as Parthenos rather than Hygieia) appeared in a dream to Pericles and prescribed a herb (subsequently called Parthenion) which cured the man, and so Pericles set up a statue to Athena Hygieia at a spot where there was already an altar. Plutarch, here again illustrating the weaknesses of late writers, speaks first of a bronze and then of a gold statue (confusion with the Parthenos) and of Pheidias, not Pyrrhos. The cult is very likely to be located at this spot, and other dedications indicate it as considerably earlier than the Periclean period. As a cynical scholar of an older generation has pointed out, the virgin successor to Athena on the Acropolis, the Virgin Mary, did better than Athena on the occasion of a similar accident; 'when the ladder broke, she held the workman suspended in mid air'.

This will suffice for the time being as an account of the deities, their assimilations and their cults directly associated with and centred on the rock of the Acropolis. The point, however, should be made, that two great heroes associated together in, for instance, the metopes of the Athenian Treasury at Delphi, have little connection with the Acropolis. They are Theseus and Herakles: the former released from imprisonment in Hades (after the episode of the attempted abduction of Persephone by Theseus and Peirithöos) by the good offices of the latter. They resemble each other in their many and colourful adventures, and in their culture-hero aspect, as ridding the world of monsters. Herakles became the Dorian hero par excellence as ancestor of the two lines of Spartan kings. He was, on the other hand, a protégé of Athena too. Not only does she appear, to his aid and comfort, on the metopes of the temple of Zeus at Olympia, but there is also an endless association of the two on Attic black- and red-figured vases, on which also his Labours are popular. Though a Dorian hero, he has a modest place in the Archaic sculptural art of the Acropolis, wrestling with a fish-bodied monster, slaying the Hydra, and being introduced to Olympos by Athena. It is curious, therefore, how much less popular on Attic decorated pottery are the exploits of Theseus, with the exception of the slaying of the Minotaur.

Athena introduces Herakles to Zeus on Olympos.
From a black-figured lip-cup by Phrynos.

The youthful Theseus,
supported by a sea creature
and attended by Athena,
in the presence
of Amphitrite.

He rarely appears in association with Athena: a well-known exception is the fine red-figured cup-interior, showing a very youthful Theseus supported by Athena in the presence, beneath the sea, of Amphitrite, wife of Poseidon. He is absent from the Acropolis. This is odd, since the festival of the Synoikia which celebrated the union of Attica under Athens commemorated the achievement of Theseus, and was in honour of Athena. It may be that he was felt to be a somewhat disreputable character who died in exile; on the other hand what purported to be his bones were brought back by Kimon with great éclat from Skyros. It could also be argued that his connection was with Poseidon; hence his descent to the sea-bed, to the realm of the sea god, the subject of the vase painting mentioned above, and of a poem by Bacchylides. It may be added that he has his place in

art on some of the metopes of the mid-fifth century temple formerly called the Theseum, overlooking the Market-place, which is in reality a temple of Hephaistos, with whom not only Theseus is associated but also Athena, as Athena Ergane, patroness of arts and crafts, appropriately enough in what was an industrial area of Athens. It is well, however, to utter a *caveat*. Arguments from pot-painters' choice of themes (which must ultimately be determined by the preference of their customers) are frequently adduced to prove this or that point of cult or mythology. Yet such evidence can be vitiated by the chances of preservation, and the infrequency of Theseus' appearances may be accidental, just as the contest of Athena with Poseidon for the land of Attica, or Poseidon striking the rock, seem rarely represented. Nonetheless Theseus' absence from the Acropolis is odd.

Besides the associations in which Athena was directly or indirectly concerned and which centred immediately on the Acropolis, the rock was the point of departure or the goal of other ceremonial in which Athena was honoured or involved.

Closer than most ceremonial to Athena and her ancient image was its decking and cleaning, involved in the festivals of the Kallynteria and the Plynteria, on the 19th and the 24th days of the Attic month Thargelion (May-June). The latter ceremony is attested in an inscription of *c.* 460 BC. Ancient literary authorities, mostly late, comment on an association with the death of Aglauros and give details of what was done. The temple in which the ancient image was kept was roped off and closed – a time when Athenians avoided undertaking business – the image was divested of its robe, and veiled; secret ceremonial was carried out by the *Praxiergidai*, perhaps originally an ancient guild. Some were appointed to wash the robe, and the image itself was conveyed, escorted in the fourth century by the *epheboi*, the young men of Athens under military training, to the sea at Phaleron, to be ceremonially bathed. It is unlikely that there was any particular connection with the sea god. After all, the initiates to the Eleusinian Mysteries bathed themselves and their sacrificial piglets similarly in the sea. After this ceremonial bathing, the image of Athena was escorted back to the Acropolis in a torch-light procession. The festival of the Plynteria seems more important, or is known in more detail, than the Kallynteria, in which it is to be presumed that the *Praxiergidai* – probably aiding the Priestess of Athena – decked the ancient statue with ornaments distinct from the *peplos* (robe), which was itself involved in the ceremonial of the Panathenaia.

These were early summer festivals (May-June); and in the height of summer (June-July) the Skirophoria was celebrated in the same month as the Arrhephoria already described. It is generally regarded as a festival belonging to the Eleusinian goddesses Demeter and Persephone (Kore), and concerned with the death and renewal of life and the fertility of the earth. But Athena had a part in it. The priestess of Athena Polias, and the priests of Poseidon-Erechtheus (carrying a sunshade) and of Helios (the sun god) processed from the temple of Athena Polias to Skiron, just outside the walls of Athens on the Sacred Way to Eleusis. It was believed it took its name from Skiros, a seer who fell in the war between Erechtheus and the Eleusinians. Athena Skiras had a temple there, and in the course of the

festival, sacrifice was made to Athena, and mystic objects – *skira* (probably cakes in the form of snakes and phalloi) – were offered to the Eleusinian deities Demeter and Kore. In the procession, too, was carried the skin of the purificatory scapegoat sacrificed to Zeus Meilichios.

This complex ceremonial was conducted by the clan of the Eteoboutadai, who provided the priest of Poseidon-Erechtheus and the priestess of Athena Polias. It was one of those ancient families of Athens, which were so much involved in the legend and ceremonial of the city, and gained thereby great prestige and influence until the fifth century and the rise of rationalism and the radical democracy, and the decline in the value of money. Pausanias gives the information that the paintings in the western section of the Erechtheum represented 'the race of the Boutadai'. The clan ancestor was Boutes, 'the ploughman', worshipped at an altar in the Erechtheum. The name recalls the ceremonial of the ox at the altar of Zeus Polieus, and is obviously associated with agriculture. So was the ceremonial of a sacred ploughing, carried out in three locations: at Skiron, at the 'Rarian field' at Eleusis, and at the 'Palladion' somewhere near the Acropolis. The ploughing at Eleusis is clearly an ancient and separate counterpart to that at Athens. Eleusis seems to have possessed a Boutes of its own, with a priesthood held by the clan of the Kerykes, a prominent family of Eleusis concerned with the Mysteries. The ploughing at Skiron was obviously at a meeting place between the cults of Athens and Eleusis. At the 'Palladion' in Athens, Athena appears again. There Zeus and Athena were worshipped, and the sacred ploughing was conducted by the priest of the deities who was a member of the clan of the Bouzygai ('ox-yokers'). Once more Athena is associated with agriculture.

In the literary texts many obscurities and variants of detail, and sometimes of reading, occur. Thus there is the ceremony of the Procharisteria celebrated when the sown seed of the corn first began to grow. The text may mean that the offerings were made 'to Athena' or 'to Kore', or possibly both. It may be correct here (and elsewhere) to identify Athena with the fertility of the soil and as an 'agricultural goddess'. The same problem arises with the festival of the Oschophoria, which included a race by the Athenian *epheboi* carrying a fruit-bearing shoot of the vine from the temple of Dionysos to the temple of Athena Skiras at Phaleron. Again it is observed that at fertile

Phlya in the plain of Athens, the cult of Athena Tithrone (a title suggesting sexual intercourse) appears with those of a number of other deities concerned with the fertility of the soil. It is questionable, however, how original the connections of Athena are with such matters of fertility. Certainly a strong case can be made for this type of association taking the Acropolis as a locality: starting from the Arrhephoroi and the secret objects they bore, clearly denoting elements of a fertility cult. It is worth pointing out that Errhephoroi ('dew-bearers') seem also to have served Demeter and Kore, and Ge-Themis. Ge-Karpophoros (Earth the fruit-bearer) was also present on the Acropolis, as an inscription indicates. There was a shrine of Demeter Chloe ('of the green or burgeoning vegetation'), and at no great distance was the Eleusinion, again belonging to Demeter and Kore. Demeter as Kourotrophos ('nurturer of youth') was worshipped in the sanctuary of Aglauros on the North Slope of the Acropolis, where from the late fourth century, if not before, young men come to maturity, the fruit of human fertility, took the oath of loyalty to Athena.

The Acropolis was associated with Boutes (the Ploughman) and with Kekrops, Erechtheus and Erichthonios, all Earth-born. One way or another they came to be associated with Athena and subordinated to her, as were Aglauros and Pandrosos. It is clear from the Skirophoria that at some time a meeting took place halfway between the deities of Eleusis and those of Athens, and Athena had her part, as she did in the Oschophoria and possibly in the Procharisteria. But was she so involved from the primitive beginnings? It is easy to see that as keeper of the city she was concerned in every aspect of its fertility: the olive, the vine and the corn, and above all the human youth. The same thing, perhaps in a lesser measure, applied to Zeus Polieus in the same capacity. On the other hand, the position of Poseidon, the third great Olympian, is quite obscure in this connection, except for his close association with Erechtheus, and the presence of the Ploughman in the same shrine. He shared a priesthood with Erechtheus, and was at the same time his slayer. There is also the question of his relationship with Athena. Contestant with her for the land of Attica, he was nevertheless closely associated with her and shared one of her temples on the Acropolis. It is worth noting that the dedicator of an offering there, in return for some unspecified but rich harvest from the sea, saw nothing odd in referring to

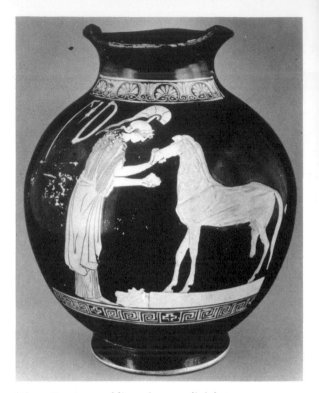

Athena Ergane moulding a horse; a link between Athena Hippia and Poseidon Hippios, and between Athena Ergane and Hephaistos.

'the ruler of the sea, Lord of the Golden Trident'. The same association existed elsewhere. Not far from Athens – at Lakiadai – Poseidon and Athena were associated together, and with Demeter and Kore; while at Kolonos Hippios – the 'White Kolonos' of Sophocles – Athena Hippia was worshipped together with Poseidon Hippios. This Athena 'of the horses' looks like a late intrusion into the sphere of Poseidon. There is here something eminently civilising about her activities: teaching the craft of managing horses to Erichthonios, and providing a bridle for Bellerophon to subdue Pegasos. All this is very different from Poseidon's Arcadian consort, the horse-headed Demeter of Phigaleia, reflecting so much that is barbarous and primitive.

Athena's association with Hephaistos (whom an ancient version asserted Hera had produced without the aid of Zeus) is less difficult to explain. Whatever the version of the begetting of Erichthonios, Hephaistos and Athena were worshipped together at the grove of the Academy, sharing the cult with that other promoter of arts and crafts for man, Prometheus, whom Athena aided in the creation of Pandora –

though not this time to man's advantage. A statue of Athena stood by that of Hephaistos in his temple on the Kolonos Agoraios, overlooking the Market-place and the industrial district of Athens which eventually stretched up to the south-west slope of the Acropolis. The association of the two went back to Solon in the early sixth century and probably earlier, but there is no doubt that the seniority belonged to Hephaistos. The festival of the Chalkeia (the bronze-workers' festival) was pre-eminently a festival of Hephaistos as smith god, but some claimed it was also the Athenaia, and during it, on the last day of Pyanepsion (October-November), 'the priestess, the Arrhephoroi and other adult women, set up the warp for the new robe of Athena'. Given Athena's quality as daughter of Metis and goddess of wisdom, the crafts – and pre-eminently the feminine ones, including weaving – were hers, and the arts such as the invention of the flute. She thus acquired, reasonably enough, the title

Ergane, which does not appear to have been a cult title, and an association with Hephaistos.

It is not an ill-judged conclusion that Athena, Zeus and Poseidon acquired a great many of their cult associations and characteristics by assimilation. Athena took over Pandrosos and Aglauros, as Poseidon took over Erechtheus. She thus replaced (not only at Athens) other local protectors and promoters of well-being, as Apollo replaced other oracle-giving powers. In the case of Athena much went, so to speak, with the Acropolis. It is also reasonable to say that Athena, as protector and patron of Athens and Attica must have been involved in promoting the fertility of the land and the people. But it would be a mistake to make a facile assertion for her of a primitive association with fertility, and consequently a remote derivation from the female powers or principles of Neolithic times, which are so widely distributed and concerned with the life of plants, animals and men. It would be

The area of new excavation below the south face of the Acropolis, showing an ancient bronze-casting pit.

equally dangerous to assert too readily the Minoan-Mycenaean culture as the connecting link. On the one hand there is the A-ta-na po-ti-ni-ja of the Linear B tablets, certainly, but also – at Mycenae and Athens – the vexed question of the relationship of this deity with Potnia Athena. It may be she was so vaguely and largely conceived that assimilation was easy. One thing is certain: because of her existence as an object of worship elsewhere, she cannot be a projection of the city. Did she then give her name to it? A good deal more will have to be revealed about Bronze Age Greece before this problem is solved.

Whatever problems of original and acquired functions and characteristics arise in connection with the other cults and ceremonies involving Athena, there can be little doubt that the greatest of Athena's festivals, the Panathenaia, was specifically directed to her glorification and that of Athens. It was asserted that it had been founded by Erichthonios as the Athenaia, and renamed the Panathenaia by Theseus on his effecting the union of the land. The great festival was not in the charge of an ancient family. It was emancipated from religious particularism, and was directed to a purely religious end. In this connection, therefore, men could look up to the Acropolis with pride and devotion, where at other times (when it was the seat of a king or a tyrant) their sentiments might be of fear or hatred. How the men of Athens would look up at Athena's domain in the great days of the fifth century BC is nobly expressed by Thucydides in the words of Pericles in his Funeral Speech in honour of those fallen in war:

'You must yourselves realise the power of Athens and feed your eyes upon her from day to day and become her lovers; and then when all her greatness shall break upon you, you must reflect that it was by courage, sense of duty, and a keen feeling of honour in action that men were enabled to win all this . . .'[27]

And the inhabitants of 'violet-crowned' Athens can never have felt so proud of their city or so conscious of its greatness and unity as when they saw the Panathenaic procession winding its way across the Marketplace, and up and through the Periclean Propylaia to the altar above. As Demosthenes says, in the sadly reduced days of the fourth century BC:

'You have heard and know this, indeed, that those who built the Propylaia and the Parthenon, and embellished the other sanctuaries of the gods after their devastation by the barbarians, left their city and were penned up in Salamis. By the ships they had they triumphed on the sea, and preserved their possessions and the city, and brought many and great blessings to the other Greeks, of which the passage of time cannot erase the memory.'[28]

Some other Greeks might feel differently, but there is no doubt about most of the Athenians. Their unity was hard won and precariously maintained; the festival must have contributed greatly to this end.

It is not known when the festival was instituted. It could be argued that Solon was the first concerned with the political unity of Athens and Attica, and marked a crisis in Athenian affairs, but no reference is made to Solon in this connection. It was believed that an important date in relation to the festival was the year 566/65 BC, when Hippokleides was chief archon, and again it was generally accepted that the intervention of the Attic tyrant Peisistratos, and of one of his sons, was particularly important. The ancient suggestion that it all had to do with the slaying of the Giant Asterios sounds like ignorance of its real origins, unless this was suggested by the woven or embroidered decoration of the robe of Athena, which seems to have portrayed the Battle of the Gods and Giants, or part of it. It is natural to assume that the robe (which was woven by the Arrhephoroi and other Athenian females), and its conveyance to the Acropolis, was an original part of the ceremonial This garment (in which the statue was clad) may imply a primitive statue of much the same sort as the Apollo of Amyklai. It is in fact described by one of the Christian Fathers, Tertullian, as '. . . Athenian Pallas . . . standing forth formless, a rough stake, a shapeless bit of wood'. This sounds like a standing figure of a very primitive sort which could be clothed, in which case the ceremonial may also have been ancient, or instituted later to embellish a primitive figure no longer acceptable in its pristine state. It can also be argued that the state management of the festival, by the *hieropoioi*, implies a relatively late date, whereas clan control would not.

It is generally assumed that in Classical times the robe was offered every four years at the greater festival, which is taken to be of later institution. Some ancient authorities, on the other hand, suggest that a robe was offered every year. From October/November to July/August seems a reasonable period for its preparation; the period of time from one great festival to another seems excessive. Yet if there was a yearly replacement, why was there a cleaning ceremonial at the Plynteria in May/June? It could be that the robe offered to Athena was laid across the knees of a seated statue, as at Troy where, in the *Iliad*[29], Theano, the priestess of Athena, receives the gift of a robe, the work of Sidonian women, and so disposes of it, praying for victory to Athena Rhusipolis (Saviour of the City). In this case, the cleansing would relate either to the statue only or to the shrine. On the other hand there is a late reference to the *Praxiergidai*, who 'dress' the statue of Athena called the *hedos* (though this does not absolutely establish that it was a seated figure).

The festival of the Panathenaia was celebrated yearly from the 28th Hekatombaion (July/August) and lasted two days. Every four years (or as the Greeks would say, every fifth), in the third year of the Olympiad, a Great Panathenaic festival was celebrated which must have lasted at least four days. The date was the traditional one for the birth of Athena. It is generally agreed that there was, for the Great Panathenaia, a progressive accretion of associated activities, and that the festival reached its fullest development in the fifth century BC or later. The date 566/65 BC might well be the time at which some athletic or vehicular contests were first introduced, and the style of the earliest known of the Panathenaic amphorae, in which the prize oil from the sacred olives was distributed to the victors, would fit in well with this date. Additions were probably made, and the festival generally embellished, again to stress the idea of union and offset clan-directed cults, in the time of the Peisistratid tyrants. Of first-class interest are two statements made in the fourth century BC: the first, that Hipparchos, the younger son of Peisistratos, first introduced the epic of Homer to Athens; and the second, from a reliable source, that only the poems of Homer were recited at the festival. The first statement has been interpreted as meaning that Hipparchos imported from Ionia the text which became official for the Panathenaia, and compelled the *rhapsodes* (epic reciters) to go through the poems, 'taking up the cues in succession' (following the official text). This seems better than to suggest a special Peisistratid recension of the text. There is evidence of musical contests from the middle of the fifth century, of flute playing, and singing to the lyre, and Pericles is credited with their institution and supervision. Other contests could well have been added later. The multiplicity of the athletic

The Warrior Athena on the Burgon Panathenaic amphora in the British Museum.

contests is attested by the Panathenaic amphorae which show on one side the striding figure of Athena (Nike?) between pillars surmounted by cocks (whose significance is disputed), and on the other, various types of competition.

Central to the ceremonial, and surely original to it, was the *pannychis* (night festival) on the night of 27/28 Hekatombaion, with a torch race (as in the festival of Prometheus), and the dancing and shouts of maidens, as described by Euripides in the *Heraclidae*:

'Thy rites we e'er fulfil
Nor fails the festival of song and dance
As months come round.
Upon thy windswept hill
The feet of maidens tread throughout the night
And shouts resound'[30]

followed on the 28th by the great procession marshalled at the Pompeion outside the Dipylon Gate under the general charge of the *hieropoioi*. From there it went by a processional route (at the side of which there seems to have been provision for grandstands) across the Market-place, from the area of the Kolonos Agoraios, past the Eleusinion to the ascent to the Propylaia, to attain the summit of the rock and the great altar of Athena by a route which passed north of the Parthenon. There the sacrifices were made, and to the Priestess of Athena, and perhaps to the *Praxier-gidai*, was handed over the *peplos* (robe) which was the centre-piece of the procession. The weaving of it, and its inception at the Chalkeia have already been mentioned. The battle of the Gods and Giants was either woven into the wool fabric, or else embroidered on it. It might have resembled the Mantle of Despoina at Lykosoura in Arcadia. Later, Plutarch says, there were added the figures of the Hellenistic rulers, successors of Alexander, Antigonos and his son Demetrios the Besieger. This was part of the distressful adulation of the great which marked Athens in the days when her greatness had departed. So, too, later, according to Plutarch:

'The Athenians gave him (Demetrios), as his lodging, the back temple in the Parthenon, and here he lived, under the immediate roof, as they meant it to imply, of his hostess Athena – no reputable or well-conducted guest to be quartered on a maiden goddess!'[31]

The robe was conveyed attached to the mast of a vehicle in the form of a ship. This ship formed part of the procession, though it does not appear on the Parthenon frieze. It is a curious feature which looks as if it had been present from an early date. It is a pity more information is not available, or illustrations of it more satisfactory than a battered remnant of a Christian sculptured frieze. There are several small references to the ship, and a fuller account from Philostratos the Sophist, of the early third century A.D. In his *Life* of Herodes Atticus, who did so much to provide Athens with amenities in the age of Marcus Aurelius, he relates:

'When he [Herodes Atticus] was offered the crowning honour of the charge of the Panathenaic festival, he made this announcement: "I shall welcome you, O Athenians, and those Hellenes that shall attend, and the athletes who are to compete, in a stadium of pure white marble." In accordance with this promise he completed within four years the stadium on the other side of the Ilissos, and thus constructed a monument that is beyond all other marvels, for there is no theatre than can rival it. Moreover I have been told the following facts concerning *this* Panathenaic festival. The robe of Athena that was hung on the ship was more charming than any painting, with folds that swelled before the breeze, and the ship as it took its course was not hauled by animals, but slid forward by means of underground machinery. Setting sail at the Kerameikos with a thousand rowers, it arrived at the Eleusinion, and after circling it, passed by the Pelasgikon, and thus escorted came by the Pythion, where it is now moored.'[32]

It is clear that this was a very special Panathenaic festival, celebrated by a man of immense wealth. The ship was special, whatever the exaggeration of the writer. It may also be said that its route might have been related to the stadium of Herodes, which has been restored in modern times and stands on Mount Ardettos on the other side of the Ilissos stream (now underground), beyond the temple of Olympian Zeus, in an area which, as Thucydides points out, was of ancient importance, where the Lesser Mysteries were celebrated 'in Agrai', and where the ancient King Kodros had his residence. Here probably was the most ancient temple of Dionysos 'in the Marshes'. On the other hand a Pythion and a shrine or a cave of Olympian Zeus existed (as has been seen) on the north-west shoulder of the Acropolis, and better suited for the observation of lightning flashes on Parnes, and for the topography of the normal Panathenaic procession.

This odd use of a ship and its mast and yard for the carriage of the robe as a sail, is attested by a writer of Attic comedy of the fifth century BC. It defies explanation. It might be added that there was, as another oddity, a 'competition of boats', though we do not know where. Possibly there was a connection with Theseus and his ship. Ships suggest the sea and Poseidon. It has been suggested that this ship is an imitation of the ship of Dionysos which, complete with wheels, appears on Attic vases. But the coming of Dionysos is closely bound up with a ship: Athena has no such connection. It might be that the ship and those who propelled it represented the fleet of Imperial Athens and the *thetes* (lower-class Athenians who rowed in it), to offset those young gentlemen who, in the procession of the Parthenon frieze, figure so largely with their splendid horses. This would imply a fifth-century date for the introduction of the ship. However, this is all purest conjecture.

Part of the Panathenaic Procession on the Parthenon
frieze showing delegates from Athenian colonies,
or Athenian citizens, with cattle as victims for the sacrifice.

Below: Four men and three rams from the Parthenon frieze.
The slab probably represents Athenian colonists leading
victims to sacrifice, as Athenians themselves did not sacrifice
sheep or rams.
Opposite: Another section of the Parthenon frieze showing
three youths carrying amphorae, possibly
for wine, and a fourth raising one from the ground.

The robe was the centre of the procession. It was attended by a great host of participants, who are represented on the frieze of the Parthenon. With them went the animals, heifers and lesser kine to be sacrificed to Athena Polias on her great altar. Probably, as in the yearly Panathenaia of the late fourth century BC, a special sacrifice was also made to Athena Hygieia and to Athena Polias coupled with Athena Nike, and certainly, as in the yearly festival, the meat of the victims was distributed to the people by demes (small, local units of population like our parishes) with some reserved for priests and officials. Sacrifices were the main source of meat for the ordinary citizen.

Both the frieze and the literary sources give the details of the participants. There were the *kanephoroi*, 'the maidens tall and stately', of noble family, who bore the *kana* (baskets). Others, too, appear on the frieze, in attendance on the robe (either the new robe or the old) held by the priest. There were the dignified old men, the *thallophoroi* (bearers of olive branches), and the resident aliens, clad in purple raiment, bearing trays of sacrificial cakes; their womenfolk, too, carried waterpots and sunshades. One would prefer to interpret their participation as an honour accorded by Athena even to non-citizens; but it might have been an obligation imposed in return for the privilege of their association with Athens, just as the colonies of Athens were required to send to the Great Panathenaia representatives offering an ox and a set of armour.

Above all, there was the cavalry of Athens, an aristocratic form of military service. On their magnificent horses they form the finest part of the great

frieze – especially the young men with their haughty, even arrogant, faces. Indeed the great glory of this procession in stone is provided by the horses rather than the men, as if Athena were appropriating to herself the attribute of her rival. But then she was also Athena Hippia. Added to these in the later fourth century were the *epheboi*, the youth of Athens coming to manhood.

It may be noted here that the Parthenon frieze cannot be just a picture of the procession. It is reasonable to take the preliminaries of marshalling and mounting as part of the procession. The slow-processing maidens and old men might just be combined with the cantering cavalry, but hardly with the chariot horses galloping at full speed and the performance of that manoeuvre wherein *apobatai* (fully armed warriors) dropped off a fast-moving chariot and joined it again: an exercise invented, it was said, by Erechtheus.

It must all have been a splendid spectacle, for the inspiration of the citizens who contemplated it from stands along the route. No doubt they did so with their characteristic mixture of ribaldry and reverence. Some of them viewed the procession and the crowning glory of Periclean Athens with divided minds, approving the glory, but deploring some aspects of the radical democracy under Pericles which had produced it all. The spiritual and political dilemma is strongly present in Aristophanes, and nowhere more so than in *The Knights*, the play named from those same horsemen of the Parthenon who form the chorus of the play. They deplore contemporary politics in 424 BC, in the difficult days – politically and militarily – of the Peloponnesian War, but in their prayers they unite Poseidon and Athena:

'Dread Poseidon, the Horseman's King,
Thou who lovest the brazen clash,
Clash and neighing of warlike steeds;
Pleased to watch where the trireme speeds

Purple-beaked to the oar's long swing,
Winning glory (and pay); but chief
Where bright youths in their chariots flash
Racing (coming perchance to grief);
Cronus's son,
Throned on Geraestus and Sunium bold,
Swaying thy dolphins with trident of gold,
Come, O come, at the call of us;
Dearest to Phormio thou,
Yea and dearest to all of us,
Dearest to all of us now.'

Let us praise our mighty fathers, men who ne'er
     would quake or quail,
Worthy of their native country, worthy of Athene's
     veil;
Men who with our fleets and armies everywhere
     the victory won,
And adorned our ancient city by achievements
     nobly done . . .

'Holy Pallas, our guardian Queen,
Ruling over the holiest land,
Land poetic, renowned and strong,
First in battle and first in song,
Land whose equal never was seen,
Come to prosper our Choral band!
Bring thou with thee the Maiden bright,
Her who greets us in every fight,
Victory!
She in the choir-competition abides with us,
Always against our antagonists sides with us,
Come, great Goddess, appear to us,
Now, if ever, we pray,
Bring thou victory dear to us,
Crown thy Horsemen today.'[33]

In the festival competition in which this play was competing, the victory is three-fold, over dramatic rivals, over what are seen to be the forces of corruption in politics, and in the current war.

Charioteer, armed warrior (*apobates*) and galloping team
from the north frieze of the Parthenon. In the British Museum.

3. The Historical Background

As has been shown in an earlier chapter, the transition from the Bronze Age to the Iron Age represented a lengthy period of upheaval in Greece. For considerably more than a century Athena (or her predecessor) and the Acropolis looked down on a scene of confusion: changes in the ruling house; the incursion of refugees, and possibly some changes of custom, such as modes of burial. Western Attica and Athens may have been more strongly affected than Eastern Attica, but eventually things settled down, and Athens emerged as the centre of Attica and – especially from the standpoint of archaeology – as a chief centre of the Geometric style of decoration in pottery. By the late eighth century Attic pottery was being turned out in large quantities. Splendid great vases were used as grave monuments, portraying funeral biers and funeral processions, chariots, ships and sea-battles in silhouette style. They were either contemporary scenes, or illustrations of the epic. Together with the burials of the seventh century in the Kerameikos cemetery and elsewhere, these monuments would seem to indicate the existence of wealthy families, controlling what was no doubt the best land in an area of Greece not very suited for agriculture, but more for olive culture. In their own eyes they were 'noble', and pre-eminently fitted to rule. They were the forerunners of the families or clans already seen to be active in cult, including the cults of Athena. But of 'history' there is nothing. Athens did not participate in the colonisation movement of the eighth and seventh centuries; nor did the social and political disturbances heard of elsewhere manifest themselves so early in Attica. Developments certainly occurred, such as the union of Attica, which was probably not completed until Eleusis was combined with Attica, perhaps in the seventh century. A few other events float dateless, and can be placed at one point or another to the taste of the historian. Later writers, in the fourth century in particular, concentrated a great deal of attention on mythical events and local cults. The problem is how much they really knew of things distant in time from them, and how they arrived at that knowledge.

Generalised conjecture tends to replace sure knowledge in the case of the Acropolis, as for other sites. It may confidently be asserted that, given the relatively primitive building techniques and the limited capacity for the accumulation of wealth before the late seventh century, public buildings and other forms of major art would be unpretentious, and on a minor scale. The buildings were of wood-framed mud brick on stone footings, and the earliest were also thatched, as certain eighth-century clay models seem to indicate. The institutions and administration which went with them were doubtless equally primitive. In principle the link between the Mycenaean palace and the subsequent worship of Athena on the Acropolis was a conviction of the sanctity of this area on the north side of the rock, rather than the unbroken development of the Mycenaean cult-chapel into the temple of Athena. On the other hand, it could be suggested that there *might* be a civic continuity, from the *megaron* or great hall of the ancient kings to the offices of the archaic magistrates of Athens – if, indeed, they were located there.

When Kodros sacrificed himself, as legend says, the kingship was abolished in his honour, and Athens, had first magistrates for life, then for periods of ten years, and then, from the seventh century, for one year only. The Athenians provided lists of names for the life and decennial magistrates and, for the seventh century, a fragmentary list of annual archons, in which some of the names are suspiciously like those of later prominent figures in Athenian affairs. In fact the kingship was never abolished: there was always a *basileus* (king) in Athens. On the other hand there was at some time a break with the reality of the ancient kingship. It has been suggested that the lineal successor of the Mycenaean king's *megaron* would be the sacred hearth of the city incorporated in the Prytaneion, and that the eastern half of the structure south of the Erechtheum (called for convenience the Doerpfeld Foundation)

Mourners lamenting at the funeral of an Athenian noble. Shoulder panel of a large Attic Geometric vase of the late eighth century, used as a grave memorial.

was just this, in fact a public building. It has also been suggested that the Boukoleion, the public residence of the *basileus*, said to be near the Prytaneion, was also on the Acropolis to the east. This theory has some attractive elements: for instance it connects with the ox of the Diipolia sacrifice, since the Boukoleion means 'the place where cattle are tended'. However, the idea must be rejected in favour of believing that, when the true kingship dwindled amid the confusion of the end of the Bronze Age, the centre of civil government was moved to the lower city. It was a natural move, and the great families of Athens would hardly have allowed one of their number, even temporarily, to hold the Acropolis. So when would-be tyrants occupied the rock, rather than attempting to hold the centre of government, they were of course concerned with its defensive potentialities, but also with the favour and support of Athena herself.

The Acropolis first comes into the light of history (or semi-history) probably in the thirties of the seventh century, when a young man of aristocratic birth, Kylon, victor at Olympia, attempted to introduce at Athens the tyranny which had appeared elsewhere, as for example at nearby Megara, where Theagenes (Kylon's father-in-law) was tyrant. With the aid of a group of Megarians and a faction of his Athenian contemporaries, Kylon occupied the Acropolis, but failed to carry the day and was besieged there with his followers. They were finally reduced by lack of food and water, and while Kylon and his brother escaped, his supporters took refuge as suppliants at 'the altar' (according to Thucydides), or 'at the image', meaning the ancient statue of Athena (according to Herodotus). They tied a line to the statue, and when this connecting link with the sanctity of the goddess was broken, they were attacked by their opponents. Some took refuge at the altar of the Semnai, which must mean the altar of the Awful Goddesses (the Eumenides) on the Areios Pagos, not far from the descent from the Acropolis. This tale, which vividly introduces the approaches to the Acropolis and the holy place of Athena, is the earliest known from literary sources. It indicates the presence of the sacred image, but reveals nothing of any building in which it might have been housed. As far as modern knowledge is concerned, a blank period stretches back from it, and another stretches forward through the economic and political troubles of the late seventh century and the reforms of Solon, through the strife of factions and attempted tyranny,

to the time (probably in the fifties of the sixth century) when Peisistratos, in his first attempt to establish himself as tyrant, seized the Acropolis with his faction but, like Kylon, failed to maintain himself there. In terms of religion it had already become the objective of the Panathenaic festival and others already described.

When Peisistratos, perhaps in 547 BC, finally and firmly established himself with the use of mercenaries, it is natural to think that the mercenary garrison was quartered there, and that the tyrant and his family lived there. If so, there is no indication in what sort of structure. The Acropolis is connected with the disarmament of the Athenian citizens by Hippias, son of Peisistratos; and whatever happened before, in the period of Hippias' oppressive rule after the murder of his brother, the Acropolis must have been his stronghold. When Hippias was attacked and blockaded in the Acropolis in 510 BC by his opponents aided by the Spartans, he seems to have been able to hold out until the capture of his children forced him to surrender. It would therefore seem that the Acropolis was defensible, even in terms of water supply, at any rate for a short time. A few years later, however, the Spartans and their Attic supporters, besieged in turn in the Acropolis, were forced to surrender, so it was clearly not very effective as a long-term stronghold.

There was an interim period, from the fall of the tyranny in 510 BC and the establishment of the limited democracy by Kleisthenes in the last decade of the sixth century, down to 480 BC. The purely historical record is largely blank, though the archaeological and architectural record is not. The event vitally affecting the Acropolis came in 480 BC. Already in 490 BC an expedition sent by Darius, the Great King of Persia, was repelled at Marathon by the Athenians and their allies the Plataians, but in 480 BC the Persians returned under the leadership of Xerxes and, driving down through Greece, entered Attica. The Athenians evacuated their city, taking the ancient image with them, while the sacred snake deserted. The Delphic oracle of Apollo had been profoundly discouraging to the Athenians, and had ultimately bidden them to take refuge in their 'wooden walls', interpreted, under the guidance of Themistokles, to mean the ships of the Athenian fleet. Their victory at Salamis justified this view. But some die-hards thought otherwise, and interpreted the 'wooden walls' as the defences of the Acropolis. It must be supposed that the ancient Mycenaean walls were augmented and strengthened by wooden stockades, otherwise the idea is an odd one. These Athenians barricaded themselves in the Acropolis, and gave so much trouble to the besieging Persians that it must be wondered whether it was not an officially organised delaying action rather than the last stand of zealots. It has been calculated that the resistance may have lasted a fortnight. The Persian attack and capture is thus described by Herodotus:

'They found the city forsaken; a few people only remained in the temple, either the keepers of the treasure, or men of the poorer sort. These persons having fortified the citadel with planks and boards, held out against the enemy. It was in some measure their poverty which had prevented them from seeking shelter in Salamis; but there was likewise another reason which in part induced them to remain. They imagined themselves to have discovered the true meaning of the oracle uttered by the Pythia, which promised that "the wooden wall" would never be taken – the wooden wall, they thought, did not mean the ships, but the place where they had taken refuge.

The Persians encamped upon the hill over against the citadel, which was called Mars Hill by the Athenians, and began the siege of the place, attacking the Greeks with arrows to which pieces of lighted tow were attached, which they shot at the barricade. And now those who were within the citadel found themselves in a most woeful case; for their wooden rampart betrayed them; still, however, they continued to resist. It was in vain that the Peisistratidai came to them and offered terms of surrender – they stoutly refused all parley, and among their other modes of defence, rolled down huge masses of stone upon the barbarians as they were mounting up to the gates; so that Xerxes was for a long time very greatly perplexed, and could not contrive any way to take them.

At last, however, in the midst of these many difficulties, the barbarians made discovery of an access. For verily the oracle had spoken truth; and it was fated that the whole mainland of Attica should fall beneath the sway of the Persians. Right in front of the citadel, but behind the gates and the common ascent – where no watch was kept, and no one would have thought it possible that any foot of man could climb – a few soldiers mounted from the sanctuary of Aglauros, Kekrops' daughter, notwithstanding the steepness of the precipice. As soon as the Athenians saw them upon the summit, some threw themselves headlong from the wall and so perished; while others fled for refuge to the inner part of the temple. The Persians rushed to the gates and opened them, after which they massacred the suppliants. When all were slain, they plundered the temple, and fired every part of the citadel. ... The day after, Xerxes collected together all the Athenian exiles who had come into Greece in his train, and bade them go up into the citadel, and there offer sacrifice after their own fashion. ... I will now explain why I have made mention of this circumstance: there is a temple of Erechtheus the Earth-born, as he is called, in this citadel, containing within it an olive tree and a sea. The tale goes among the Athenians, that they were placed there as witnesses by Poseidon and Athena, when they had their contention about the country. Now this olive tree had been burnt with the rest of the temple when the barbarians took the place. But when the Athenians, whom the king had commanded to offer sacrifice, went up into the temple for the purpose, they found a fresh shoot, as much as a cubit in length, thrown out from the old trunk.

Meanwhile at Salamis, the Greeks no sooner heard what had befallen the Athenian citadel, than they fell into such alarm that some of the captains did not even wait for the council to come to a vote, but embarked hastily on board their vessels, and hoisted sail as though they would take to flight immediately.'[1]

The account given by Herodotus contains a number of interesting points, not least the statement that the fall of the Acropolis was greeted with alarm by the Greeks on the ships, which might indicate that it was an official holding operation. Speaking of the assault, Herodotus refers in a very confused fashion to 'the front of the citadel, but behind the gates and the common ascent', but it is quite clear that he is speaking of the North Slope, and despite problems of what might or might not be guarded, it is more likely that the assault was made from the upper part of the staircase in the cleft near the Arrhephoreion rather than further west where the path descends to the terrace of the caves and possibly to the enclosure of the Pelargikon. The fact that the defenders rolled down stones from above on the attackers at the gates suggests that the wall defences here were a good deal less than complete. Above all, this passage of Herodotus, mentioning as it does the temple of Erechtheus, introduces problems of the utmost importance concerning the nature of the buildings standing on the Acropolis at the time of the Persian invasion.

The initial sacking of the Acropolis is recorded in this passage. After the defeat of the Persians at Salamis and the precipitate retreat of Xerxes himself, his lieutenant Mardonios withdrew into Thessaly for the winter of 480 BC and reoccupied Athens in 479 BC. When it became clear that he could not persuade the Athenians to come over to the Persian side, and that the Spartans were on the march against him from the Peloponnese, Herodotus states that 'he resolved to burn Athens, and to cast down and level with the ground whatever remained standing of the walls, temples and other buildings'. Thus after the battle of Plataia, which was another great victory for the Greeks, the Athenians returned to a totally ruined city. As Thucydides says:

'The Athenian people, after the departure of the barbarian from their country, at once proceeded

to carry over their children and wives, and such property as they had left, from the places where they had deposited them, and prepared to rebuild their city and their walls. For only isolated portions of the circumference had been left standing, and most of the houses were in ruins; though a few remained, in which the Persian grandees had taken up their quarters.'[2]

In the event, political problems of relations with their allies forced them, using every resource of material and labour, to construct walls for the city, which, it is generally agreed, had been without them before. The rest had to wait: and the Acropolis stood in fire-blackened ruins for a considerable time. Herodotus, telling the story of how the Athenians defeated the men of Chalkis in 506 BC, relates that they bound their captives in chains, which they afterwards dedicated on the Acropolis, where he saw them still surviving some sixty years after, 'hanging from walls blasted with fire by the Medes, in front of the western *megaron*'. Parts of the columns and entablature of an Archaic temple

The north wall. Built-in unfluted column drums seen from the inner side of the wall.

appear built into the north wall of the Acropolis, as are also the unfluted column drums of a temple which was in course of construction on the south side of the Acropolis when the Persians came. And so either immediately, or some time after their departure, the Acropolis wall which they had destroyed was rebuilt, at any rate on the north, on approximately the same line as its Mycenaean predecessor.

From the mid-sixth century into the later fifth, five great names are associated with Athens: Peisistratos, the tyrant who laid the foundations of Athenian greatness; Kleisthenes, who established the framework of Athenian democracy; Themistokles, who built up the fleet and wedded Athens to the sea; Kimon, who used that fleet to extend the Delian League founded under the leadership of Athens after the repulse of the Persians; and Pericles, founder of the radical democracy and personification of Athenian greatness. Of these it is certain that Peisistratos must have embellished the Acropolis first. No record remains of an artistic or architectural contribution by Kleisthenes. Themistokles, who saw to the fortification

Fig. 6: The Acropolis and surrounding area in the early fifth century BC, before the Persian sack.
(Solid shading indicates structures existing or assumed to exist in 480 BC; \\\\\\\ indicates buildings under construction (for Older Parthenon see *fig. 11*); ///////// indicates conjecturally located buildings; broken lines indicate later structures.)
1 Eleusinion. 2 Theseion (?). 3 Prytaneion (?). 4 Bouzygion (?). 5 Boukoleion (?). 6 Thesmotheteion (?). 7 Anakeion (?). 8 Cave of Aglauros. 9 Klepsydra fountain. 10 Python. 11 Olympicion. 12 Area of Pelargikon/Pelasgikon. 13 Suggested Enneapylon. 14 Descent to lower terrace. 15 Ancient temple of Athena. 16 Kekropion. 17 Altar of Athena. 18 Older Parthenon. 19 Temple of Dionysos. 20 Sanctuary of the Nymph. 21 Propylaia. 22 Temenos and altar of Athena Nike.

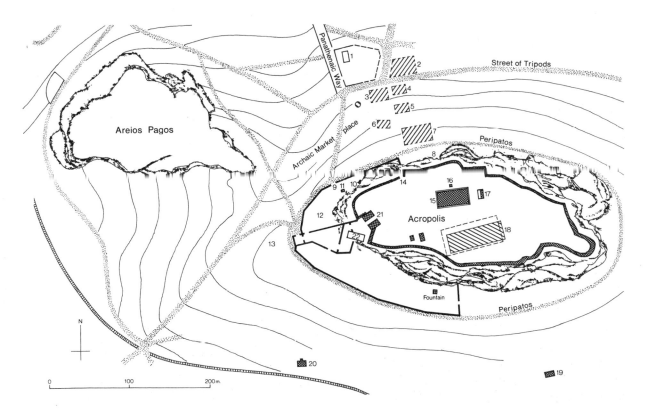

of the harbours of Athens and secured the construction of a wall round the lower city after the retreat of the Persians, seems too active in public affairs not to have made his contribution to the Acropolis. It is difficult to believe he did not play a part in the preparations for the construction of a great temple on the site of the later Parthenon. He may have constructed the north wall with its incorporated fragments. On the other hand, as one who would very willingly have moved the centre of Athenian life down to the Piraeus, he may not have favoured further building at the ancient centre of Athens.

There is no doubt, however, about Kimon, who was active in extending the power of Athens in the seventies and sixties of the fifth century BC. Tradition gives him a great deal of credit for extending the amenities of Athens in terms of tree-planting and landscape improvement, and a walling of the Acropolis is specifically ascribed to him. Pausanias mentions this vaguely; Plutarch more specifically mentions the south wall of the Acropolis (now hidden by a mediaeval one) as erected from the spoils of the battle of Eurymedon, his great defeat of the Persians which probably took place in 469 BC. He is also credited in modern times, though on no very certain grounds, with a simpler predecessor of the Periclean Propylaia or entrance gate, of which traces remain. As in the case of Themistokles, it is difficult to believe that Kimon would not wish to honour Athena, who was so far housed in a ruined Acropolis. An obvious plan would be to resume the project to construct a temple on the south side of the rock (where it sloped down to the Mycenaean wall), utilising the platform already constructed. The Kimonian wall, built outside the Mycenaean, was part of such a plan. But the scheme was not completed since Kimon was exiled in 462 BC and the ascendancy of Pericles began.

From the very departure of the Persians in 479 BC Athens had been intensely involved in the affairs of Greece, developing her naval power and her leadership of the Delian League for reprisals against Persia and the deliverance of those still subject to the Great King. To this activity, in which Kimon had a conspicuous part, Athens added hostilities with members of the Peloponnesian League and Sparta shortly after the exile of Kimon. Athens was not content with establishing undoubted authority in the Delian League. She attacked Persian power in the Eastern Mediterranean and in Egypt, and at the same time sought to be the dominant power in mainland Greece.

All this taxed the resources of Athens, and the apparently tireless Athenian effort ultimately ground to a halt. In 454 BC, by reason of Athenian reverses in Egypt, the treasury of the Delian League was transferred from the island of Delos, which was vulnerable to Persian attack, to be stored on the Acropolis at Athens. From this year a 'tithe' of one sixtieth of the allied contributions was paid to Athena; earlier it had probably been paid to the Delian Apollo. Athens thus had in her hands a very large sum, which was not hers but the League's, and a lesser sum annually passing into the treasury of Athena, in effect the treasury of Athens. In 451 BC a truce was made with Sparta for five years, and in 449 BC (after a campaign against Persia by Kimon, who had returned from exile) peace was made with Persia. For the time being, therefore, there was a lull in Athens' activities, before they were renewed in 446 BC.

It is at this time that Athens under Pericles (but not necessarily under Pericles only) considered the question of replacing the temples destroyed by the Persians – replacing rather than restoring them, since the Greeks were not yet antiquarian-minded in terms of art. This is one of the projects mentioned by Plutarch[3] as the subject of a Panhellenic conference which may be dated to this time, proposed by Pericles, but rejected by Sparta since it was an Athenian initiative. The proposal was 'to take counsel concerning the Greek shrines which the barbarians had burned'. In effect 'Greek' meant 'Athenian', and when the conference proposal was rejected, Athens still went ahead, and a great controversy began. Ostensibly it was concerned with the expenditure of allied money on Athenian buildings: it could be pointed out that if this involved a temple for Athena, she was indeed a Panhellenic goddess, but it would perhaps have been better, in view of the Ionian membership of the League, if it had been a temple of Apollo. The issue was in fact a stick intended by a political opposition to beat the contemporary political regime. Kimon, with his conservative sympathies and connections with the Athenian upper class, was dead, but his mantle had fallen on a member of the same family, Thucydides the son of Melesias, an honest and

The Parthenon at sunrise, showing the rock surface between it and the Propylaia.

well-intentioned man who opposed Pericles and the development of a radical democracy. But under that mantle gathered a whole spectrum of politically animated individuals from moderate democrats to extreme oligarchs. They had now, as later, one thing in common in the matter of public expenditure: concern with the questions of who was to provide the money for public expenditure and who was to benefit from it. They shared this attitude with the wealthier members of the states of the Delian League, which was now fast becoming an Athenian Empire. Most of these states, like Athens, were divided into factions shading from radical democratic to oligarchic. But it was the rich who, directly at any rate, produced the money which paid the contributions to the League treasury. They resented it, and class solidarity felt by the same element in Athens led them to oppose Pericles and the radical democracy. Ultimately it came to a referendum and it was Thucydides who went into exile and Pericles who remained. Thus the Parthenon and other buildings became a political issue. It may be pointed out that another, and eternal, moral principle was involved. Is it morally justifiable to use for such an end – however splendid – money which is wrung from the unwilling, which might be better distributed for the material good of individuals or not exacted at all? Shall the few decide for the many: the citizen population of Attica, or a portion of it, for the inhabitants of the Empire?

The whole issue and its background, including the involvement of Pheidias as a friend of Pericles, is set out by Plutarch in his *Life of Pericles*. It must not be expected that a Greek of the second half of the first century AD bent on edification and by no means reliable in detail, can be taken as a writer of accurate history (if there is such a thing). However, the general impression given by his narrative is probably dependable enough, built as it is on authorities, including writers contemporary with Pericles – and especially the Old Comedy – available to Plutarch but not to modern scholars. In the quotation which follows there are manifest inaccuracies. For example it is doubtful whether there were any 'one-thousand-talent-temples'. It is certain that Pheidias did not die in Athens in prison or by poison. But the general atmosphere is probably well reproduced:

'That which gave most pleasure and ornament to the city of Athens, and the greatest admiration and even astonishment to all strangers, and that which

now is Greece's only evidence that the power she boasts of and her ancient wealth are no romance or idle story, was his [Pericles'] construction of the public and sacred buildings. Yet this was that of all his actions in the government which his enemies most looked askance upon and cavilled at in the popular assembly, crying out how that the commonwealth of Athens had lost its reputation and was ill-spoken of abroad for removing the common treasure of the Greeks from the island of Delos into their own custody . . . and how that "Greece cannot but resent it as an insufferable affront, and consider herself to be tyrannised over openly, when she sees the treasure, which was contributed by her upon a necessity for the war, wantonly lavished out by us upon our city, to gild her all over, and to adorn and set her forth, as it were some vain woman, hung round with precious stones and figures and temples, which cost a world of money."

Pericles, on the other hand, informed the people that they were in no way obliged to give any account of those moneys to their allies, so long as they maintained their defence, and kept off the barbarians from attacking them; while in the meantime the allies did not so much as supply one horse or man or ship, but only found money for the service; "which money," said he, "is not theirs that give it, but theirs that receive it, if so be they perform the conditions upon which they receive it." And that it was good reason, that, now the city was sufficiently provided and stored with all things necessary for the war, they should convert the overplus of its wealth to such undertakings as would hereafter, when completed, give them eternal honour, and for the present, while in process, freely supply all the inhabitants with plenty. With their variety of workmanship and of occasions for service, which summon all arts and trades and require all hands to be employed about them, they do put the whole city, in a manner, into state pay; while at the same time she is both beautiful and maintained by herself. For as those who are of age and strength for war are provided for and maintained in the armaments abroad by their pay out of the public stock, so, it being his desire and design that the undisciplined mechanic multitude that stayed at home should not go without their share of public salaries, and yet should not have them given them for sitting still and doing nothing, to that end he thought fit to bring in among them,

The east end of the Parthenon. Fragment of a large
Ionic capital, of which the *torus* and necking rings are
decorated with palmettes.

with the approbation of the people, those vast
projects of building and designs of work, that
would be of some continuance before they were
finished, and would give employment to numerous
arts, so that the part of the people that stayed at
home might, no less than those that were at sea or
in garrisons or on expeditions, have a fair and just
occasion of receiving the benefit and having their
share of the public moneys ...

As then the works grew up, no less stately in size
than exquisite in form, the workmen striving to
outvie the material and the design with the beauty
of their workmanship, yet the most wonderful
thing of all was the rapidity of their execution.
Undertakings, as any one of which singly might
have required, they thought, for their completion,
several successions and ages of men, were every one
of them accomplished in the height and prime of

one man's political service. ... For which reason Pericles' works are especially admired, as having been made quickly, to last long. For every particular piece of his work was immediately, even at that time, for its beauty and elegance, antique; and yet in its vigour and freshness looks to this day as if it had just been executed. There is a sort of bloom of newness upon those works of his, preserving them from the touch of time, as if they had some perennial spirit and undying vitality mingled in the composition of them.

Pheidias had the oversight of all the works, and was surveyor-general, though upon the various portions other great masters and workmen were employed. For Kallikrates and Iktinos built the Parthenon. ... The Propylaia, or entrances to the Acropolis, were finished in five years' time, Mnesikles being the principal architect ...

When the orators, who sided with Thucydides and his party, were at one time crying out, as their custom was, against Pericles, as one who had squandered away the public money, and made havoc of the state revenues, he rose in the open Assembly and put the question to the people, whether they thought that he had laid out too much; and they saying: "Too much, a great deal." "Then," said he, "since it is so, let the cost not go to your account, but to mine; and let the inscription upon the buildings stand in my name." When they heard him say thus, whether it were out of a surprise to see the greatness of his spirit or out of emulation of the glory of the works, they cried aloud, bidding him to spend on, and lay out what he thought fit from the public purse, and spare no cost, till all were finished. At length, coming to a final contest with Thucydides which of the two would ostracise the other out of the country, and having gone through this peril, he threw his antagonist out, and broke up the confederacy that had been organised against him ...'[3]

None the less he was vulnerable through his friends and associates, and one of these was Pheidias:

'Pheidias the Moulder had undertaken to make the statue of Athena. Now he, being admitted to friendship with Pericles, and a great favourite of his, had many enemies upon this account, who envied and maligned him; who also, to make trial in a case of his, what kind of judges the commons would prove, should there be occasion to bring Pericles himself before them, having tampered with Menon, one who had been a workman with Pheidias, stationed him in the market-place, with a petition desiring public security upon his discovery and impeachment of Pheidias. The people admitting the man to tell his story, and the prosecution proceeding in the assembly, there was nothing of theft or cheat proved against him; for Pheidias, from the very beginning, by the advice of Pericles, had so wrought and wrapt the gold that was used in the work about the statue, that they might take it all off, and make out the just weight of it, which Pericles at that time bade the accusers do. But the reputation of his works was what brought envy upon Pheidias, especially that where he represents the fight of the Amazons upon the goddess's shield, he had introduced a likeness of himself as a bald old man holding up a great stone with both hands, and had put in a very fine representation of Pericles fighting with an Amazon. And the position of the hand which holds out the spear in front of the face, was ingeniously contrived to conceal in some degree the likeness, which meantime showed itself on either side. Pheidias then was carried away to prison, and there died of a disease; but, as some say, of poison, administered by the enemies of Pericles, to raise a slander, or a suspicion at least, as though he had procured it.'[4]

There is much in this which sounds simple-minded. There are other sources of information. A late commentator on a passage of Demosthenes quoted above speaks thus:

'... they built the Propylaia and the Parthenon. After thirty-three years they began to build the shrines, subsequent to the Persian war. They also had made the image [agalma], in the archonship of Euthydemos [431 BC] on the motion introduced by Pericles that the Athenians should make use of [kinein] the five thousand talents in the public treasury brought together from the tribute [raised] according to the assessment of Aristeides.'[5]

This commentary illustrates the difficulties inherent in all such: the figure of years after the Persian war should be thirty-two (447 BC); the archon's name should be Euthynos (450–449 BC); it might be that 'public treasury' should be 'League treasury'. The point of importance is that under the impulse of Pericles the Athenians set out to spend on their city's embellishment the sum of five thousand talents, either the money of the League or a transfer to their own, that is, to the treasury of Athena. This sum was far more than the accumulation of the 'sixtieth' could be from 454 BC on. Hence the outcry and the opposition. A number of inscriptions are contemporary evidence of activity connected with the Acropolis and the two great Periclean constructions of the Parthenon and the Propylaia. There are fragments of Parthenon building accounts from 447–6 BC to 433–2 BC (the last). They give account of purchases of material,

salaries of officials, wages of quarrymen, transport of marble, and payment of sculptors. In 438–7 BC the great gold and ivory statue of the Parthenos was dedicated. Fragments of the accounts concerned with its materials and construction survive. Its dedication implies that the temple was almost structurally complete by that date, and it is reasonable to suppose that the main building activity was transferred to the Propylaia, for which there are fragmentary accounts from 437–6 BC to 433–2 BC. In these accounts there

The eastern (inner) façade of the Propylaia.

The north wall, showing built-in column drums
below the Erechtheum.

are indicated direct payments from the administrators
of the tribute (the 'tithe' to Athena) and other small
payments ultimately from the same tribute source.
The same was probably true earlier of the Parthenon,
in both cases a clear indication of the origins of at
least part of the money spent on these buildings. The
latest accounts of the Propylaia (433–2 BC) coincide
with the preliminaries of the Great Peloponnesian
War. In effect the great gateway was never finished,
but this rather for religious reasons which will be
considered later.

The other two important buildings on the Acropolis – the Erechtheum and the temple of Athena Nike

– are not so clearly dated. The latter, standing on the
south-west bastion of the Acropolis, occupied a site
of a cult of some antiquity. An inscription, the subject
of much debate in relation to its letter forms and date,
provides for the appointment of a priestess to be
chosen democratically from all Athenian women, the
construction of a door to an existing precinct, and
the construction of a temple. The inscription may be
dated to 450–445 BC, in which case there is a long and
odd interval between the decree and the construction
(which has led some to down-date the inscription),
since there is no doubt that the charming little Ionic
temple standing on the south-west bastion is to be

dated *c.* 425 BC, on the grounds of the style of its figured frieze. Later a balustrade with figures of Nikai (Victories) was erected on the edge of the bastion.

The Erechtheum presents a similar problem. The very complex issue of its building centres on an inscription of the year 409 BC, when a commission was appointed to see to the renewed construction of the temple, to report on its unfinished state, and to make an inventory of the materials lying on the site. A large part of this report is preserved on a marble *stele* found by Chandler on the Acropolis in 1765. It shows that the construction of the building was resumed in 409 BC. This was after an interruption caused, in all probability, by the disastrous Sicilian campaign of 415–413 BC. It might be suggested that this complex structure had been started either in the last years of the Periclean era or during the Peace of Nikias after 421 BC, when a considerable degree of euphoria must have prevailed in Athens. After 409 BC and the report of the commission, there are accounts for 409–8 BC and on to 405–4 BC, giving details of those concerned and the amounts they received for the construction of what is, in these accounts, called 'the temple . . . in which is the ancient image'.

Apart from these buildings, so significant for the religious life of Athens, there were other improvements: the strengthening of the Acropolis against runaway slaves (seeking sanctuary?) and robbers. There was also supplementary work concerned with the security of the Acropolis in 434–2 BC, doubtless, like other arrangements, in expectation of war.

The Great Peloponnesian War was won and lost: at intervals in the course of hostilities, in 425 BC (related to the victory at Sphakteria), in 421 BC at the Peace of Nikias, and in 409 BC after the deceptive victories of 410 BC, the Athenians with their usual confidence and optimism engaged in the embellishment of the Acropolis. Then came the final disaster of Aigospotamoi, the ultimate defeat of Athens, the establishment of an oppressive oligarchy, and the occupation of the Acropolis by a Spartan garrison. Soon after – by 403 BC – democracy once again triumphed.

The latter years of the Great Peloponnesian War had cost private individuals and the state dear. Athens had to melt down dedications, including the gold-covered Victories which may have been modelled on the one held by the gold and ivory statue of Athena Parthenos. These were replaced in the fourth century BC by the democracy after the Battle of Knidos, when a flood of Persian gold, ironically enough, came to Athens.

In the fourth century BC there were no outstanding changes involving the Acropolis. Under the regime of Lykourgos – the Eteobutad statesman who was by his family connection closely associated with the Erechtheum in particular – a number of public works were undertaken, but none on the Acropolis.

It had by that time essentially assumed the arrangement which was to be maintained through the Hellenistic period to the Roman era. But from the period of Philip II and Alexander onwards, the Acropolis, like Athens as a whole, was fated to be a victim of greater powers, and its treasures and dedications liable to be converted to other uses than the glory of Athena.

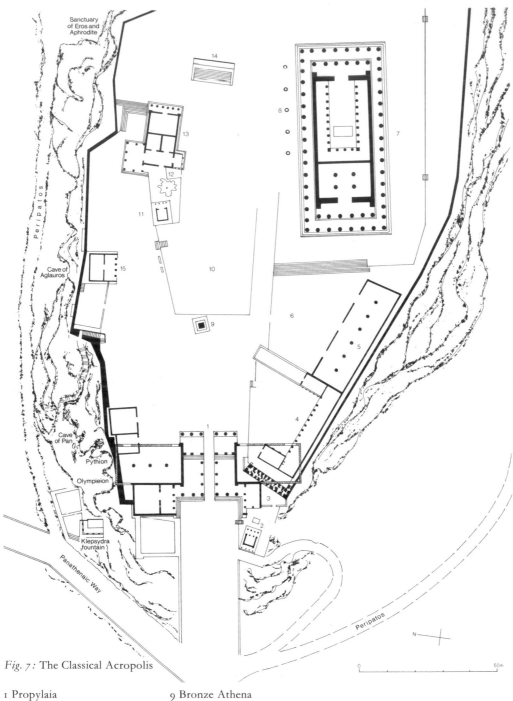

Fig. 7: The Classical Acropolis

1 Propylaia
2 Temple of Athena Nike
3 Mycenaean wall
4 Artemis Brauronia
5 Chalkotheke
6 West court of Parthenon
7 Parthenon
8 Cisterns
9 Bronze Athena
10 Suggested Cyclopean enclosure
11 Pandroseion
12 Kekropion
13 Erechtheum
14 Altar of Athena
15 Arrhephoreion

4. The Buildings

There are three major buildings, of the Classical period, on the Acropolis, two connected with religion (the Erechtheum (13) and the Parthenon (7)), and one secular (the Propylaia (1)). It has been said that the Athenians felt the greatest pride in the Propylaia (Demosthenes, for instance, mentions it first and the Parthenon second), because while the Parthenon was indeed a splendid building – 'grandeur in a temple need cause no surprise' – the Propylaia was 'grander in relation to its function. Such magnificence in a secular building was a splendid extravagance.' Both

a centre of cult and associated with the sacred places of the Acropolis. It stood in a region of the rock clearly of very ancient occupation. So any quest for other ancient vanished temples, with which might be associated the fragments of Archaic architecture and sculpture found on the Acropolis, must first be directed to the Erechtheum and its vicinity. One earlier temple has not wholly disappeared: the foundations of a building of some complexity still remain to the south of the Erechtheum and in very close proximity to it [6, 15]. It has been called the Archaic

A model of the Classical Acropolis.

were more than glories of Athens, they were Hellenic glories, and as such perhaps one way of justifying the fact that they had been paid for (in part at any rate) by Hellenic money.

Demosthenes does not mention the Erechtheum, which was essentially an Athenian shrine, and there was a difference between it and the Parthenon. It was

Temple of Athena. It is perhaps better to refer to it as the Doerpfeld Foundation, from the archaeologist who exacavated it (see Page 47).

On the other hand, the Periclean temple of Athena, which housed the gold and ivory statue made by Pheidias, was not a centre of cult. It served to glorify Athena and Athens and the Hellenic people. The

Below: Gold and enamel earring medallion with relief head
inspired by the Athena Parthenos of Pheidias. Found
in 1830 in a Scythian tomb at Kul Oba in south Russia.
Opposite: Looking west from the Propylaia.

sculpture which decorated it served as a 'picture book': two great events associated with Athena in the pediments; other lesser associations on the metopes, which mainly illustrated the hard-fought triumph of civilisation and culture over barbarism and savagery, and of Greek heroes over barbarians; and the frieze represented Athena's greatest festival. The temple housed the statue of the Parthenos, officially called an *agalma*, a term of wide application meaning a glorious gift or offering. That it commanded the wonder and admiration of Antiquity is well known, but it is doubtful whether it inspired the awe and reverence felt for the crude, ancient statue, housed elsewhere,

Previous page: looking north-west from the Nike Bastion, with the temple of Hephaistos in the distance.
Opposite: The temple of Athena Nike: frieze, architrave and Ionic capital.
Below: Turkish inscription on a stone in front of the Erechtheum.

and ultimately in the Erechtheum, for which the *peplos* was offered to Athena.

It seems reasonable, therefore, to ignore chronological order, which would mean starting with the Parthenon, and to look first at the Erechtheum.

THE ERECHTHEUM

As was noted above, the date when the construction of the Erechtheum began is, within certain limits, a matter of conjecture. On the other hand, a report of a committee set up in 409 BC to examine the state of the unfinished building (the Chandler Inscription, so called after its finder) gives a wealth of detail about the materials, construction (including the wooden ceilings) and decoration (including colour and gilding). It also shows the stage reached when work ceased temporarily, perhaps in 415 or 413 BC. For instance the South (Caryatid) Porch was more or less

The Caryatid removed by the agents of Lord Elgin from the Maiden Porch of the Erechtheum and now in the British Museum.

completed, and so was the *cella* at the east. The document presents some problems, however, and does not solve others relating to the building. Incidentally it makes clear that the name of the temple in 409 BC was 'the temple in which is the ancient image'. It has been suggested that this anticipates the transfer of the image from elsewhere, but this is not a necessary conclusion. It is also clear from the Chandler Inscription that the whole of it was thought of as a temple of Athena. The name Erechtheion (whence the Latin Erechtheum) is of very rare occurrence. The study of the building is complicated by damage and changes of use suffered at various times. It was damaged by fire shortly after its completion, and again in the late first century BC. There are therefore Roman restorations following the original scheme and, in addition, in the late first century AD modifications in structure. It was converted into a Christian church dedicated to the Virgin, and then in the period of Latin domination incorporated in the palace of the duke of Athens. Under the Turks it became partially and temporarily a dwelling house. Those seventeenth-century European visitors who sought to check on some ancient details found themselves much impeded by the fact that a Turk's harem was housed in the western portion of the building. At the beginning of the nineteenth century the Turkish military commander resided in the building in dangerous proximity to a powder magazine in the North Porch. This official use impeded Elgin's agents in their activities, but ultimately he was allowed to carry away a Caryatid, the north angle column of the East Porch, and the *anta* (pilaster) capital and other fragments. At the clearance of the Acropolis the Erechtheum was partially reconstructed in 1837–46, and rebuilt as far as possible in 1903–9.

The curious plan of the Classical Erechtheum [8] was determined by the configuration of the rock on which it stood, and probably by the terracing which existed previously. It has been suggested that an earlier structure stood on the eastern part of the site, but there is no evidence for this or for a special sanctity of this area, though an altar of Dione stood in front of the temple. She was the ancient consort of Zeus, who as Zeus Hypatos had an altar perhaps on the lower level east of the North Porch [8, 5], down to which a staircase descended from the higher level of the eastern portion [8, 2]. Of particular importance were 'the signs', the marks of Poseidon's trident, and

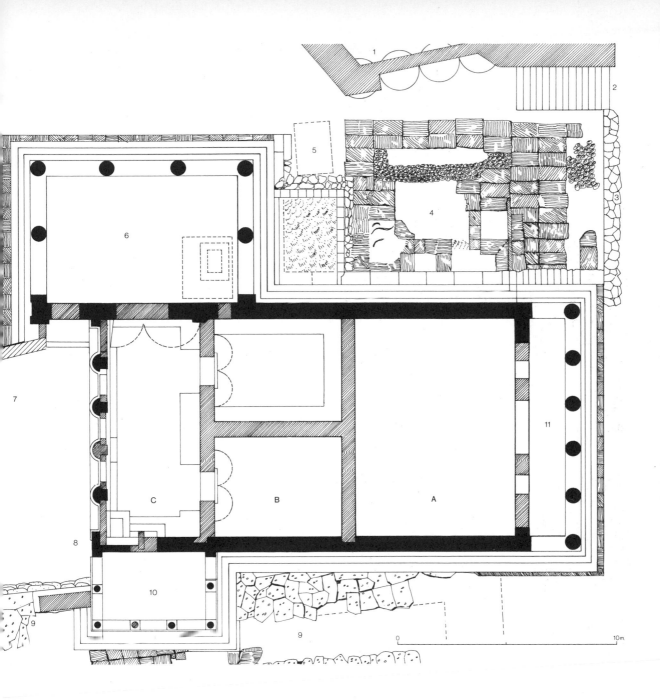

Fig. 8: The Erechtheum – A,B,C the three sections of the
cella. 1 Portion of the north wall of the Acropolis with
built-in column drums. 2 Modern steps to north court.
3 Modern wall. 4 North court and paving. 5 Altar of
Zeus Hypatos (?). 6 North Porch with roof and pavement
openings. 7 Pandroscion. 8 Kekropion. 9 Substructure
of Archaic temple of Athena. 10 Caryatid Porch.
11 East Porch.

the so-called 'sea' or salt well, both mentioned by ancient writers. It has already been noted that there was the complication of multiple cult, of Athena, Poseidon-Erechtheus, Boutes (son of Poseidon and Oreithyia, daughter of Erechtheus), and Hephaistos. It may be noted that in this cult Poseidon, as *Gaieochos*, was particularly connected with the Earth.

Basically the building consisted of a rectangle (hereafter called the *cella*), divided unequally by north-south walls into three sections, which from east to west may be denoted A, B and C [8]. Externally the platform on which the temple stood is approximately 24 m. long and 13 m. wide. On the east was a portico of six Ionic columns with entablature and triangular pediment [8, *11*], and coffered stone ceiling. Behind it was a door in the east wall with an ornamental frame and flanked by two windows with finely carved frames. It gave access to the (largest) eastern section of the *cella* (A). This east wall suffered very severely from the construction of the apse of the Christian church, but there seems to be evidence on the inside of it that a shrine or baldacchino stood inside section A, the significance of which will be considered later. It is generally agreed that this eastern room was concerned with the cult of Athena and ultimately housed the ancient image. It is a moot point, however, whether there was any connection between it and sections B and C. Pausanias' story of the passage of an intrusive dog through the temple is difficult to understand if there was not, and so some have postulated a door and stairway between A and B, but there is no material evidence for it. If it ever existed it vanished in the construction of the nave of the Christian church.

The western division, C, was entered by a notable North Porch with four Ionic columns on the front [*6*], and one on the return behind each of the corner columns. The columns were surmounted by an entablature and pediment. Inside the porch was a fine doorway with frame, lintel and consoles (partially restored in the Roman period) leading to the interior. The eastern wall of this section was pierced by two entrances to the middle section B, which suggests that the latter was divided into *adyta* or shrines, though there is some debate about this, and more still concerning the possible division into two of the westernmost section C, which Pausanias might seem to suggest. The western side of the North Porch projected somewhat beyond the western façade of the main structure so that an entrance at the back of

Above: Architectural detail from the Erechtheum.
Opposite: Looking through the Erechtheum from the eastern porch.

the porch could be made penetrating to the enclosure west of the temple [8, 7]. This enclosure, prior to the construction of the Erechtheum but after the Persian sack of the Acropolis, seems to have had an entrance of its own.

To the south-west corner of the main structure was attached the famous Caryatid Porch [8, 10]. It stood on a southward extension of the temple platform proper, which in turn rested on other foundations to the south [8, 9]. It consisted of a balustrade on which stood the celebrated figures of *peplos*-clad and statuesque young women. In the inscriptions relating to the building of the temple they are called *korai* or 'maidens'. They belong to a tradition of the Aegean and Asia Minor, as is clear from the Cnidian and Siphnian treasuries at Delphi. Later they were called Caryatids, named – so it is said – from Karyai in Laconia, which was famed for its statuesque women. Four stand on the south front of the balustrade, and one on either return. A cast replaces the one removed by Lord Elgin which is now in the British Museum. They support a flat roof, again with a coffered stone ceiling. At the north end of the eastern side of the balustrade there is an entrance to the interior of the porch. The three steps of the temple platform and the sill make it too high for common use.

Before tackling the fascinating problems which are concerned with detail, it may be said that it is likely that the completed building was not as it had originally been envisaged. Aside from everything else, there seems reason to believe that the west wall was intended to lie ·61 m. further west, with conse-quent modification to the Caryatid Porch whose supports are at present unsymmetrically placed. It has been suggested that the building was intended to extend as far to the west on the axis of the North and Caryatid Porches as it does to the east. This would have made a very odd building indeed, and one quite unnecessarily long. On the other hand, it is hard to resist the idea that the North Porch should have been at the west end, though there would have been difficulties of construction. As for the Caryatid Porch, its peculiar form with the balustrade or podium supporting the 'maidens' can be explained by the particular problems of construction at the south-west corner, and the need to provide an entrance – clearly not for common use – into section C, by a narrow staircase of awkward character. The need for this staircase descending from a higher south level into section C is the best argument for a division of this

Opposite: The North Porch of the Erechtheum with the Propylaia beyond
Below: A column of the North Porch of the Erechtheum.

section into two: one part commonly frequented and entered from the north; the other an inner shrine approached from the south.

Once conjecture has gone so far it is a short step to ask why a temple was erected in this area at all, given the fact that another erected in the sixth century or earlier [6, *16*] had been placed further to the south, and did not take into its area the 'signs' incorporated in the Erechtheum. For this reason it has been suggested that the original intention had been to replace this temple, destroyed by the Persians, with another on the same site, but an important use

had been found for the repaired western section, while the fire-blackened eastern part stood as a memorial of Persian vandalism, in keeping with the oath supposed to have been sworn before Plataia, that 'the sanctuaries which have been burnt and thrown down by the barbarians' were not to be rebuilt, but to be left 'as memorials of the impiety of the barbarians'.

It is clear enough that clashes of plan and of religious interests, and of progressive and traditional views, such as those which affected the southern portion of the Periclean Propylaia, operated here also,

to frustrate a design which could truly satisfy the
intentions of the architects (who may have been
Mnesikles and Kallimachos) and force them back on
an elaboration of detail. For while the overall form
is odd and unattractive, it is possible for the least
expert in Greek architecture to perceive the elegance
attained by the Ionic style in this building: the refine-
ment in the minutely curved profile (*entasis*) of the
columns 59 mm. high in the North Porch, the elegance
of the mouldings and decoration in column capitals,
necking rings and bases, cornices and wall-crowns,
and door frames. Much else in terms of colour,

Opposite: The base of an Ionic column from the
Erechtheum.
Above: The Erechtheum. The North Porch and the door
into section C. The mouldings are partially a Roman
restoration.

gilding and woodwork (especially in the coffered ceiling) can only be guessed at, though in the cable-band beneath the capitals of the North Porch beads of glass, of various colours (red, blue, yellow, purple), were preserved until quite recent times.

On the other hand, the frieze inserted between the architrave and the horizontal cornice, and carried round the main structure and the North Porch at two different levels, was a dubious success. While the technique might have an archaic forerunner on the Acropolis, it was not used again later as far as is known. This frieze, ·683 m. high in the North Porch, and ·617 m. high elsewhere, consisted of a band of black Eleusinian stone to which figures in white marble were attached. Its style and subject matter will be a matter of later consideration. As for the Caryatid Porch, the figures of the 'Maidens' combine charm with the monumentality necessary to their function. It is not too fanciful to think that the artist who designed them, whether he was Kallimachos or another, knew of the practice in Archaic times of dedicating the fine flower of womanhood to Athena, and resolved to do something similar as a part of her temple.

In the details of its construction the Erechtheum has been the object of endless controversy. What remains is frequently hard to interpret in detail for the reasons given above. The report of the commission of 409 BC adds some problems, and so does the description of Pausanias, who is at his most careless and obscure here. After leaving the Parthenon, he deals in very summary fashion with the east end of the Acropolis, and in describing his approach to the Erechtheion (as he calls it), he leaves us in considerable uncertainty as to how he entered it. It is really a matter of fitting Pausanias' description to the temple plan as we have it. He describes the altar of Zeus Hypatos 'in front of the entrance ... on which no living thing is sacrificed', and it can reasonably be located in the court to the east of the North Porch. He then goes on to mention the altars of Poseidon-Erechtheus, Boutes and Hephaistos, the wall-paintings relating to the Boutadai, the salt-water 'sea' and the marks of Poseidon's trident. It is generally thought that he entered by the North Porch, yet he then mentions 'the gold lamp dedicated to the goddess', the work of Kallimachos, burning for a year with its asbestos wick, and with a chimney of some artistic importance. This sounds, in all common sense, like a return to section A.

Thereafter he goes on to describe the objects of religious and historic interest in the 'temple of [Athena] Polias', then the sacred olive, the 'temple' of Pandrosos contiguous with the temple 'of Athene', and the Arrhephoroi 'who dwell not far from the temple of the Polias'.

If Pausanias had set out to cause confusion he could hardly have been more successful. He speaks in turn of the Erechtheion and the Polias temple, but it is not clear from him whether there were two buildings or one. If he entered the building under discussion by the North Porch he might sensibly have spoken of sections B and C as the Erechtheion, since Poseidon-Erechtheus was worshipped there. He goes on to mention the ancient image (which, in common with the Chandler Inscription, he calls the *agalma*) and the ever-burning gold lamp. It is most reasonable to assume they were in the easternmost section (A) of the building. Do we assume he got back somehow to this portion of what he has so far called the Erechtheion? Then he goes on to speak of the Polias temple and the historic bric-à-brac it contained, including an ancient statue of Hermes. Then, most abruptly, he turns to the sacred olive of Athena (without locating it) and the 'temple' of Pandrosos; adding, as noted already, that the Pandroseion is adjacent to the Polias temple, and not far away is the residence of the Arrhephoroi. He is manifestly speaking, therefore, of the area to the west of the building now called the Erechtheum, and it must be concluded that he uses the Greek form Erechtheion, first, and then the phrase 'temple of Athena Polias' for the same building or parts of it. This is the sensible explanation, preferable to the alternative, namely that he in fact passed to the ancient temple which stood further south, which undoubtedly was once the temple of Athena Polias and housed the sacred image. Today it is represented only by the so-called Doerpfeld Foundation. It was ruined by the Persians, and whatever the problems of its repair, and the duration of its preservation, it is difficult to believe that it survived until the second century AD especially as the part of it associated with Athena and the sacred image is least likely to have been restored after the Persian sack.

Pausanias' confusion twice confounded serves only too well to illustrate the difficulty of extracting sense from a late literary text. The same type of problem arises when, after describing the altars in the Erechtheum, he adds: 'the building being double, within there is a well containing sea water. .... There is also the imprint of a trident on the rock.' The question immediately arises, what building is double, and where in relation to it are the salt well and the trident marks? Pausanias does not make these points clear.

The three-fold division of the temple *cella* has been described. It has been made clear already that section A was on a much higher level than sections B and C, though one unbroken horizontal roof covered them all. Descent from the higher eastern level to that of the North Porch outside the building was by a staircase, as it is today (the existing stair is modern). The interior is a sorry mess of walls and native rock, due to the conversion into a Christian church, which reduced section A to the level of B and C, used section C as the narthex of the church and B and A as the body of it with nave and two aisles, with the apse destroying the east wall of A, but leaving the columns of the Eastern Porch intact. It has already been pointed out that in this way any material evidence for a way of communication between A and B has been destroyed.

The main entrance to sections B and C was by the North Porch. The various uses that the building has been put to, and Pausanias' confused description, have combined to obscure the answers to problems of internal arrangement in this area of ancient cults. It may be pointed out, incidentally, that there is no need to postulate an earlier building or buildings on the site to match the undoubtedly ancient cults of Poseidon-Erechtheus, Boutes and Hephaistos. Unroofed precincts and open-air altars were common enough at all times.

The western façade may be taken first. It has already been explained that the North Porch continued further west than the western façade of the *cella*, so that it was possible to pass through a door in the back of the porch and descend to the surface outside the western façade. It was equally possible to descend to the same area through a door in the wall of the western façade, the threshold of which is slightly above the floor of the North Porch. Access was thus given to the Pandroseion, located in an enclosed *temenos* in this area. Further to the south

The west end of the Erechtheum with the North Porch, and the area containing the Pandroseion and the Kekropion.

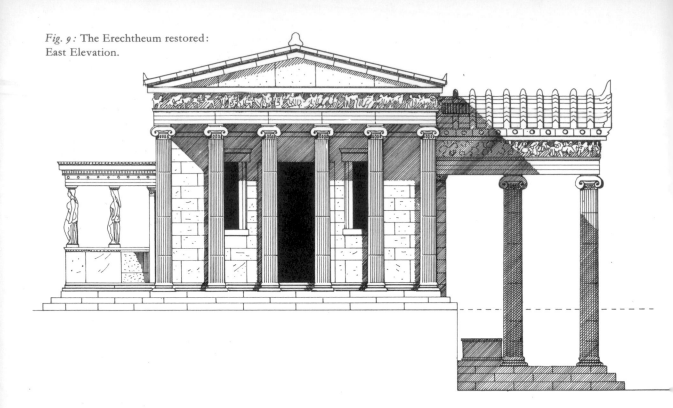

Fig. 9 : The Erechtheum restored:
East Elevation.

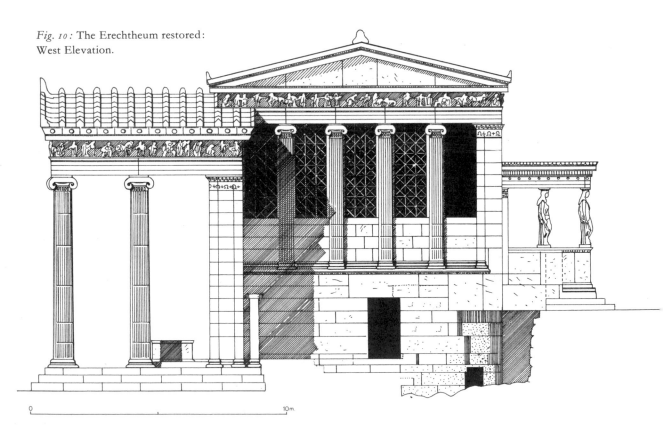

Fig. 10 : The Erechtheum restored:
West Elevation.

0   10 m.

there is an opening partly beneath the south-west corner of the Erechtheum *cella* and partly underneath the Caryatid Porch, bridged by a great block, while the wall is cut back behind it. The surface of the wall to a certain height at the south-west corner was clearly not intended to be seen, neither was the surface of the substructure on which the Doerpfeld Foundation stands. At the present this area is one of confused debris, but it is not difficult to see that there must have been some structure of great sanctity here which could not be moved. Allowance had to be made for it in the substructure of the Erechtheum which over-laid it in part. Had the temple been further extended to the west it would have been covered completely. It is reasonable to suggest that this structure was a mound covering some piece of an ancient building – not necessarily a tomb – which was identified as the Kekropion, the tomb of Kekrops. It must have been bordered with some sort of kerb, and to the north and west of it was a paved enclosure entered more or less on a level from the North Porch. This has been identified as the Pandroseion, and part of an enclosure appears still to survive. Here are certainly two older sites of sanctity and cult to which the Erechtheum was adapted. In the same area, it is generally assumed, was the sacred olive (which, burned by the Persians, sprouted again with miraculous speed), and possibly the sacred snake of Athena.

The western façade, as now exposed to view, is composed of various elements: first the wall in which is the door (described above), with a great lintel block, the equivalent of two courses on either side; above this is a horizontal moulding, on which stand four Ionic columns (or rather half-columns), on the exterior, backed by pilasters in the interior. The bases of these are original; the columns and the rest are Roman. It would appear that the intervals between these columns and between them and the *antae* (pilaster wall-ends) of the *cella* were walled approximately to the height of four courses, and above this wall the apertures were closed with wooden grilles to the height of the architrave. These grilles are clearly attested in the inscriptions concerned with the construction of the temple. Above was the usual Ionic architrave, the frieze and a pediment. Later, in the Roman period, the columns were restored (as was a good deal else), the grilles were removed, the walling was carried up to the architrave and three windows were left between the columns. It appears that, originally at any rate, the aperture

The engaged columns and windows of the western façade of the Erechtheum.

between the most southern column and the south *anta* was not filled, even by a grille. The interior of section C seen from the North Porch door presents a confusing spectacle since the floor-paving, originally flush with the floor of the North Porch, has disappeared. Beneath the level at which it must be located is a large cistern occupying the whole area. There may have been a smaller cistern or something like it in ancient times, but such a large area could not have been spanned by floor slabs, supported solely at their edges. In its present form the cistern is certainly later than the Classical period. In general, despite the obscurities of ancient authorities (including Pausanias) there is a disposition to locate the 'sea' or salt-water well in this part of the building. Some scholars would place it centrally in section C. In that case traces of it have gone beyond recovery. On the other hand, in the south-west corner of the same part is a well-like sinking in the rock. The southernmost opening in the west wall, between a column and the south pilaster, was not closed by a grille. In the south-west corner, in the south and west walls, there is a niche diagonally roofed over. It is possible to explain it as a device to lighten the load on the great stone bridging the gap beneath at the Kekropion. On the other hand, it is difficult to resist the suggestion that this is an important sacred site, and that the salt well or 'sea' may have been in this corner. The report of 409 BC mentions a *prostom-iaion*, an antechamber, as it were, to a *stomion* or aperture. This would be a justification, first, for a division of section C, and secondly an explanation for the narrow right-angled staircase from the Caryatid Porch to an inner section of C, but there is no way of proving this.

The eastern wall of section C and the general arrangement of the middle chamber have been badly affected by the construction of the Christian church, and before that by modifications carried out in the Roman period. The building inscriptions seem to substantiate the existence of two doors into the central chamber from the west, and it seems likely that the wall was not carried up to its full height, thus providing lighting for the middle chamber. The doors seem to indicate that this was divided into two, and it is natural to place the altars, already mentioned, in these two divisions, and to see in them the 'double' shrine mentioned by Pausanias, rather than to divide the western section C for this purpose.

The last problem relates to the North Porch. Near its south-eastern corner there was an aperture in the roof and ceiling, and a corresponding opening (now of irregular shape) in the pavement of the porch, thus exposing the surface of the rock. In this are a number

The Erechtheum. Aperture in the roof of the North Porch.

of holes, which might be accepted as the marks of Poseidon's trident. It may be, however, that these traditional trident marks have disappeared and were elsewhere (near the 'sea' is the obvious suggestion). The opening in the roof might suggest that these marks were thought of as those of a thunderbolt, perhaps to be connected with the altar of Zeus Hypatos in the court to the east. The inscriptions relating to the construction of the Erechtheum refer to an altar 'of the Thyechöos' in the North Porch, which may have been adjacent to the aperture in the pavement. The surface of the rock here is accessible also from beneath the floor of the central chamber of the Erechtheum. There is no obvious reason for this, but it is suggested that offerings were cast down onto the surface of the rock, and access was necessary for their removal from time to time. It has also been suggested, with more assurance than is justified, that here – rather than at the Kekropion – was the haunt of the sacred snake or snakes, if indeed there were such creatures.

THE ANCIENT TEMPLE OF ATHENA (THE DOERPFELD FOUNDATION)

The problems connected with this complex building are not yet exhausted. It has already been seen that Pausanias, in his slipshod and inadequate description, speaks first of the 'Erechtheion' and then of the temple of 'Athena Polias'. If these are not the same and the equivalent of the existing Erechtheum, he must mean by the second phrase the structure of which the surviving foundations lie to the south of the Erechtheum. It must be recalled that from the high point of the Acropolis to the south-east of the Erechtheum the rock slopes north, south and west. The east-west slope accounts for the difference in level between the eastern chamber of the Erechtheum and the central and western, and the south-north slope in part for the difference in level of the eastern and northern porches. The same sloping surface of the rock necessitated the creation, immediately to the south of the Erechtheum, of a levelling structure, the imposing north side of which can be seen to the south of the western façade of the Erechtheum, where in Antiquity some of it would have been concealed by the Kekropion. On the surface thus formed and levelled Doerpfeld discovered the ground-plan of a temple, on much the same site, it should be recalled, as the putative palace of the Mycenaean rulers of Athens.

The north peristyle of the Parthenon, looking towards the Erechtheum.

What can be seen today on the Acropolis amid the disconcerting jumble of stones south of the Erechtheum are the foundations of the *cella*, interior walls, and peristyle of this temple. Two elements are distinguishable: the foundations of the *cella* and interior walls of Acropolis limestone, and the foundations of a peristyle (as it is interpreted) of Kara limestone from Mt Hymettos. The quality of the working and laying of the interior foundations is not high; that of the peristyle foundations is superior. To a certain extent it has been possible to agree on the ultimate form of this temple, but how it attained this final form is a different matter. There are problems of dimensions, involving the use in its reconstruction of fragments partly built into the north wall of the Acropolis and partly found buried at points on it and elsewhere. Some are of *poros* stone, some of marble: fragments of columns with attached capitals – these latter of broad archaic form, fragments of architrave, triglyphs, horizontal and raking cornice and *sima* fragments colourfully decorated, and plain metopes.

To add to the jigsaw puzzle there is the ascription to the building of fragments of coarse limestone, again brightly painted, which some have sought to place in the triangular pediments at either end of the building. The task is made no easier by the conviction of other scholars that these fragments (or some of them) come from an early temple on the site of the Parthenon, which scholarly ingenuity determines as one hundred Attic feet long, and therefore the proper candidate for the name Hekatompedon ('the hundred-foot temple') a name which others would apply to the building under consideration which stood on the Doerpfeld Foundation.

This temple was Archaic Doric. It has already been made clear that there are problems of its dimensions. There are others relating to the stone-mason's tools used, as a means of dating. The problem of dating would also be helped if certainty could be attained on the nature of the sculpture which decorated it. The following details are, however, relatively uncontroversial. It was a temple 21·34 m. by 43·44 m. including the peristyle, and 12·30 m. by 33·50 m. for the *cella* and its porches. The peristyle had twelve columns on the long sides and six at either end. The interior foundations seem to indicate shallow porches – too shallow, some think, for columns to stand between the *antae* (wall-ends). The alternative is an arrangement of four columns in front of each end. Behind the *prodomos* or eastern porch a door gave entry to a room slightly less than half the *cella* proper. Three columns may have stood at either side to divide it into nave and aisles. This room was entirely cut off from the western portion of the temple, which was entered from the western porch and consisted of two parts: the westernmost single, the inner portion divided into two, each of these rooms being entered by a door from the west. It will be seen, therefore, that leaving aside the placing of the western entrance, the Erechtheum reproduces the layout of this temple, a closer approximation in fact than the classical Parthenon to which some have also compared it. The attic foot is variously given as ·328 m. or ·2957 m. In the former case the *cella* and porches at 33·50 m. might roughly be called 'a hundred foot structure' — Hekatompedon — as being 102 Attic feet. In the latter case its length would be between 113 and 114 Attic feet, and it is hard to believe that even in common parlance, and still less officially, this could therefore be called 'the hundred-foot temple'.

The name occurs in a fragmentary decree inscription engraved on two of the marble metopes which some ascribe to this temple – others were used as a dado in the pre-Periclean Propylaia or entrance gate to the Acropolis, and one lay about until the mid-fifth century for an idler to scratch a name on it. The decree or decrees, to be dated to 485–484 BC, enact regulations relating to the Acropolis, and obviously connected with sacrifices and cult matters. They are important for understanding problems of the organisation of the Archaic Acropolis. There are references to bronze vessels and their listing 'except those in the sealed rooms' (*oikemata*, which might mean treasuries); regulations necessary to control the mess resulting from animal sacrifices and cult practices in certain areas of the Acropolis: 'in front of the temple; to the eastward of the great altar; to the south of the temple; within the Kekropion; the whole area of the Hekatompedon.'

It is clear from this inscription that the Hekatompedon is distinct and separate from 'the temple'. This 'temple' must be the temple of Athena Polias under consideration, enjoying the prestige of containing the ancient image: therefore the temple *par excellence*. It will be convenient hereafter, following certain official usage to call it the 'ancient temple'. It is tempting to see the inner part of the western section as the *oikemata* to be opened at set times, but there is insufficient evidence to identify them or the whole as the Hekatompedon.

On the question of the building of the 'ancient temple', amid the many disagreements in detail, it seems agreed there were two stages: an early temple of the first half of the sixth century (not to be too specific as to date), and a later version, on which there is general agreement that it was the work of the Peisistratid tyrants of Athens, perhaps in the eighth decade of the sixth century. One view assumes that the earlier temple was without a peristyle, having only the two porches and no side columns, the entablature being set on the *cella* walls. Another opinion is that this temple possessed a peristyle as many of the most ancient temples did. Whichever view is chosen, the Peisistratid alterations meant considerable changes of architectural detail and the modification of the pediments to take, in the eastern one, the famous group of Athena and the giants in marble. It has been put forward that the use of island marble was natural for the tyrants, since they had connections with the Aegean islands; but scholars are now less confident than they were that it is possible to identify different kinds of marble with accuracy. Four Ionic columns, which may have stood in each porch, are seen as an instance of the penchant of the Peisistratids for this order, as in the great temple of Zeus begun by them. Possibly there was a sculptured frieze around the *cella*, foreshadowing the Parthenon. An alternative suggestion is that the whole of the earlier temple was pulled down, the foundations reworked, and a new temple built: the kind of action which might be expected of the tyrants, rather than a tinkering with an older structure.

This, then, was the ancient temple of Athena Polias; as some would have it, the only large temple on the Acropolis in the sixth century, successor to 'the strong house of Erechtheus'. This must be, in the account by Herodotus[1] of the siege and burning of the Acropolis, part of the *hiron* ('sacred area') in which some Athenians took refuge, and the *megaron* in which they were ultimately slain must be the temple. It is significant that in another place he claims to have seen on the Acropolis the chains, with which

Fragment of a late Archaic relief from a rectangular
building, showing a charioteer mounting.

the Athenians bound their Chalcidian captives in 506 BC, hanging on a wall 'scorched by the Median flames, opposite the *megaron* facing west.' This might be the eastern portion of the ancient temple or, as one scholar has suggested, a surviving Mycenaean wall, on the west of which the Bronze Athena later stood. 'And,' adds Herodotus, on the Persian sack, 'having plundered the sacred place they burned the whole Acropolis.' He goes on to say that Xerxes bade the Athenian exiles, who returned with him, sacrifice on the Acropolis, and he then introduces another apparent problem:

'I will now explain why I have made mention of this circumstance: there is a temple of Erechtheus, the Earth-born, as he is called, in this citadel, containing within it an olive tree and a sea. The tale goes among the Athenians that they were placed there as witnesses by Poseidon and Athena, when they had their contention about the country. Now this olive tree had been burned with the rest of the sacred place when the barbarians took the place. But when the Athenians, whom the king had commanded to offer sacrifice, went up into the sacred place for the purpose, they found a fresh shoot as much as a cubit in length, thrown out from the old trunk.'[2]

Herodotus, it seems, is not very well informed. There is no mention of the trident marks, and according to later tradition the olive tree grew in the precinct of Pandrosos. Herodotus consistently uses the term *hiron* (*hieron*) in his account, except in this one case of the 'temple' of Erechtheus. This must be a slip and no proof of the existence of an earlier Erechtheum, of which there is no evidence on the ground.

The Acropolis was burned (as far as it was combustible) by the Persians, and the structures actively cast down at the second occupation in 479 BC. There is a limit to what can be done without explosives, though mud brick with a timber framework is vulnerable enough. It must have looked a sorry mess, and there is a particular problem concerning the 'ancient temple'. The primitive image had gone with the Athenians when they evacuated Attica. It had now returned, either to the ancient temple hurriedly repaired (in despite of the oath before Plataia) or to some temporary shrine elsewhere, which is the most likely event. It is also to be assumed that valuable dedications (which might be few in the earlier days)

were removed at the evacuation of Attica, and brought back afterwards, if they were not utilised for expenses. They had to be stored somewhere on the Acropolis. The ancient temple was in ruins. Any *oikemata* or treasuries which might have existed previously, decorated with some of the Archaic sculpture found buried on the south side of the Acropolis, were also destroyed. If the Hekatompedon had really existed as another building, distinct from the 'ancient temple', it had been pulled down between the two Persian wars to make way for the pre-Periclean Parthenon which had not progressed very far by 480 BC. It is an interesting problem which students of architectural archaeology tend to dismiss as 'purely' historical.

The name 'ancient temple' appears after 480 BC. In an inscription earlier than 460 BC it is recorded that the moneys of the Eleusinian Goddesses are to be deposited 'in the back of the ancient temple of Athena on the Acropolis'. Even though 'ancient' is here restored in the inscription, 'temple' can refer only to one building, the only one in existence on the Acropolis at that date. Another inscription of very considerable interest was formerly dated to *c.* 460 BC, but is now regarded as belonging to the period 431–421 BC, after the completion of the Periclean Parthenon. It refers to the 'ancient temple' in a decree concerning the Plynteria festival, naming the Fates (*Moirai*), Zeus their leader (*Moiragetes*), and the Earth, and also mentioning the putting of the *peplos* on the statue. This is a piece of evidence on which the contention could be based that the whole of the ancient temple was restored after 480–479 BC. Next the historian Xenophon puts on record that 'in the archonship of Kallias [406 BC] the ancient temple of Athena was burnt.' This was just at the time of the completion of the Erechtheum, and there is reason to believe that it suffered in the fire. This is a crucial piece of information because the orator Demosthenes[3], speaking of those committed to prison for various reasons, mentions 'the treasurers in whose period of office the Opisthodomos was burned, both those of the Goddess and of the other Gods.' Is this the same conflagration, or a later one in the fourth century? This is of interest since an inscription which might possibly be of the fourth century, dealing with jewellery and dedications connected with the statues of Artemis Brauronia, refers to the 'ancient temple'. Is the date incorrect, or did the temple survive to the fourth century; or was the Erechtheum sufficiently old to be so called? It was, of course, in the time of Strabo (first century BC–AD), who mentions the Parthenon and 'the ancient temple of the Polias' containing the gold lamp – clearly the Erechtheum, if any trust is to be placed in Pausanias' description.

But there is a greater problem, namely the term *Opisthodomos* used by Demosthenes, the word for the back porch of a temple *cella*. It is very commonly applied to the western porch of the Parthenon. It should be noticed that, after its completion, the Parthenon became an increasingly used storehouse of dedications, some of them very curious bric-à-brac. It was in the charge of annual commissioners who carefully recorded objects (and sometimes their weights), and handed on their charge to their successors of the next year. These, in epigraphical parlance, are the *traditiones* 'handings over' which start in 434–3 BC, and diligently set down the inventories divided between the *pronaos*, or eastern porch, the *hekatompedos neos* (which was not a hundred feet long and must have got its name from an earlier temple) which was the eastern *cella*, and the *parthenon*, the place of the Virgin (or perhaps of the virgins). There is no mention among these of the Opisthodomos. On the other hand a celebrated inscription, the so-called Decrees of Kallias, which most scholars would date to *c.* 434 BC, mentions the money of the Goddess stored on one side of the Opisthodomos and that of the Other Gods on the other. An inscription of somewhat later date (possibly 418–17 BC) shows that the Opisthodomos had doors, and the records of the Eleusinian overseers for 408–406 BC speak of 'gold in the Opisthodomos in a bronze chest from the fourth cupboard'. There are lists of accounts which mention the Opisthodomos for 425–4 BC, and they continue down to 406–5 BC. Yet another inscription, of the second half of the fifth century, mentions the setting up of 'a pillar on the Acropolis, behind the Opisthodomos.' None of these references is older than the Periclean Parthenon, and there is no reason why the Opisthodomos, if that name is applied to the western porch of the Parthenon, should not be closed with grilles, as the *pronaos* was, and made a repository for strongboxes.

Since different officials and different lists were concerned there is no reason why the Opisthodomos should be mentioned in the *traditiones*, yet it is odd that it is not more closely identified with the Parthenon. That is why some scholars, taking account of the references to the 'ancient temple' after 480–479 BC, locate the Opisthodomos of Demosthenes in the western portion of the 'ancient temple' conveniently supplied with two minor chambers to fit the division between Athena and the Other Gods in the financial arrangements referred to. The Caryatid Porch of the Erechtheum, which was almost completed by 409 BC overlapped the foundations of the peristyle of the 'ancient temple'. The peristyle, therefore, must have been removed by then. But it has always been objected that it would be intolerable if this beautiful porch were masked by the old dilapidated building. Some would suggest that the whole had been removed on the construction of the Erechtheum between, say, 421 BC and 415 or 413 BC. The usual explanation of the later references to the old temple is, of course, to say that the rear portion was left and repaired as a storehouse of treasure. It was in effect the 'rear building'. If Demosthenes' reference is to the fire of 406 BC, it ties together the 'ancient temple' and the Opisthodomos. An inscription, possibly of 418/17 BC, refers to an improvement of the Acropolis. If the ruined eastern section of the ancient temple was tidied away, then the Caryatid Porch would be exposed to the east of the Opisthodomos, and there could be little objection to the retention of the latter, as long as it was serviceable. It is hard to believe it remained in this state much later than the end of the fifth century or the early fourth, or that it survived to the time of Pausanias.

THE 'UR-PARTHENON'

The objection that an 'ancient temple', without a peristyle would not be wide enough to take the Archaic sculpture group which it is thought should go with it, and another objection that a peristyled temple (which would be wide enough to take the sculpture) has to be given surviving fragments of side entablatures which should properly stand on walls and not on a peristyle, have led some scholars to use much the same fragments to construct yet another Acropolis temple. There is also the question still remaining of the *hekatompedon* the 'hundred-footer', a term which can only be applied inaccurately to the 'ancient temple'. This introduces in turn the Periclean temple of Athena Parthenos and the problems concerning the structures which stood or may have stood earlier on the site, which was itself considerably modified in the fifth century by the construction of the great platform on which the Parthenon stands.

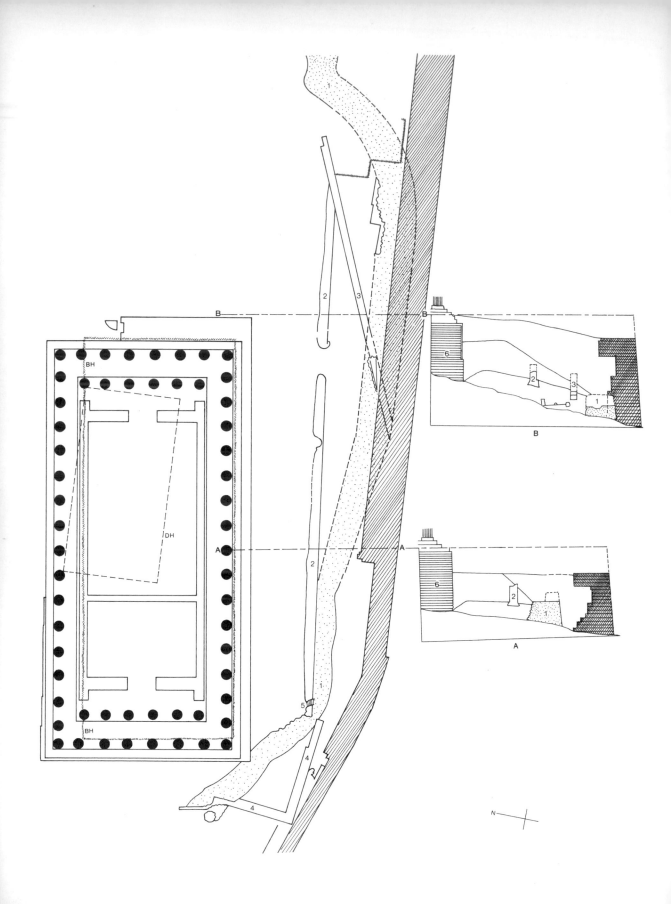

Fig. 11: Plan of the Parthenon area showing
(DH) Hekatompedon, (BH) Older Parthenon, Periclean
Parthenon and the complex of walls not now visible
except at 5.
A = section at AA, and B = section at BB on the plan.
1 Mycenaean (Late Helladic IIIB) = 'Pelasgian' wall
2,3,4 Terrace walls to be associated with building activity
5 Staircase in wall 2
6 Temple platform

The temple about to be discussed has been called by German scholars Ur-Parthenon (the 'grandfather Parthenon'). There are cuttings in the Acropolis rock to form the bedding for a building along the north side of the Periclean temple platform. On the south and west the terracing necessary to augment such a rock-cut platform has disappeared, but must have existed. The cuttings have been taken to indicate the presence of an oval, or, more likely, a horseshoe-shaped building, one hundred (Attic) feet long, 29·57 m., which was replaced by a rectangular building. Opinions are divided on the interpretation of the evidence. An oval or horseshoe-shaped plan would indicate a structure of very considerable antiquity, and it is perhaps better to accept the idea of an early rectangular temple, which one scholar argues was founded or dedicated in 566 BC, which he takes to be the date of the first quadrennial Panathenaic festival. This explanation of the date is not universally acceptable, and since the architectural and sculptural fragments are not connected with this building with absolute certainty, its date is in fact quite uncertain, even if that of the fragments is agreed.

The rectangular Ur-Parthenon, it is suggested, was a temple with three-column porches at either end, like the porch of the fountain house on the famous Attic black-figure mixing-bowl, the François Vase. This type of porch, it is argued, is evidenced by the jointing of the corner blocks of the architraves, but other archaeologists would question this. To this temple, as noted above, are ascribed architectural fragments and sculpture otherwise assigned to the earliest stage of the 'ancient temple'. As in the case of the latter, it is disputed whether the Ur-Parthenon had a peristyle or not. It is contended that the entablature of the temple flanks must have rested on solid walls, and not on a colonnade. There are a great many fragments of the *sima* (crowning moulding), which have been ascribed to the earliest stage of the 'ancient temple', which seem to fit better here. They were colourfully decorated with lotus and palmette chains, chevrons and chequers. With them must go the fragments of the underside of a sloping cornice with incised and gaily coloured flying birds (seen from the underside) and stylised lotus flowers. Between the triglyphs on the flanks and rear of the temple were blank marble metopes with stylised Doric leaves on the upper border in alternate red and blue. To the metopes of *poros* stone on the front were attached couchant marble leopards and lions in relief. In the two pediments of this reconstruction there are placed, at the front, two lions on a fallen bull in the centre, and the Triple-bodied Monster, Herakles and Triton at the corners; at the rear, a lioness devouring a calf, and another lion-group, with large snakes at the corners. Other elements on the flanks were false cover-tile ends (antefixes) decorated with stylised lotuses and palmettes, and pipe-shaped waterspouts. If it existed, this temple must have presented a colourful spectacle of Archaic art, but it is an assemblage of *poros* and marble fragments, many of which have also been used to reconstruct the 'ancient temple', and have no direct link with the ground. In the same way its pedimental sculpture also has been largely ascribed to the 'ancient temple': Herakles and Triton and the Triple-bodied Monster on the front of it, with 'Athena and a sea-maiden' possibly in the centre; and at the back, a lion killing a deer (?) and the large snakes. Similarly, the marble flying Gorgon (of which the head survives) is either ascribed to the apex of the Ur-Parthenon or, with the panther remnants, placed as pedimental corner ornaments on the 'ancient temple'. The allotment of *poros* fragments (with others of marble for the finer architectural elements such as the crowning mouldings and the roof tiles) to these various structures presents some tantalising problems. Nothing is known of the interior of the Ur-Parthenon, but if this is the building called the Hekatompedon by reason of its length, in the famous inscription already mentioned, it had a *cella*, and *oikemata* (interior chambers) for the storage of treasures rather than a multiple cult.

This temple, it is thought, was intentionally demolished about seventy-eight years after its dedication (therefore at about 488 BC) to be replaced by another. The date is suggested by the extent to which the successor was in fact constructed at the time of the Persian sack of the Acropolis in 480 BC.

THE OLDER PARTHENON

On the subject of this successor there is little or no conjecture, except in the matter of the date of its inception. There are two possible occasions: in the late sixth century after the expulsion of the tyrants and the establishment of the Cleisthenic democratic constitution – a great turning point in the history of Athens – or after 490 BC and the Battle of Marathon, the victory of Athens over the Persians and crowning glory of the Athenian democracy. Since it stood on a great platform of limestone, the process of construction on the south side (where the Acropolis slopes downwards) involved excavation and the building of a terrace wall. The date of the latest pottery sherds associated with this indicates a date after 490 BC, and when the Persian sack came the scaffolding – still in place – was destroyed by fire, which left its marks on the stones. The temple did not occupy the whole area of the platform, which was intended to raise the temple on an exposed base so that it could be seen properly from the city below; and it has been well suggested that the extension for the Periclean Parthenon made it visible also from the north.

Except for the third step, the building was to have been entirely of marble. By the time of the Persian destruction the columns were well advanced, but the interior *cella* had not progressed beyond the bases of the walls. Enough evidence remains to establish that the temple stylobate measured around 72·67 m. long and 26·87 m. wide over all, with six columns at front and back, and sixteen on the sides. The interior structure, the *cella*, had porches at east and west with four columns standing before them. The *cella* was divided into two: the eastern *cella* proper with nave and aisles, formed by two rows of ten columns as interior colonnades, and a more or less square room approached from the west, possibly with four supporting columns. This was the forerunner of the *parthenon* proper of the Periclean temple. Enough fragments of this temple have been found at various points on the Acropolis to give an idea of its form, and in particular some of its column drums were built into the northern wall of the Acropolis. Some material survived the Persian sack, and could be used in the Periclean Parthenon. It has even been suggested that certain dimensions of the latter were determined by the use of the earlier material.

THE PERICLEAN PARTHENON

This unfinished building was followed by the Periclean Parthenon, of which the political and financial background has already been outlined. Its form was more or less foreshadowed by the earlier building. The platform was extended to the north; the temple base was not so long from east to west as the substructure, but the temple was both longer (69·51 m.) and broader (30·86 m.) than its predecessor. Pheidias, the close friend of Pericles, had over-all supervision,

The Typhon (Triple-bodied monster) group of Archaic sculpture.

and Kallikrates and Iktinos were the architects. The latter wrote a book (now lost) about it, since it was his greatest achievement. The temple was entirely of marble, including the roof tiles; wood was used for the inner ceiling, the doors and the door frames. The peristyle had eight columns on front and back and seventeen on the sides, so that the proportions were slightly more than a double square. There were two porches, each with six columns standing before them, with coffered marble ceilings. The interior building (apart from the porches, the *pronaos* and *opisthodomos*) was divided into two: the *cella* proper, the *hekatompedos neos* (possibly inheriting its name from the Ur-Parthenon, or being roughly one hundred Attic feet long [29·57 m.]), and the more or less square *parthenon* entered from the west. The *cella* proper was divided into a nave and two aisles by two rows of ten Doric columns. Behind the great gold and ivory statue of Athena were five transverse columns, so that it was possible to pass behind it.

The temple was the most splendid and refined example of the Doric order, but like the 'ancient temple' it incorporated Ionic elements, first and foremost the sculptured frieze around the outside of the *cella*, placed some 12·192 m. high (which should be remembered when it is contemplated at eye-level in

Opposite: The south peristyle of the Parthenon.
Below: Interior of the Parthenon *cella*, looking west.

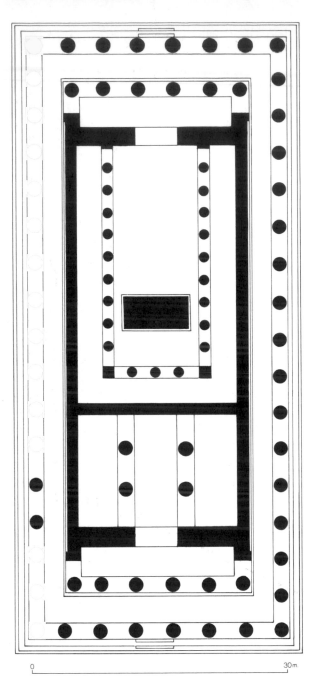

0   30m.

Above: Fig. 12: The Parthenon.
Opposite: Looking north-west across the interior of the
Parthenon to the Erechtheum beyond.

the British Museum), and four columns – probably
of the Ionic order – were placed two on either side in
the rear chamber. The rear chamber, so divided,
could be adapted for treasury purposes in the same
fashion as the rear chambers of the 'ancient temple'.
Dedications and treasure could be sealed in contain-
ers and placed in cupboards or on shelves, and in this
way, with the use of grilles, the *prodomos*, the *parthenon*
proper and the *opisthodomos* could be used as treasuries.
It is quite clear from the inscription already cited that
the *prodomos* was used in this way. The same arrangement could have been applied to the *opisthodomos*,
which was, in effect, the western porch of a double
temple.

The temple within, and especially the *cella* proper
(the so-called *hekatompedos neos*), had a wooden
ceiling supported on a second range of small columns
above those dividing the *cella* into a nave and two
aisles. Given the evidence of the Erechtheum inscription, such woodwork was probably highly
decorated and gilded. It may also be stressed that
colour was much used, as it had been in Archaic times.
This use of colour is worth comment in the whole
context of Greek Classical architecture. As A.W.
Lawrence points out:

'An alternative method of decoration (i.e. to
sculpture or earlier painted terracotta), by painting
on the stone, supplanted terracotta before the end
of the sixth century. The colours were applied after
the designs had been incised upon the stone, which,
if rough or absorbent, was given a coat of limewash
or marble-dust stucco, and very bright colours
were then obtainable; the detail, however, had to
be on a larger scale. That mattered little, however,
because it was soon realized that the old finicky
patterns were less effective than a combination of
flat washes in general with a few bold designs at
specially important parts. As a rule such major
features as the cornice face, the architrave, and the
columns were left pale (either uncoloured or
slightly toned down to reduce glare); the rhythm
of the frieze was emphasized by black or dark blue
triglyphs, regulae and mutules, against the red that
was applied to the plain surface of metopes, the
bed-mould and the underside of the cornice. The
broken lines of the sculptured figures on metopes
and pediments were still more broken by the
application of various colours to drapery and other
accessories; on the other hand, the carved ornament

of such parts as the gutter and capitals received the utmost clarification, its detail being picked out in contrasting paints, sometimes with the addition of gilt.

The colours in general were crude and appear too vivid in restorations, but when toned down by strong sunlight they must have fulfilled their purpose admirably.'⁴

The bronze adjuncts to sculpture would not be much to the modern taste, but these features and the colour must be borne in mind when contemplating the sculptures of the Parthenon as displayed in a modern museum, and the ruins on the Acropolis.

The other important aspects of the Parthenon are its architectural refinements, again well related to the over-all architectural concept by Lawrence:

'The whole design of a temple is a matter of contrapuntal relationships; it depends ultimately on the clear demarcation of its parts, which must be so shaped as to keep the spectator's eye continually on the move. Every part must be rightly proportioned in itself as well as in relation to the rest, but none may attract more attention than another. Each line points towards one which turns at a different angle and obliges the eye to follow it: some lines, moreover, ought to be so constructed as to lead in either direction simultaneously. The Egyptians had long contrived to get that effect with columns, designing them against exclusively upward movement by

The east front of the Parthenon.

making the shaft bulge as it rises and contract again before it meets the heavy capital; the Doric column needed to be more subtly designed, though on the same principle. The columns in Egypt were almost invariably in the interior of a building, either bordering the sides of a court or supporting the ceiling of a hall, and their relation to what came above and below them offered a far less difficult problem. The tapering shafts of a Doric pteron have to link the peaked superstructure with the platform in such a manner that the eye will travel both up and down them, and eventually that requirement was fulfilled by an almost imperceptible convex curvature of the side in conjunction with an inward slant of the whole column, gently anticipatory of the gable.'⁵

If this seems unduly subtle, the effect of the curvature of the stylobate is obvious enough, and so too, that of the curvature or *entasis* of the corner columns.

The Parthenon, apart from these refinements in architectural skill, was the great monument of Athenian glory. It may be said again that the pediments record the vital moments of the Athena legend; the frieze the greatness of Athens and her inhabitants, and the metopes principally the triumph of civilisation over barbarians.

TEMPLE OF ATHENA NIKE

Another clearly important area of the Acropolis from Bronze Age times was the south-western bastion, flanking and defending (when defence was necessary) the entrance gate. With this area, as seen already, is to be associated the warrior Athena who figures on the Panathenaic amphorae, the prizes of victory in the great festival. The warrior Athena could also be taken as promoter of the victories of the state in war. The evidences of an early cult are: a polygonal retaining wall for an early enclosure; two successive altars of which the first bore an inscription of the mid-sixth century, and the remains of a small shrine going back to an early date and perhaps rebuilt after the Persian Wars. A decree of 449 BC, which some would connect with the so-called Peace of Kallias with Persia, made provision for an entrance to the enclosure, and for the erection of a temple. The architect was to be Kallikrates, who was associated with Iktinos in the building of the Parthenon. It is likely enough that the problems connected with the construction of the latter building, and with the plan of the Propylaia, delayed the building of the Nike temple, which is indicated as later than the Propylaia by the overlap of the structure of the former on the latter. The small temple was probably completed between 427 and 424 BC. It would be tempting to connect it with the Athenian victory over the Spartans on the island of Sphakteria in 425 BC – a turning-point in the course of the first decade of the Great Peloponnesian War – but the temple was probably started earlier and discontinued for a period. With the construction of the temple went a rewalling of the bastion, which also received a parapet (surmounted by a grille) decorated with reliefs of Victories, commonly dated in the last decade of the fifth century.

The charming small Ionic marble temple, so well placed on the bastion, has been twice restored after its components had been used by the Turks in their fortification of the Acropolis. It takes the form of a *cella* or walled room, with four *antae* (pilasters) at the four corners. The base and capital mouldings of the pilasters are continued around the walls. At either end are four Ionic columns standing in front of the *cella*, and the whole stands on a three-stepped platform measuring some 8·268 m. by 5·64 m. There is no door from the *cella* into the back porch; the front is open, with two pillars between and matching the *antae*. A partly enclosed porch was in fact formed by joining the *antae* to the corner columns of the front, and to the pillars by grilles. The columns are Ionic, with capitals which are later than those in the interior of the Propylaia, and with bases which some believe to be of an earlier type. Above them was a three-fascia architrave and a frieze. Fragments of the horizontal and sloping cornices, the gutter-mouldings, lion-head spouts and *akroterion*-bases survive. The horizontal gutter-moulding was painted with a lotus and palmette design, and there are indications that at least one of the pediments contained figures. With the Erechtheum, which in detail is close to it in style and construction, this small temple represents a charming exposition of the Ionic order.

The precinct of Athena Nike and the adjoining precinct of the Charites form a useful link with the Periclean entrance gate of the Acropolis, since they imposed limitations on the plan of the latter.

Opposite: The southern section of the Propylaia, with the bastion and Temple of Athena Nike.
Below: The Temple of Athena Nike: anta capital, column capital, architrave and frieze.

THE PROPYLAIA

The Mycenaean entrance gate and the problem of the Enneapylon have been mentioned in an earlier context. Various opinions have been held on the possible construction of a gate in the Archaic or early Classical periods, to replace this survival of Bronze Age antiquity. The story of the defence of the Acropolis against the Persians in 480 BC certainly involves a gate in the Acropolis walls, and there is the curious oracular reference to a 'wooden wall'. The wall on the south side of the Acropolis is ascribed to Kimon and the spoils of his victory over the Persians at the Battle of the Eurymedon. The north wall, with the built-in architectural fragments, some from the pre-Periclean Parthenon and some earlier, has been dated to the same period, but it has also been associated with the fortification activity of Themistokles immediately after the Persian retreat. It is natural to expect that such wall-building would include a new gate, at whatever date it took place; it is likely, however, that a gate would be associated more closely with the south wall than with the north, and suggest a connection, therefore, with Kimon. There are in fact, preserved to the south of the Periclean Propylaia, the remains of an earlier and simpler entrance gate orientated more

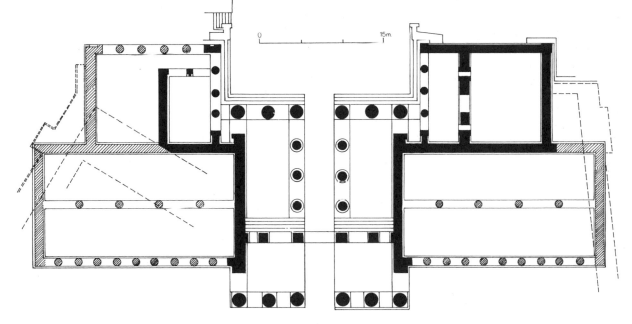

Above: Fig. 13: The Propylaia.
Opposite: The eastern (inner) façade of the Propylaia, also showing the rock surface of the Acropolis.

to north-east and south-west and clearly integrated with the well preserved section of the Mycenaean wall. The remains consist of two marble steps, a portion of the pavement, two blocks of a marble pilaster related to *poros* limestone walling, and a series of marble slabs backing a bench. The structure is thought to have been a porch, with four Doric columns on either side of the wall gateways [13]. Other indications of the north side and of the north-east corner have been found in the passage-way of the Periclean Propylaia and under the floor of its northern portion. Outside the Archaic gateway was a forecourt, seemingly of hexagonal shape, one side of which was formed by the Mycenaean wall joining the south-west corner of the outer portico. Against this wall, and also at right-angles to it beyond the south wall of the Periclean south-west wing, are dado slabs (in fact metopes from an Archaic temple) and a marble bench on three rock-cut steps.

These remains show traces of fire which must be the result of the Persian sack of 480 BC. The Archaic

Below: Looking out from the temple of Athena Nike to the Propylaia and the Parthenon.
Opposite: The western façade and north wing (Pinakotheke) of the Propylaia, seen from the front of the temple of Athena Nike (on the left).

Propylaia were therefore built before that date, but the re-use of the metope slabs (possibly belonging to an earlier stage of the 'ancient temple') do not necessarily date the gate to the sixth century, since at least one of these slabs was left lying about the Acropolis until well into the fifth century BC. On the other hand, the fire marks make a date about 465 BC, and the connection with the Kimonian south wall of the Acropolis too late. It is best to place the construction after Marathon and contemporary with the older

Parthenon. Marble and *poros* limestone were used in the construction of this gate and also, the remains indicate, mud brick and stucco with vertical timbers, to which horizontal planks were attached, which might be interpreted as the 'wooden walls' of the Delphic oracle.

This relatively modest entrance gate was replaced under Pericles and almost wholly obliterated by a grandiose structure conceived by the architect Mnesikles to occupy almost the whole of the western end of the rock. The Periclean Propylaia were built in five years, from 437 BC to 432 BC. Though the structure was one of the greatest glories of Athens, or, indeed, the greatest, it is difficult to believe that the cost was 2012 talents, drawn from public sources, including funds from the Hellenotamiai or Stewards of the Imperial Tribute, and from private contributions. The sum seems excessive if modern calculations of the cost of the Parthenon (mentioned below, on page 178) are taken into account.

Overleaf: The eastern façade of the Propylaia

Basically the building was intended to be a five-fold gate in a wall, with a ramp for animals, and with wings on the north-west and south-west, and larger halls on the north-east and south-east. The north-west wing and the central gate structure were completed; the south-west wing was curtailed by the Nike precinct. The north-east and south-east halls hardly reached even a beginning of the plan intended.

Seen from the ramp, which ascended in zig-zag fashion – the present arrangement is a considerable alteration dating from Roman times and later – the central unit of the gate proper and the north-west and south-west wings stood on a four-stepped platform, three of Pentelic marble and the lowest of dark Eleusinian stone, to warn the unwary of the rock below. The same intention is apparent at the top step of the five at the actual entrance gate.

Some basic measurements give an idea of the dimensions involved: the width of the actual Propylaia was 18·125 m., and the depth from front to back 25·04 m. This latter measurement includes a west porch 15.243 m. deep, a wall 1·295 m. and an east porch 7·358 m. deep. The central door measured 7·379 m. by 4·185 m. and the rock-cut central passage-way was 4 m. broad, later replaced by a stepped ramp fitted with a rain-water drain. The set of pivot-holes for the main doors of the gate still remains, and a metal track for the wheel under one of them.

It has been said that in this gateway, on rising ground the problem was 'how to make a coherent and harmonious effect of the roofing which called for great architectural ingenuity, since the eastern part of the central section is higher than the western, and all the wings had to be separately provided for' with a hipped roof.

The most compendious and clear description of this complex building is that given by D. S. Robertson (quoted here with some omissions):

'In essence the traditional plan was retained – a roofed porch projecting from both the outer and inner sides of a gate in a wall: but the scheme was here complicated by the addition of wings, and by the elaboration of the porches themselves. The full plans were never executed, partly through religious conservatism, which refused to sacrifice ancient sanctuaries to mere magnificence, and partly through the financial stress of the Peloponnesian War. Enough, however, was executed to indicate the architect's intentions, and the main lines of the original scheme have been recovered notably by the observations of Dörpfeld. At the head of the winding chariot-road which led up the steep western slope, the visitor found himself faced by a hexastyle Doric façade crowned with a pediment. It stood upon a platform of four steps, except between the two central columns, where the road passed; this intercolumniation was wider than the rest, and carried two triglyphs. The façade was that of a huge prostyle porch; close behind each of the angle columns was an *anta*, which in each case formed the end of a side-wall, common to both the outer and inner porches. If the visitor passed through the central intercolumniation, he found the rising road-way on which he stood flanked to right and left by the platforms (the true floor of the porch), on each of which stood three Ionic columns, carrying a marble architrave level with the triglyph frieze of the outer façade. These two architraves helped to carry a system of marble beams and cofferings, decorated with golden stars on a blue ground, which covered the whole porch. This marble ceiling and a similar one in the inner porch were still unrivalled in the days of Pausanias. At the back of the outer porch a solid wall ran right across the structure: the chariot road passed through it by a great gate about twenty-four feet [7·314 m.] high and nearly fourteen feet [4·267 m.] wide: the inner width of the whole porch was nearly sixty feet. If the visitor preferred to mount the steps of the western façade, and to pass through one of the outer inter-columniations, he found himself on one of the raised platforms already mentioned, between the Ionic columns and the side-walls. In front of him the great cross-wall was pierced by two doors, a larger and a smaller, at the top of a flight of five steps, the top one of black Eleusinian limestone. There were thus four doors for foot passengers, in addition to the chariot gate. Beyond the cross-wall lay the inner porch, which was exactly like the outer one, except that it was much shallower and had no inner columns: the depth of the outer porch, from anta-face to cross-wall, was between three and four times as great as the corresponding measurements of the inner porch.

Opposite: The south door of the Propylaia with the Erechtheum beyond.
Overleaf left: The Propylaia. Doric and Ionic column shafts.
Overleaf right: The Parthenon colonnade.

The façade of the inner porch was almost identical in size with that of the outer porch: and since its stylobate stood between five [1·524 m.] and six feet [1·829 m.] higher, there was approximately the same distance in level between the two sections of the roof. Consequently the inner porch had a pediment at its back which rested on the cross-wall between the two porches: the raking cornice of this pediment was complete, but the horizontal cornice and tympanum were partly masked by the roof of the outer porch. The whole of this awkward junction was little in view, and if the complete scheme had been executed, it would hardly have been visible from any angle. The part of the gate-wall entirely concealed between the roof of the outer porch and the ceiling of the inner was lightened by a large opening, to relieve the pressure on the lintel of the central gate. Precautions were also taken to relieve the pressure on the architrave over the central intercolumniation in the eastern porch and doubtless also in the western one, though here evidence is lacking ... the architrave was reinforced with iron bars. Of the supplementary structures which flanked the porches only one was fully executed, the north-west wing, which the visitor saw above him to the left as he approached the outer porch. This was a rectangular building, at right angles to the porch, with the steps and stylobate of which its own were continuous. In plan it resembled a temple, having a porch with three Doric columns *in antis*, connected with the main room by a door and two windows; but it had no pediment (its low roof had three slopes) and it was linked to the north wall of the western porch. It seems to have been a picture gallery. The south-west wing was designed, in the main, on the same lines, with the difference that for its west wall an open colonnade was perhaps to be substituted, in order to give easy access to the bastion and temple of Athena Nike. In fact, however, this wing was seriously curtailed, though the portion executed approximately balances the north-west wing: some details seem intended to remind the spectator of the architect's disappointment. It is clear that there were also planned two larger halls flanking the eastern porch. The south wall of the north-eastern hall and the north wall of the south-eastern hall would have been formed by the north and south walls of the central building, while a great part of their west walls would have been formed by the east

Opposite: The curve of the Parthenon stylobate.
Below: South (inner) side of the Propylaia, showing the lifting bosses on the wall blocks.

walls of the north-west and south-west wings. An open row of Doric columns would perhaps have given free access to each of these halls from the Acropolis, while half-way back a more widely spaced row of Ionic columns would have helped to support the roof, which would probably have sloped from west to east. Neither hall was ever built, but preparations had been made for the insertion of the roof-beams and rafters of the northern one.'[6]

Some differences of detail have been suggested: the south-west wing may have had a solid wall on its west side, and the north-eastern and south-eastern halls may have been intended to have solid walls with doors on the eastern side. This may well have been so if they were intended for storage, with cisterns beneath. Had they been built, the Acropolis rock would have been even more densely occupied with buildings than it was, presenting a very different aspect from that of today. For while this completes the tale of the largest and most important buildings on the Acropolis, there were other buildings and precincts which have left less evidence of their existence and character, while for the Archaic period there are buildings surviving only in fragments of architecture or sculpture in the Acropolis Museum.

THE HOUSE OF THE ARRHEPHOROI

Some mention had already been made of the building on the north side of the Acropolis, to the west of the Pandroseion. In it the maiden Arrhephoroi lived,

The north-east section of the Propylaia showing the wall of the unfinished north-eastern hall, with lifting bosses and beam sockets.

played and carried out their ritual described earlier. The ritual had early origins, and there must have been some earlier building on the site. The stairway down to the North Slope would be closely related to it. There was a *stoa* in this region of the Acropolis, and on part of it was constructed in the fifth century a large rectangular building with a two-column portico *in antis*, which can reasonably be identified with the Arrhephoreion.

THE PRECINCT OF ARTEMIS BRAURONIA

On the south side of the Acropolis an important area stretched from the Propylaia and the precincts of Athena Nike, and those of the Charites and Hekate, eastwards to the south-west corner of the Parthenon. It was enclosed on the south by the Kimonian Wall, and because of the configuration of the rock-surface it was (and is in part) a made-up area. In it was buried a portion of the Mycenaean Wall. Beyond it was the terracing to the south of the Parthenon. On the west the ancient precincts – and particularly those of Athena Nike and Artemis Brauronia – have already been mentioned as limiting the full development of the Periclean Propylaia. The precinct of Artemis Brauronia, enclosed by the massive Mycenaean Wall on the west and by a wall with an entrance gate in it on the north, has not yielded remains of a temple. The chief centre of worship was at Brauron in East Attica, where the ancient wooden image was kept, but two statues of the goddess are recorded on the Acropolis, one Archaic and the other by Praxiteles. There were in the enclosure two *stoai* (porticoes), one probably of the same date as the Kimonian Wall and the other probably thirty years later. The older of the two was on the south side with ten Doric columns forming the open side facing north. It also had a northward projecting room at either end. The other was on the east of the precinct, aligned with the east room of the southern *stoa*. It may have had five Doric columns on its open west side, but the restoration, from scant evidence, is tentative. The toilet objects and woollen and silk garments of various colours, or embroidered, which were dedicated by women to the goddess and listed in inscriptions, may have been stored elsewhere.

THE CHALKOTHEKE

To the east of the precinct of Artemis the now concealed remains of the substructure of a large

building partly resting on the Kimonian Wall were excavated. These remains seem to indicate a rectangle, slightly irregular, 42·977 m. and 41·504 m. long and about 14·021 m. wide. They are restored as a large room, its roof supported inside by six columns. A portico on the north side (its east wall not properly aligned), with eighteen Doric columns on the front and three on the returns, was added later. The older part has been dated to *c.* 450 BC, and identified with the Chalkotheke – also known from official records as a storage place of arms and other material. It is hardly likely that the much debated Opisthodomos is to be identified with this building.

Again to the east there was the area between the Kimonian Wall and the Parthenon. Excavation of the Acropolis revealed walls of various periods, and associated deposits, related to building activities culminating in the construction of the Parthenon [12].

Base of a black-glazed mug found at Olympia in the 'Workshop of Pheidias', inscribed 'I belong to Pheidias'.

THE WORKSHOP OF PHEIDIAS

Amid this complex of supporting walls there were also the remains of a large building which, it has been suggested, was a workshop connected with the construction of the Parthenon, especially for those operations which had to be carried out under cover. At Olympia tradition spoke of a workshop of Pheidias; remains preserved under an early Christian church have been identified as this, and recent excavations have yielded not only scraps of materials used for the great gold and ivory statue of Zeus, moulds for the shaping of its garments in gold, and for the casting of glass spangles, but also goldsmith's tools, and an authentic indication of the presence of Pheidias. It would be tempting to think of Pheidias as employed on the gold and ivory statue of Athena in this building on the Acropolis, but there is no similar evidence.

SERVICE BUILDINGS, THE SANCTUARY OF ZEUS POLIEUS AND THE PANDION

Some structures on the Acropolis, of which foundations have been discovered and reburied, are identified as 'service buildings', a useful phrase to conceal ignorance of their purpose. Furthermore centres of ancient cult, considered earlier, have to be located, and to this end a close scrutiny has been made of scant remains, or of cuttings in the rock. The sanctuary or precinct of Zeus Polieus must be found somewhere. Cuttings and postholes at the highest point of the rock suggest the existence, north-east of the Parthenon, of a barn-like structure and an enclosure in which could have lived sacred cattle connected with the festival of the Diipolia and the curious ritual of the Bouphonia ox-slaying, but it is all uncertain and evokes a curious picture of the Classical Acropolis. There is the same obscurity about the sanctuary of Pandion, not the ancient king whose sons contested the rule of Attica with Theseus, but an earlier figure in the series of Attic culture heroes, probably deriving his name from the festival of the *Pandia*, the 'all-embracing god'. Remains at the south-east end of the Acropolis are better identified as this sanctuary than others in the north-west corner, but it is all a matter of conjecture.

MINOR STRUCTURES

Finally, as a return to the Archaic period, there is the question of the architectural and sculptural fragments discovered in the Acropolis excavations of the last century now exhibited in the Acropolis Museum. They have been found in great numbers, and while many have been used more or less convincingly in the reconstructions of the 'ancient temple' and the Ur-Parthenon, much remains over. Many of the fragments come from buildings of small size, with quite small dimensions, as far as these can be determined from the fragments, or estimated from the number of columns *in antis* conjectured on the façade.

The German archaeologist Wiegand distinguished five buildings, lettered A, B, C, D and E. The first of these has been divided into two, A and Aa, and to the latter has been ascribed a painted pediment: of special interest because the pediment has a composition of animals executed not in sculptural relief but merely in painting, the animals being light on a dark ground like the red-figured vases of later times. The size of these structures has caused some of them to be identified as 'treasuries' of the sort which must have existed on the Acropolis. Building A is calculated to have a gable floor length of 3·798 m., in which case it is difficult to see that it can be given four columns between the *antae*. The surviving fragments are of *poros* limestone, and to it has been ascribed the 'olive-tree pediment' (see below, page 147), and at the rear perhaps the smaller Herakles and Triton group.

Entablature of *Poros* Structure A, reconstructed in the Acropolis Museum.

To judge from the clamps used to fasten the building-blocks together, it is the oldest of this group of buildings, and may belong to the mid-sixth century. Building B with its gable-base length of 8·915 m. is of exceptional interest. Fragments of it were built into the north-west wing of the Periclean Propylaia, and it seems established that it had an apsidal end. Its length is unknown, and it may have had a façade of three columns between *antae*, or alternatively a solid wall-front pierced by a door. Buildings C, D and E are calculated to have gable measurements of 6·680 m., 5·156 m. and 4·267 m. respectively. The number of columns in the façades is assumed to be four on the basis of the estimated gable measurements. Some fragments of C were found in the Kimonian Wall, others in the north-west wing of the Propylaia. The dating is uncertain, but generally in the second half of the sixth century: C is contemporary with B,

Fragment of a late Archaic relief showing a male figure (Hermes or a mortal) in tunic and *petasos*. Identical in dimensions and style to the relief shown on page 113.

E is younger than the Peisistratid Athena temple, and D still younger. Details in all these buildings were picked out in bright red and blue which, unhappily, have almost completely faded. E shows remarkable skill in the effecting of repairs to the stonework.

The finding of masonry from B in the foundations of the north-west wing of the Propylaia, coupled with the discovery of a fragment of a curved base in the same area, might seem to suggest the location of this building in that vicinity. On the other hand, fragments of C have been found in the Kimonian Wall as well as in the Propylaia, and one of D near the Agrippa monument outside (where it was possibly moved by the Turks), so that the place of discovery of fragments is of little evidential value. Again some of the sculpt-

ure which must be from buildings of this size and nature – including the 'Herakles and Hydra' and 'Introduction' pediments – were found on the south side of the Acropolis. For this reason B, C and E have been located by some to the west of the Hekatompedon (Ur-Parthenon). In addition there has been a tendency to think of the *oikemata*, mentioned in the Hekatompedon inscription, as such structures. It is tempting to locate the apsidal building B inside the ancient wall at the west end of the Acropolis. This might be so, but it is unjustifiable to suggest that it may have survived to the period of the construction of the Periclean Parthenon. The Persian sack must have seen the end of these small structures, and the problem arose of storing their contents elsewhere. Fragments were either buried fairly soon, or were left lying on the surface for decades, like some fragments of the larger buildings.

5. The Sculpture

The Acropolis was the setting for a great quantity of sculptural art; in gold and ivory, bronze, stone of various sorts, and wood. It comprised individual figures of deities and dedications of idealised youths and maidens, men and women, heroes and heroines, and animals: the associations were religious or mythological, or historic. There were great statues such as the gold and ivory Athena Parthenos of Pheidias, and the great Bronze Athena commonly called the Athena Promachos. The sanctuaries and the open spaces of the rock must have displayed a forest of sculptures, and the dedicatory inscriptions which went with them provide both epigraphical and historical records of immense importance. There were also inscriptional records in stone and bronze: substantive enactments relating to the cults of the Acropolis, and to the construction and administration of its shrines. Beyond all this, on the buildings which were erected at various times, was the decorative sculpture in pediment, metope, frieze and *akroterion*.

Opposite: Detail of the northern part of the east pediment of the Parthenon (see page 162).
Right: Head of a sphinx cut out and incised on a slab of marble. An Akroterion of the early sixth century.

Altogether we have a picture book – though an imperfect and battered one – of the sculptural achievement of Attica and places beyond.

ARCHAIC REMAINS

The Archaic temples and small structures discussed in the previous chapter were decorated with sculpture, and the assigning of this excavated sculpture and consideration of the sites where it was found form part of the problem of their reconstruction. It is useful to commence with the one example of a painted pediment, of what has been called 'Temple Aa': a composition of animals executed not in sculptured relief but in painting, the animals being rendered in light colour on a dark ground like the red-figured vases of later times. This is in the tradition of the late seventh-century painted metopes of Thermon in Aetolia, and also of the brightly painted architectural detail of the Archaic period. The logical development is, first, to

Below: Detail of the archaic Hydra Pediment (Herakles,
Hydra, Iolaos, chariot, crab), showing Iolaos and the chariot team.
Opposite: The so-called Introduction Pediment (the
introduction of Herakles to Olympos by Athena) from an
Archaic building on the Acropolis. Zeus seated to right,
Hera facing, (Athena missing), Herakles and possibly Iris.

introduce relief and to develop increasing skill in adapting sculptured figures to the pedimental triangle and, second, to attain increasing depth of the relief until at last the figures are entirely detached, a process ultimately promoted by the use of more costly and finer stone for the figures than for the pedimental wall. The first stage is represented by the pediment which shows Herakles' combat with the Hydra, whose snaky body is admirably suited to fill one corner, while the chariot of Herakles with the horses facing to the angle, their heads bent to sniff at a great crab, help to fill the other. The relief is only 25 mm. in depth – the first

called the 'Well House' or 'Olive Tree' pediment. Apart from a tiny maiden figure of doll-like, Archaic charm and the indication of an olive tree, the most important feature is a building with a wall before it, variously interpreted as a well house (if so, the subject might be the ambush of Troilos and Polyxena by Achilles), or as a primitive Erechtheum, in view of the presence of an olive tree. The building is thus described by the American scholar Dinsmoor: 'A mythological scene of architectural importance because of the meticulously detailed representation of a building with pseudo-isodomic coursing of the wall

stage, as it were, beyond a picture incised in stone. It has been suggested that, in the other gable of this building, or in the following, there was a primitive-seeming representation of Herakles wrestling with the sea-monster Triton.

Other elements which link sculpture with painting are the non-human, non-animal background and architectural representations, which are rather rare. On the Acropolis there is a small pediment variously

masonry, mutular cornice, and tiled hip roof.' The subject is, in fact, quite uncertain. It is still a miniature pediment, but the relief is ·254 m. deep.

Again somewhat deeper in relief, and larger, is the 'Introduction Pediment', of which the subject also appears in vase-painting. It is appropriate to the Acropolis, since it represents the introduction by Athena of her hero-favourite, Herakles, to the assembly of the gods, including Zeus seated to right

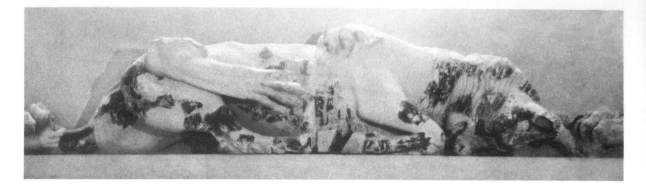

Above: Archaic *poros* group from the Acropolis.
Two lions attacking a bull.
Below: The Acropolis Hound.

and Hera facing. The coarse stone shows incised
detail and the remnants of bright colour.

To the larger Archaic temples on the Acropolis are
allotted, in various permutations and combinations,
the truly monumental sculptures in *poros* limestone
representing lions or lionesses attacking bulls or
calves which formed admirable heraldic groups for
the centre of a pediment, with snakes at the corners.
There is also another, and larger, Herakles and Triton
and a snaky-tailed 'Triple-bodied Monster' grasping
what are possibly intended to be the symbols of fire,
water and air. How these are to be combined is a
matter of debate, but here one should note their
artistic character, and in particular the brightly
coloured decoration of the stuccoed surface of the
coarse stone.

Finally, there is from the second half of the sixth century the sadly battered eastern pediment of the Peisistratid temple of Athena. The figures are in marble and are no longer attached to the pediment wall. It is a disaster that the surviving figures are a mosaic of fragments reconstructed in plaster. Athena, striding to the spectators' right, stood in or near the centre of the pediment. While she was undoubtedly engaged in striking down a Giant, the fallen semi-recumbent figure, with the awkward anatomical transition between upper and lower body, was not closely related to her, as it was in the earlier arrangement in the Acropolis Museum. The recumbent Giant has now been reassembled (and shortened) and placed at a greater distance from Athena, while the other two forward-crouching figures fit into the corners. Their battered state conceals the great achievement they represent. It has been said of them by the late Humphry Payne, who had a superlative understanding of Greek art: 'in force of movement they are the only Archaic statues really comparable with the west pediment of Olympia.' They show, he believed,

the highest Archaic precision of form, in common with the celebrated Acropolis Hound. There are also fragments of a marble group of lions devouring a bull, which may belong to the western pediment of the same building.

From this same building – at a period perhaps somewhat before 520 BC – come other fragments, which serve to introduce the not inconsiderable amount of Archaic sculpture, not pedimental, found on the Acropolis. There are fragments of a Nike *akroterion* and of a ram's head waterspout, and the superb lion's head waterspout, which some have sought to associate with the Hound, and therefore by a great master. More uncertain are fragments of a frieze with a figure which could be male or female, Apollo or Artemis, mounting a chariot, and another which might be Hermes. They could be parts of a frieze of the Panathenaic procession. It has been

Sima block and lion's head waterspout. From the Peisistratid reconstruction of the Archaic Temple of Athena (?) of about 520 BC.

suggested that these are fragments of a frieze around the *cella* of the Peisistratid temple. The style could be said to be too late for this, but it would be ill-advised to distinguish too nicely between 520 and 510 BC.

Much earlier is a splendid Gorgon mask, which, with some fragments of her body, represent a main central *akroterion* of a building of *c.* 570 BC, matching a Perseus of which a large fragment is also preserved. To the same period and to one of the early buildings on the Acropolis belong the bodies and heads of panthers which may have been used to decorate a frieze or metopes, and the remains of a facing chariot group. The four heads of the horses are symmetrically out-turned, two to the left and two to the right, in an ambitious attempt at a rendering which is an alternative to the more common side view. The full frontal rendering appears elsewhere in vase-painting and relief metalwork, and strikingly in the eastern pediment of the Archaic temple of Apollo at Delphi, and in a metope from a Sicilian temple. Its artistic value is dubious, but the Greeks themselves seem to have appreciated it as a tour de force.

The Archaic architectural sculpture from the Acropolis is not only battered, but also wholly detached from its context, since the buildings it decorated have disappeared. This is not so true for the Classical period. The buildings still stand, and although they are ruined, and the decorative sculpture is in large measure separated from them, its placing, if not the arrangement of some of it, is well established. On the other hand, what survives – again in a battered state – is a good deal less than the original total, and many problems of interpretation and detailed arrangement arise. Three Classical buildings on the Acropolis were decorated with sculpture which in part survives. In chronological order they are the Parthenon, the temple of Athena Nike and the Erechtheum.

THE PARTHENON

The Parthenon sculptures are incomparably the most important. From early on they attracted the attention of travellers and artists, and to this we owe the many drawings which, with varying degrees of accuracy, indicate the state of the sculpture (especially the pediments) at varying dates. These records, together with the vicissitudes undergone by the Parthenon and other buildings on the Acropolis, will be considered later. The present account is concerned with the

sculptures as they survive in Athens, Paris, London (and possibly elsewhere), their original state, and their interpretation.

The two pediments of the Parthenon were filled with some fifty sculptured free-standing figures. Unfortunately the central group of the eastern pediment was destroyed by the creation of an apse, when the Parthenon was converted into the Christian church of the Holy Wisdom. The western pediment suffered from the explosion of 1687, and from Morosini's subsequent attempt to remove a central portion of the sculpture. The eastern and western metopes survive to this day *in situ*. Besides the wear and tear inflicted by time and weather, many of the metopes also suffered deliberate defacement, certainly before 1674, and possibly at the time of the conversion to a Christian church, or later. The metopes of the south side escaped this treatment, as did the most westerly metope on the north side, containing two female figures and it has been suggested that it received a Christian interpretation as a representation of *The Annunciation*. In similar fashion the became part of Christian symbolism, and so the south metopes were spared. If this is true, one wonders why the frieze and the figures of the pediment were left undefaced.

The great explosion (of 1687) blew out the central portions of the north and south colonnades, and so largely dismounted the metopes on these sides. The same disaster affected the frieze, which stood above the inner colonnades of the porches on the east and west and above the wall of the interior chamber on the north and south. The frieze is happily preserved *in situ* at the west end of the temple, thus giving some indication of its artistic effect and the degree to which it was visible from the level of the temple platform. The rest was displaced from the building, and the eastern, northern and southern sections had already suffered in the construction of the early Christian church.

A considerable number of damaged figures and fragments survived from the outer angles of the pediments. The arrangement of the centre of the eastern pediment is wholly a matter of conjecture, since it is totally lost. The same is largely true of the centre of the western pediment, though some small fragments of the central group remain. Of the ninety-two metopes originally decorating the building, twenty-eight survive *in situ* on the east and west, eleven on the north side, and one on the south.

Above: Centaur and Lapith on a metope from the
Parthenon and now in the British Museum.
Overleaf: The Parthenon. Interior looking east.

Fifteen metopes of the south side are in the British Museum, one in the Louvre and one in the Acropolis Museum, which also has two northern metopes, and fragments from which two more southern metopes can largely be reconstructed. Thus sixty-one survive. The draughtsman employed in 1674 by the Marquis de Nointel drew all the metopes of the south side, and so there is evidence for twelve more slabs which have now vanished. He did not draw the metopes of the other three sides because they had been deliberately defaced.

The frieze (about one metre high) was originally approximately a hundred and sixty metres long. Roughly 128 m. of it survive: and a further 17 m. are known from drawings. Thus comparatively little has been lost of this supremely great work of art, and what has been lost disappeared at an early date, since the central portion of the east front, and slabs on the north and south sides were affected by the conversion of the temple to a Christian church.

The construction of the Parthenon is partly documented by contemporary account inscriptions, which give evidence of dates and other details, though, unlike the Erechtheum accounts, little of craftsmen and their work or remuneration. Costs are given for quarrying and rough hewing at the Pentelic quarries; for loading on wagons; for transport and for the dragging of the blocks to the workshops, presumably on the Acropolis. There are sums for wood for the construction of the wagons (but no details of the oxen which drew them), and it is probable that the cost of road construction was also covered. The accounts start in the year 447/6 BC. By 440–438 BC there is reference to doors and woodwork, and by 439/8 BC to ivory, silver-work and gilding. In 434/3 BC surplus gold and ivory were being sold, and the last surviving account is dated 433/2 BC, the eve of the Peloponnesian War. As far as these accounts are preserved (and a great deal is missing) only the pedimental sculptures appear from 438/7 BC onwards to 434/3 BC. They could not have been placed in position until the roof was on the building, and it is generally assumed that this stage had been reached by 438/7 BC when, according to an emended comment (quoting a fourth-century Attic historian) on a line of Aristophanes, the great gold and ivory statue of Athena was set up in the temple (unemended the date would be 432/1 BC).

There is a series of ten very fragmentary inscriptions which give the accounts for 'the golden statue', and record the purchase of ivory and gold. The fourth-century source mentioned above gives the total weight

The Parthenon frieze.

of the gold as forty-four talents, which is approximately 1151 kilos. It is interesting to note that one source of the gold was 110 gold coins of the Lydian King Croesus, used for this purpose a century or so after their issue. None of these accounts for the statue is dated, but as there are ten, and the statue was set up in 438/7 BC, it is assumed the work on it commenced in about 447 BC, at much the same time as the work on the temple. Its construction must have been a complicated process. This was a decade in which Pheidias was certainly in Athens, working on the statue and exercising general superintendence. Following on the dedication of the statue in 438/7 BC came the attacks on Pericles through his friends, the charge of embezzlement of the gold, Pheidias' departure into exile, and his period of residence at Olympia to work on the great gold and ivory statue of Zeus. The finds on the site of the 'workshop of Pheidias' at Olympia, and especially the style of the moulds found there which were used to make metallic drapery, seem to confirm this chronology.

Therefore after 438/7 BC Pheidias was no longer in Athens, but the work on the pedimental sculpture went on to 434/3 BC, and possibly to 433/2 BC, which might also be the date of Pheidias' death. In 434/3 BC the sum of 16380 drachmai was paid out to sculptors, but it must be admitted this gives no clue to the number employed or their quality and prestige. It is greatly to be regretted that we do not have more detail; that we do not know how Pheidias was remunerated, or the other well-known sculptors who must have worked with him. The position is different in the Erechtheum building inscriptions of 408/7 BC and the following years, in which a great quantity of detail is given on wages. Here there is clearly a craftsman's daily wage of one drachma per day. On the other hand, sculptors did piece-work in the preparation of the frieze of marble figures pegged to the band of Eleusinian stone which ran round the building. These figures were probably somewhat less in height than the ·683 m. of the stone background, and therefore very minor. One suspects that the eight sculptors employed were also relatively undistinguished. The record of their work is set down thus: in the case of single figures, 'the man holding the bridle, 60 drachmai'; 'the man leaning on a stick beside the altar, 60 drachmai'; for double or treble

figures the payments are 80 or 120 drachmai. There seems to be a unit of payment, which reduces the work from the artistic to the journeyman level.

In these Erechtheum accounts the total payment for one prytany (or tenth of the year) is 3315 drachmai. When the sum of 16380 drachmai, paid out in 434–3 BC for the Parthenon sculpture, is looked at, it is not unreasonable to conclude that by that year the massive pediments of the Parthenon were largely finished. They were therefore approximately the work of the years from 438 BC to 433 BC. Since the backs of the figures are clearly finished in detail, they must have been carved on the ground and hoisted into place. This would not preclude final touches *in situ*, or repairs necessitated by damage suffered in the difficult operation of hoisting the massive figures into place. The metopes had to be slotted in between the triglyphs, and thus positioned before the roof was put on. It is therefore generally agreed they were made between 447 BC and 439 BC, but here, if the figures were roughly blocked out, and the necessary margins reduced to the thickness required for placing between the triglyphs, the rest of the carving could be done *in situ*. However, the planning of the figure decoration for each metope would have to be done before 439 BC. In the same way the frieze blocks had to be placed in position before the roof, but in this case the whole work could have been done *in situ*, and indeed this is asserted for the north and south sides. Nevertheless some scholars claim that the west frieze was carved on the ground. It is not very clear why this should have been so, unless it was a matter of the organisation of 'work flow'. If this view is correct, the west frieze would have been carved between 447 BC, when the temple was started, and 439 BC when the roof was probably put on, while the long sides were executed in the years from 439 BC to possibly 432 BC. Indeed it is entirely feasible that a plan of work marshalled craftsmen, stone masons, carpenters and sculptors together at the beginning in 447 BC, and organised their work on the ground and then *in situ* on the building as it rose, and also progressed from west to east (or the reverse).

Thus the various groups of sculptures were produced in relatively limited periods of time, but the determination of the length of time in each case is complicated by the considerations outlined above. In general it may be said that the contrast between what is old fashioned (as in the metopes) and new in terms of the development of Greek art (as in parts of the frieze and in the pedimental sculptures) may well mean the employment of older or younger artists within a short period, rather than the development of the same personalities over a longer period.

As in the rest of Classical Greek sculpture and the later copies of it, archaeologists have played the game of detection of styles in the case of the Parthenon sculptures. Sketches and models must have been produced under the over-all supervision of Pheidias, though he can hardly have executed them all. These sketches and models, subject to the approval of the building commissioners, can have reflected only the ideas of other true artists associated with the Master. On the other hand, the detailed sculptures were the direct work of expert craftsmen, working under supervision but permitted some freedom in detail. Thus it is idle to attempt to detect the work of Pheidias' older or younger contemporaries, especially as no original and clearly attested works by them survive.

Before the Parthenon sculptures are considered in more detail, certain points may be made which are frequently overlooked. The tradition of 'marmoreal whiteness' current from the Renaissance in Western Europe obscures the fact that Greek architectural sculpture relied on colour, as well as gilded bronze. Colour was used for considerable areas, such as backgrounds for metopes and frieze, and also for details. Frequently details partly represented in relief were continued in paint. The bronze adjuncts must have supplied a good deal to the interpretation of figures, as for example in the pedimental sculptures. Their lack has made it difficult for modern scholars to identify certain figures in the pediments. It is clear from roughened areas of the marble that the use of gilded bronze plating as for shields was quite extensive.

There is one final preoccupation of the modern scholar. Some aspects of the sculptural decoration such as the backs of the pedimental figures, could not be seen by any human person, so here it is better to assume an extreme perfectionism rather than the gratification of the Gods. The sculpture of the temple must have been difficult to see, except at a distance, and therefore detail of a refined sort was irrelevant, unless we assume incredibly good eyesight in the Athenians of the fifth century BC, as we must in the mediaeval viewers of stained-glass windows. This problem is nowhere better illustrated than in the

An Erechtheum Caryatid.

frieze which, less than one metre high, was placed some twelve metres above the platform of the temple. The relief of the upper part is deeper, to compensate, it is always said, for the extreme angle of view. Indeed it must have been very difficult to view it at all satisfactorily, though the coloured background no doubt helped. It was also very strongly illuminated by reflected light from below without obscuring of detail. In general the clear bright light would tend to throw strong shadows, and thus provide a contrast with the relief. In any case, leaving aside all argument on sight lines, unlike the metopes and the pedimental sculptures which were a representation in stone of certain figurative but unreal events, the frieze was a record of something the Athenians could see in the flesh, as it were, at regular intervals. If they knew it was there, this would suffice, even if it could not be adequately seen. It was the supreme glory of Athens, laid up for all to think about, if not to see.

Opposite: The western porch of the Parthenon showing the position of the frieze.
Below: The 'Carrey' drawings of the eastern pediment of the Parthenon.

The decorative sculpture of this great building received but scant attention in Antiquity. Only Pausanias gives a brief comment: 'At the entrance to the temple which they call the Parthenon, all the figures, as many as are placed in the pediments as they are called, relate to the Birth of Athena, and at the rear is the Contest of Poseidon with Athena for the land'[1]. He then goes on to describe, not without some striking irrelevance, the gold and ivory statue of the Parthenos. Even so this is better than the case of the metopes and frieze, of which there is no mention whatsoever in Antiquity. However brief the description of Pausanias, it serves to remove any doubt on what is represented in the pediments; doubt which would otherwise arise, since the central portion of both is missing. Even so, the eastern pediment was once interpreted as the Contest for Attica.

The Pediments

In the eastern pediment the centre may well have been taken by a great figure of Zeus enthroned. Since it is inconceivable that Athena was represented issuing from the head of Zeus in the Archaic manner, she had

to be shown fully developed, but suitably enough, of lesser stature than her father. The central placing of Zeus is thus better than a central Athena flanked by lesser figures of Zeus and Hera. It is, however, doubtful for the solution of the problem what value is to be placed on the so-called Madrid Puteal, a circular altar converted into a well-head. It is decorated with a relief showing Zeus seated to the right, with Hephaistos behind his throne on the left; Athena before him crowned by Victory, and the Three Fates, Klotho, Lachesis and Atropos. It is uncertain how far this relief is to be trusted; in one particular it certainly cannot represent the arrangement of the pediment. A three-dimensional Zeus seated to the right would be an unsightly arrangement from some angles of view. Therefore Zeus must be envisaged facing, and thus receiving a prominence suitable to the King of the Gods, even on Athena's temple. Or his seated figure and chair could be so arranged as to conceal the illogical combination of frontal and profile renderings. On his left Athena would then appear crowned by Victory, matched on his right by Hephaistos with his axe. Or Victory could be an ornament of Zeus' throne. An inferior and subordinate Hera would not be unsuitable to the relationship of the two goddesses.

For the rest it is difficult to decide how far any canonical figures in Archaic representations, such as the Fates and Dionysos, appeared also on the Parthenon. To a great extent the attendant figures must have been determined by Pheidias and the commissioners representing the Athenian people. Thus (and the same is true of the western pediment) the battered, headless torsos and fragments of heads and bodies are difficult to identify, especially as they are now deprived of their attributes, which were originally in bronze. It should be added that the vicissitudes to which the Parthenon has been exposed from the Early Christian period onwards have progressively worsened the state of the sculpture up to the time of the investigation of the Acropolis as an archaeological monument. Hence the importance of sketches and drawings made over a long period by visitors to Athens or commissioned by them: not only general sketches of the Acropolis and the Parthenon by travellers such as Spon and Wheler in 1676, and many others down to Dodwell, Gell and Smirke in the first years of the nineteenth century, but also drawings of sculpture, and particularly of the pedimental sculpture. Most important are the drawings made for the Marquis de Nointel in 1674, shortly before the great

Below: The floor of the eastern pediment of the Parthenon, showing the fastenings for the pedimental sculpture.
Opposite: A figure from the southern half of the eastern pediment of the Parthenon now in the British Museum. Possibly a personification of Mount Olympos, but more likely Dionysos.
Overleaf: Three figures from the northern portion of the eastern pediment; possibly Hestia, Dione and Aphrodite. In the British Museum.

explosion – though the centre of the eastern pediment had disappeared long before – and those made in the eighteenth century by Dalton (1749) and Pars (1765), which illustrate the damage and loss suffered after 1674, and between 1765 and Elgin (1799). It may also be noticed that for figures which survive, and were recovered from the ground at either end of the temple, the site on which they were discovered is important to determine their original placing: so too is the existence and nature of weathering, and the marks of fastenings on the pedimental floors.

In the southern corner of the eastern pediment, what is generally taken to be Helios (the Sun) rises with his chariot team from the rippling water. From the northern end of the pediment there is a female

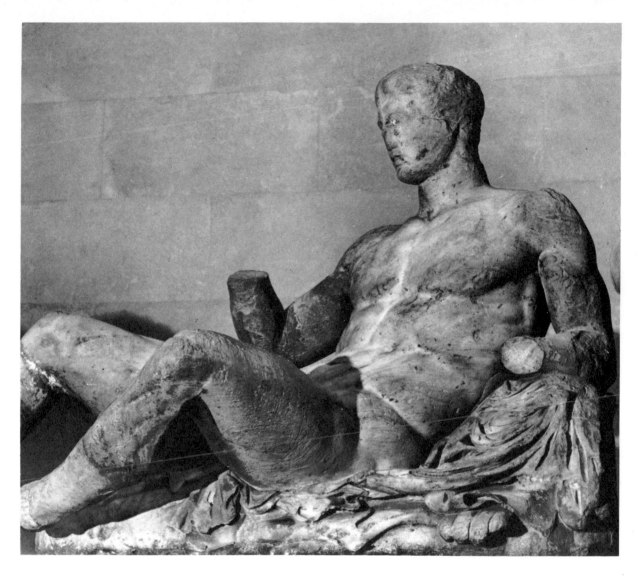

torso, clad in charioteer costume, and the heads of a team of horses (one of which, Goethe's '*Urpferd*', must surely be the finest ever) which seems to be a counterpart to Helios. It is probably meant to represent Selene sinking into the sea with her weary horses or else Night. A head which seems to come from the Parthenon has been associated with the Selene torso, but it does not appear in the Carrey drawing and was in fact found in front of the western face of the temple. These corner groups seem to identify the time of the Birth. It is not unreasonable, therefore, to expect an indication of place. It is with this association of ideas that the male figure, three quarters facing to the south, once quite inappropriately taken to be Theseus, has been identified as a personification of Olympos, the scene of the event, illumined by the rays of the rising sun. Another favoured suggestion is Dionysos, in Archaic art frequently present at the Birth of Athena. Yet if this is correct, it is difficult, except on grounds of fitting the figures into the pedimental triangle, to explain why he turns his back on the scene. He quite certainly cannot be Herakles though this has been strongly argued by one scholar.

The female figures next in order, seated on chests, are clearly very closely associated. The second of them has an arm raised towards the centre of the pediment. It is problematic whether these are Demeter and Kore (and certainly difficulties arise in the case of the latter) or two of the three Horai. Next seems to come the figure of a youthful, wingless female running to

Above: Late Greek *hydria* (water-jar) in the Hermitage Museum, Leningrad, showing the contest of Athena and Poseidon for the land of Attica.

The 'Carrey' drawings of the west pediment of the of the Parthenon. *Below:* The southern section. *Opposite:* The northern section.

the left, but turning her head (now lost) to the centre. She held her upper garment billowing behind her, and may be intended to represent that outward wave of interest or emotion which unifies the scene. Beyond this figure may have been the Three Fates, elsewhere represented as present at the Birth.

To the north of the lost central group, in the right-hand section of the pediment, are three massive female figures seated on a rock, the folds of their garments, and the body beneath, superbly rendered. The first sits almost frontally, but turned somewhat to the centre, the second is turned more to the right, her lower legs drawn back, and beyond her the third figure reclines, her right arm and shoulder on the lap of the second. In 1674 the first two still possessed their heads. They cannot be the Three Fates, and they are unlikely to be Clouds or Hesperids. The first is commonly identified as Hestia; the second and third as Dione and Aphrodite, or perhaps Gaia and Thalassa, Earth and Sea. It is all rather obscure, and the attribution of other pieces is even more dubious and disputed. A torso in Athens may be Hephaistos or Poseidon; other fragments may represent Eros, Herakles, Hermes, Ares, Apollo, Artemis and Leto: material for the diverse restorations of the pediment.

The pediments of the Parthenon represent two aspects of the legend of Athena, one of which is oecumenical – her birth from the head of Zeus – and relevant to all Greeks; the other intensely local – the Contest between Athena and Poseidon for the land of Attica, in which she produced the olive tree and Poseidon the sterile gift of the salt spring. In this Contest, in the western pediment, although (with the aid of coins, a red-figured vase in the Hermitage and a Carrey drawing) the arrangement and identity of the central figures can be determined with some certainty, the figures in the angles present very considerable problems of identification, since they are connected with the local legends of Attica.

The pediment suffered from the explosion of 1687 and from Morosini's attempt to remove part of the centre. What survives is a mass of battered torsos and smaller fragments. A number of the figures are known only from drawings. The centre was probably occupied by the olive tree, encircled by Athena's snake, with Athena on the left of it and Poseidon on the right. Behind each of them was a chariot team. That of Athena was the object of Morosini's ill-starred attempt at removal, while that of Poseidon had already disappeared when the Carrey drawing of the western pediment was made. Fragments of the olive tree and snake, and of Athena's chariot team survive, but not really enough to judge the quality of the horses in comparison with those of the eastern pediment. There is also the upper torso of Poseidon, and a portion of the upper torso and head of Athena. Poseidon still possessed his head in the Carrey drawing, but had lost it by 1749. The charioteer of Athena, probably to be identified as Nike, survives only in a drawing, but there are fragments of the charioteer of

Poseidon, who may be identified as his wife Amphitrite. Beneath is a sea monster to underline the association of the two deities with the sea, or else to suggest the salt spring. For Athens of the time the sea was particularly important. Behind Athena's chariot a male figure which possessed its head until 1674 now survives only as a torso, and is probably to be identified as Hermes. Dalton's drawing of 1749 shows this figure overthrown in the pediment; by Elgin's time it had fallen to the ground and been built into a Turkish house. Matching Hermes on the side of Poseidon was a female figure represented by the celebrated torso in the British Museum with its remarkable clinging draperies. It was winged, and probably to be identified with Iris.

It is unfortunate that there is little or nothing of a canonical version of the Contest in other art forms. Indeed the myth does not appear in art before the period of the Parthenon, and in literature before Herodotus.[2] Some small copies of figures from the pediment have been found in the excavations of the Athens Market-place and at Eleusis.

It is not unreasonable to believe that the male torso, with its outstandingly skilful anatomical rendering, in the left (northern) angle represents a river of Attica, possibly the Ilissos. If so, then it is possible to match it in the right-hand (southern) angle by identifying the figures as the Kephissos or Eridanos in the case of the corner male figure, and the fountain Kallirhoe in the case of the female figure still reclining *in situ*. Alternatively the northern angle figure could be identified as one of the ancient heroic figures of Attica: Kranaos, Aktaios, Amphiktyon, Boutes or Bouzyges. Similarly the figures of the south corner could be Kephalos and Prokris, with a certain lack of mythological accuracy. There was an Athenian Kephalos, son of Hermes and Herse, or of Hermes and Kreousa, who was beloved of Eos (the Dawn) or of Hemera (Day) who carried him off. This event was represented in the Athenian Stoa Basileios, and may be hinted at on the Parthenon if these corner figures are Kephalos and one of his goddess pursuers.

Kephalos then provides a link with the rest of the side figures – the heroes or heroines of ancient Attic saga. From the left (north) there followed after the figure of the angle, another, preserved only in a drawing of Pars; hard to identify and perhaps another heroic character, or the wife of the first. Then came what is probably the figure of Kekrops, but not shown as snake-bodied, and a daughter (Pandrosos?).

The heads of both survived to 1765, and that of Kekrops to 1795. It should be noted that Kekrops played some part, as spectator or judge, in the Contest. After this point in the northern half, drawings and fragments may represent Herse, Aglauros, and the child Erysichthon. In the southern half, beyond Iris and possibly Aphrodite, fragments of an adult female figure and of a child could be identified (originally with two children) as Oreithyia, daughter of Erechtheus – her garment appropriately billowing in the blast of her husband Boreas, with her children Zetes and Kalais. There follows Ion on the lap of his mother Kreousa (another daughter of Erechtheus) and Praxithea, his wife, and beyond her another daughter and her child. The next crouching male figure (preserved as a battered torso, but possessing its head in the Carrey drawing) and the reclining female *in situ* have already been discussed. This is altogether a complex and intensely local subject, excellently adapted to the triangular pediment. The western pediment clearly illustrates also the importance of drawings as records of elements now lost. Some of the vanished heads must survive in modern museums, having passed from the possession of private owners. The head of Kekrops, for example, was in the possession of the English traveller Dodwell, while a Frenchman, Fauvel, owned the head of the daughter. The celebrated Laborde Head (in the Louvre) may have come from one of the pediments and is possibly the head of Amphitrite.

It is natural that efforts should have been made to detect the work of different hands, but there is very little justification for attaching famous names. In the eastern pediment the style of Hestia is different from that of Aphrodite and Dione, and the latter can be related in style to Iris, but it seems highly dubious to identify here (and in a horse head) the style of Agorakritos, and even more so the style of Kolotes in the Hermes torso of the western pediment. Again it is reasonable to seek the same sculptural hands in elements of pediments, metopes and frieze, and even to give names such as the Helios Master, but not to go further. The dangers of subjectivity are illustrated by the fact that some distinguished authorities believe that the western pediment is later than the eastern,

The eastern façade of the Parthenon.

which infers a construction from east to west, while another asserts that the construction took place in the opposite direction. Here we know too little of work methods to argue from such considerations.

The other two categories of sculptural decoration of the Parthenon may be treated in briefer fashion. Something has already been said about the date of the metopes and the frieze in relation to the construction of the building. The theme of the frieze was also outlined when cult ceremonial was described.

The Metopes

It is natural to assume that in determining the events to be represented in the metopes, priority of importance would be given to the east front. The theory of a 'peaceful' subject in the pediment did not preclude strife in the metopes. Here, therefore, was represented the Battle of the Gods and Giants, in which Athena played a notable part, as she did earlier in the marble pediment of her ancient temple, and contemporaneously on the inside of the shield of her gold and ivory statue. It reminded Athens of her own struggles. In the words of one commentator: 'The struggle of Athens was linked to Athena's own by joining to this myth the battle of the Gods and Giants in the east metopes of the temple and on the inside of the shield of the statue.' At the west end of the temple appeared the Battle of Greeks and Amazons. Not all the metopes here and at the east end show two combattants. On the south Lapiths and Lapith women resist the wanton attack of the Centaurs at the marriage of

Head of a centaur from a southern metope
of the Parthenon.

Peirithöos; a subject represented earlier by a great master in the western pediment of the temple of Zeus at Olympia.

The subject or subjects of the northern metopes present more difficulties. Greeks, Trojans and Gods appear, but some episodes and figures are very difficult to interpret, as for example the westernmost metope, which was possibly taken by early Christians to represent *The Annunciation*, and thus escaped defacement. The various struggles may be regarded as symbols of Greek resistance to the barbarians, recalling especially their historic stand against the Persians. These episodes of mythology, with symbolic intent, appear again and again in Attic art. Thus the Centaurs and Lapiths were seen on the shield of the great bronze Athena, and earlier in the temple of Hephaistos; the Amazons and the Sack of Troy in the famous Stoa Poikile or Painted Porch in lower Athens (where they were coupled with the representation of a historic event, the Battle of Marathon); and the Amazons again in the temple of Hephaistos.

The relief in the metopes is sometimes excessively high. The style varies considerably – as does the skill displayed in composition – from excellent to poor. It is obvious that the high relief and the limited field presented a considerable challenge. The usual group in the surviving metopes is of two figures, though there are rare cases of three and one has four. On occasions background and 'landscape' elements are indicated. As in the frieze, it is clear that there were many adjuncts in gilded bronze, such as weapons, harness, and the covering of shields. Details (partially in relief), in both the metopes and the frieze, were augmented and continued in paint which has disappeared. Colour was also used for the background. It is difficult to envisage the effects of these additions which have to be mentally supplied when the sculptures are contemplated in the modern museum setting. It is to be doubted whether the overall effect would have been to modern taste, but bright light and distance must have been factors of some importance in the ultimate impression.

As in the pedimental sculptures, scholars seek to detect different hands at work in the metopes, as well as parallels in other sculpture, and the style of great artists. There is certainly a wide spectrum of style in the metopes, and the question of the limits of date within which these sculptures were produced has already been mentioned. Aside from the question of greater or less technical competence, there is the fact that, in relation to the date of execution, some 'old-fashioned' styles appear, and some which are more modern. Three of the names mentioned are those of Kritios, a sculptor already active around 480–470 BC; of Myron, creator of the *Diskobolos* and an older contemporary of Pheidias; and of Pheidias himself. The detection of the same unnamed hands in metopes, and in slabs of the frieze is less debatable, as is also the quest for relationships with the sculptures of the Hephaisteion (the so-called Theseum) on the edge of the Market-place. This was the temple which the goddess as Athena Ergane (in which quality she appears on the Acropolis also) shared with Hephaistos, the god who secured her delivery from the head of Zeus. He has been described as 'working partner to the new-born goddess of work', and this relationship is implicit in the myth of Pandora on the base of the great gold and ivory statue in the Parthenon.

The Frieze

Finally there is the frieze, in effect the best preserved element of the sculptural decoration of Athena's temple. It has already been commented on for its subject and artistic relationship to the pedimental sculpture and the metopes. In its subject and in the continuance of the same theme around all four sides of the building it seems to be unique and it has been suggested that this was an innovation of Pheidias himself. He must also have superintended the general lay-out, but the more detailed organisation of the four sides would have to be left to other masters, and a detailed execution to pupils and craftsmen. Broad differences of style between the sides, and variations in details of rendering and degrees of competence, all indicate the employment of a large number of sculptors, perhaps as many as seventy, to carve the band which is some 158 metres long and one metre high. The result of this complicated undertaking is one of the world's greatest works of art: certainly not without its deficiencies, but in general a miracle of skill, especially in the number of overlapping planes contrived between the front surface and the background within a remarkably limited depth.

The observation has already been made that the greater depth of relief at the top than at the bottom, adjusted to the position of spectators from below, would seem to indicate that the frieze was intended to be seen and appreciated. It has also been claimed that careful account was taken of sight-lines, especially from the platform at the west end of the temple. None the less it cannot have been easily seen on the north and south sides in the crammed and constricted state of the Acropolis, when all the structures were fully preserved – whatever advantage was obtained from reflected light. A view of the frieze would also have been interrupted by the columns of the peristyle, but this interruption might have given an effect of motion. It has already been suggested that the human viewer did not so much matter. The Athenians could contemplate the living reality of the Panathenaic procession every year, and the grander version every four years, and so the frieze could be interpreted, like the statues of youths and maidens dedicated on the Acropolis, as primarily an offering to the goddess. The frieze did not represent the whole procession, still less the whole festival. Nor is it the procession as it was after the Panathenaic ship had been left at the foot of the Acropolis. The well-organised western frieze, in which some have detected an 'Ionic' influence, and which certainly shows a more open style illustrates the preparations for the cavalcade and its marshalling, which took place in the Pompeion, the building at the Kerameikos Gate from which the procession set out. It is unlikely that cavalry and chariots ascended to the restricted area and narrow processional route on the Acropolis, despite indications of grooves on the processional way on the Acropolis, and the provision of a ramp up through the Propylaia, which, in any case, was replaced by a staircase paved with marble in the Roman period under Claudius. On the other hand the hoplite foot soldiers of Athens could have made the ascent, but they are not represented on the frieze. It might be suggested they would be far more difficult to diversify artistically than cavalry and chariotry. The Assembly of the Gods and the figures of old men who may represent the Athenian tribal heroes, in whose presence the robe of Athena is handed over to be placed on the ancient image, form the focus of the ceremony, but are not part of the festal procession. The whole must be taken to be a choice of incidents to symbolise those aspects of the ceremonial best fitted to demonstrate respect for the gods, the glory and ideal unity of Athens, and the skill of her artists – especially in the rendering of human and equine forms.

The problem of organising the procession, commencing at the west, dividing on the north and south,

Four riders and parts of five galloping horses
from the north frieze of the Parthenon and now in
the Acropolis Museum.

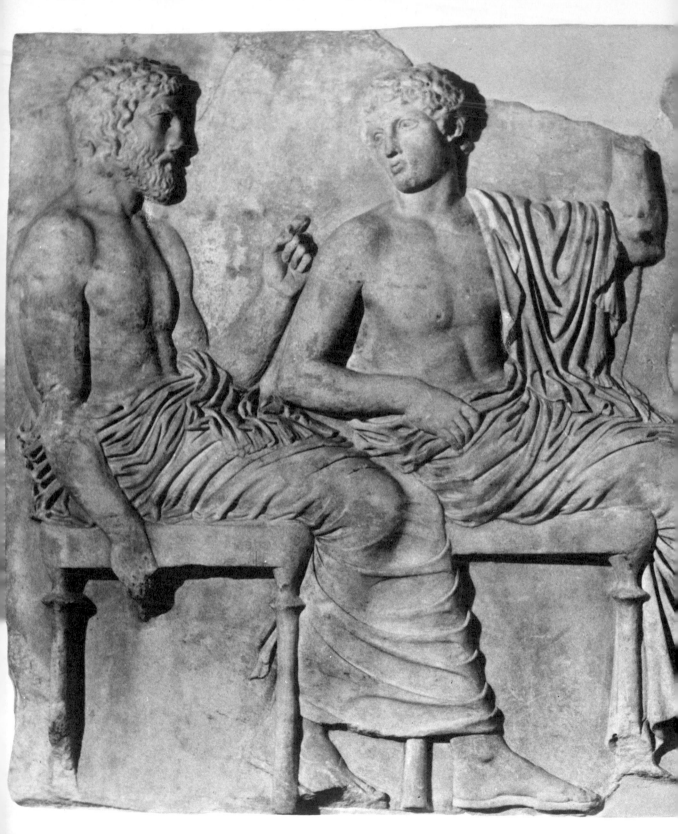

Slab from the eastern frieze of the Parthenon,
showing part of the Assembly of the Gods. Poseidon
(his trident formerly added in paint?), Apollo or
Dionysos, Peitho or Demeter. In the Acropolis Museum.

and meeting in the east is skilfully met. As P. E. Corbett puts it:

'... it was possible to go around the south west corner, but the most convenient and natural route lies on the North. Thus most people would see the West end and part of the North side at the same time, but they would not normally see the South and West sides together, so that the South-west corner is the most unobtrusive position for the division between the two streams into which the relief is divided.'[3]

The central point of the east frieze is easily determined, as the same writer points out, even if details of the composition and rendering are weak:

'At the East the artist has set above the main entrance a group that is worthy of its position; in a

Opposite: A dedicatory maiden-statue.
Below: Slab from the eastern frieze of the Parthenon, showing the setting of seats for the Gods, and *either* the folding of the old peplos *or* the receiving of the new.

magistrate with the *peplos* and the priestess with the stools we see the moment of greatest solemnity at which the procession reaches its natural end. The necessity of bringing together the two streams which run along the North and South of the building lends itself to the formation of a unified composition that guides the eye to the middle; the seated divinities enclose the central group, lifting it above the plane of normal human life; their presence also creates a wide interval between the two converging lines of maidens, thus avoiding the awkwardness of a head-on meeting.'[3]

The western frieze presents a more difficult problem, the organisation of divergence, not convergence, and the avoidance of an obvious central division. To quote the same scholar:

'... the central point is marked out by a group of exceptional liveliness and quality – the man controlling a restive horse – and there are a number of standing figures which provide a static element; several of them face to the right and save the side

from being unidirectional, while the last three slabs on the right include a horse which is heading in the opposite direction from all the rest; this animal, with the two men nearest the corner, facilitates the transition to the South side.'³

Particularly striking is the variation of movement, from the static figures of the Gods, the magistrate and the priestess, the old men and the maidens in the eastern frieze to the slow motion of the participants in the procession and the sacrificial animals; in the cavalry and chariots all the variations from dismounted and static to motion at the canter and gallop – the latter a quite impossible part of the procession.

The point has already been made that the frieze, like the metopes and the pediments, represents much artistic work done in a relatively limited time, and the work of many individuals. It is natural to seek that of Pheidias among them, and to him have been ascribed the group of Zeus and Hera among the Gods of the eastern frieze, and the scene of the handing over of the *peplos*, matched, perhaps, in the pediment above by the seated figure of Zeus, now lost. It is hard to see how this could be any more than conjecture, like the ascription of the group of tribal heroes to another known artist, Demetrios of Alopeke.

The frieze was the fine flower of the greatest occasion of the greatest Greek city, offered to the goddess like the fine flower of youth, the marble young men and maidens, who stood on the Acropolis. It is greatly to be regretted that we do not possess, as we do for the Erechtheum, some detail on the organisation of its carving and the mode of payment. In the case of the Erechtheum the figures tend to be single or grouped simply. The Parthenon frieze, with its complexities and overlapping figures of men and horses, would not lend itself to payment in the same manner for single figures or groups. The work must have been allotted and paid for by the slab. Attempts have been made to calculate the cost of the Parthenon, on the basis of the accounts already mentioned, with the addition of such other evidence as seems relevant. If in fact the frieze cost twelve talents and the metopes seventeen, and we calculate the cost of the frieze per foot at 137 drachmai, we are little forward, except that

Left: A dedicatory maiden-statue found on the Acropolis.
Opposite: A dedicatory statue of a youth found on the Acropolis and now in the Acropolis Museum.

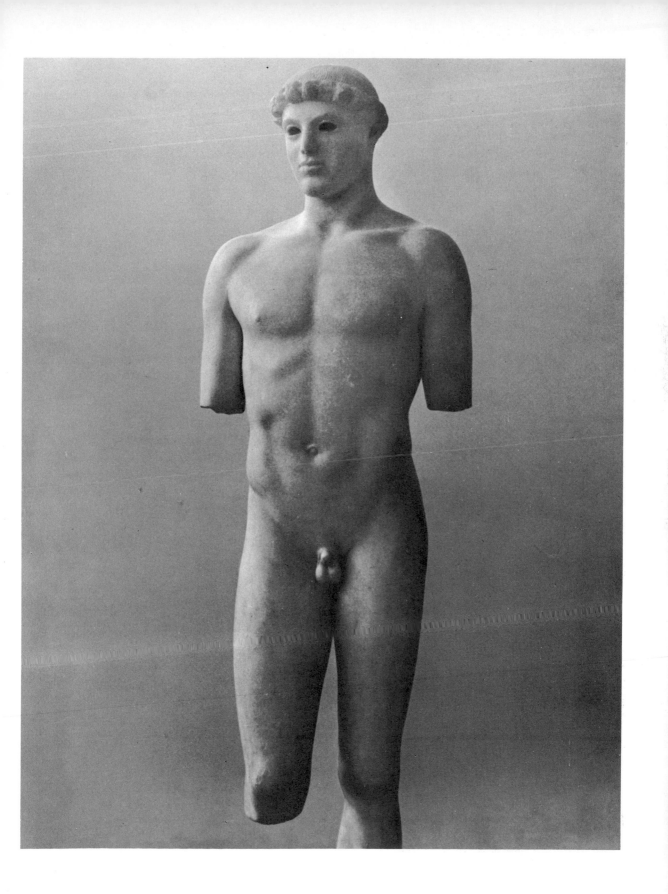

these costs seem high in relation to the 17 talents allotted to the pediments and *akroteria*. If they have any validity then we must assume that there were considerable differentials in payment between the craftsmen and the supreme artist. It may be added that walls, colonnade, pavements and core of the temple are reckoned to have cost 365 talents; the ceiling, roof and gates a further 65 talents. The total, 469 talents, falls far short of the 'thousand-talent temples' of the jibe against the profligate Periclean democracy.

Entablature and columns of the Athena Nike east front.

THE ATHENA NIKE SCULPTURE

The rest of the architectural sculpture on or from buildings on the Acropolis can be dealt with more briefly.

The small temple of Athena Nike was decorated with a frieze above the architrave, while the dangerous drop from the bastion was fenced by a balustrade. It has already been noted that the inscription founding a priesthood of Athena Nike and proposing other arrangements, including the construction of a temple, poses problems by its date of 448 BC. There are those

who suggest that the base of the Nike temple overlaps the structure of the Propylaia, and so conclude that, despite the decree, the Propylaia was constructed first, though the previously existing structures relating to the cult of Athena Nike affected the plan of the south wing of the Periclean entrance gate. It is then suggested, on the style of the frieze, that the Nike temple was begun about 425 BC to celebrate the victory of the Athenians at Sphakteria. Others, again, see the column bases of Athena Nike as earlier than those of the Ionic columns in the Propylaia, while regarding the capitals as later. It is accordingly suggested that the temple was started sometime after 448 BC, its construction interrupted during the building of the Propylaia, 437–432 BC, and resumed again around 421 BC. It could be suggested some slabs of the frieze were put in hand in the first phase of construction, just as the frieze of the Parthenon – or at any rate the west frieze – may have begun in the workshop when the building of the temple began.

The Nike temple frieze (·47 m.) remains for the most part in Athens as an element of the reconstructed building. Some slabs, removed from the Turkish fortifications by Lord Elgin, are in the British Museum, and casts replace them on the building. The subject is obscure. There may be an assembly of the Gods on the east side; on the others there are battles of warriors. If these represent contests of Greeks with Greeks and with Persians, then they mark an unusual departure from the symbolism of the Parthenon metopes. From antiquity the temple remained unaffected except by the passage of time until AD 1685 when the Turks built it into a defensive bastion. The frieze has suffered badly from this use.

The style of the frieze presents interesting problems. Some elements of it are in deep relief, with statuesque figures largely isolated from one another. Overlaps are avoided as far as possible, as are motives reminiscent of painting except of the primitive sort. This 'traditional' style contrasts with another, very clearly different, which has been compared with the frieze of the temple of Apollo Epikourios at Bassai in Arcadia, and associated with the name of the sculptor Kallimachos. This style avoids the statuesque poses and symmetry, and employs overlaps and multiple planes. In this respect there is something of the technique of the north frieze of the Parthenon, but the effect is quite different; the figures are much more spread out, and there is much more free background into which shields and drapery recede. Carl Blümel

sees in the first style an older 'Dorian-influenced' art, and in the second 'Ionian' influence. The same description of 'Ionian' has already been given by another German scholar, Ernst Langlotz, to some characteristics of the west frieze of the Parthenon which, however, shows close resemblances to the first style of the Nike temple sculptures. Indeed there is little to prevent them being carved at the same time, if the Nike frieze is regarded as first put in hand around 448 BC. On the other hand, tracing the origins of styles and disentangling them is hazardous in the extreme, especially in the second half of the fifth

Gravestone of the Periclean period, now in the National Museum, Athens.

century, when so many artists and craftsmen flocked to Athens, the great centre of artistic activity, to work on the temples, produce other works of art such as gravestones, and mingle their styles, as, for instance, in one or two cases on a single slab of the Parthenon frieze.

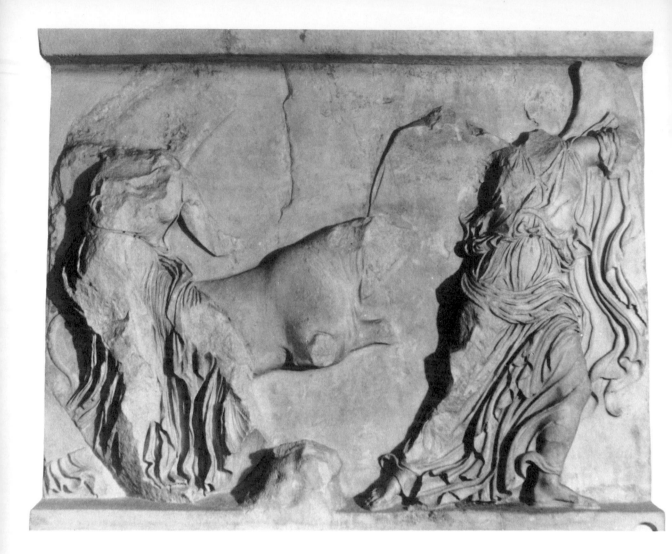

Above: Two winged Nikai and a bull from the Nike Balustrade.

Opposite, left: Slab with winged Nike from one end of the Nike Balustrade frieze.

Opposite, right: Nike fastening her sandal. Also from the Nike Balustrade.

In its second style the frieze looked forward to the fourth century. The balustrade also carried further the innovation seen particularly in the statue of Iris on the western pediment of the Parthenon and later in the figures of the Nereid Monument from Xanthos, now in the British Museum.

The balustrade, which almost enclosed the Nike 'bastion' as it may be called, stood on a cornice and was topped by a bronze rail: otherwise the temple area, approached either from the south-west portion of the Propylaia or by a small staircase in the bastion, would have been a highly dangerous place. The balustrade (1·06 m. high, and about 41 m. long) was decorated with panels showing winged Victories engaged in various activities, including sacrifice. It may have represented a unified whole, broken at intervals by two, or possibly three, seated figures of

Athena Nike. It is customary to date these splendid figures in their clinging draperies to the last decade of the fifth century, though 'lingering Phidian influence' has been detected in the seated Athena figures. The reliefs represent a considerable piece of work; they must have been put in hand fairly early in the period of the completion of the temple. It is unlikely that they were a rapidly conceived and executed celebration of the triumphant return of Alkibiades from exile. Variations in drapery style, movement and figure-rendering seem to indicate the work of at least two artists.

THE ERECHTHEUM SCULPTURE

Of very much less importance is the frieze of the Erechtheum. Its peculiar technique, the pegging of

Part of the Erechtheum Frieze showing three male figures.

relief figures in white marble on to a band of dark Eleusinian stone ·68 m. high, has already been mentioned. It was not a very successful idea, and was not used again as far as we know. Because of the technique, the frieze seems to have suffered damage and replacement of the figures at an early date, and there was a fire in 406 BC. The figures are of two sizes, the larger on the North Porch. The relief varies considerably in depth from the front to the flat-tooled back, which fitted against the background. The whole appears to have been composed of groups or episodes with a limited number of figures. The subject or subjects are difficult to identify, and only two heads survive. It is natural, however, to think of cycles of Attic myth involving Gods, heroes and mortals, as being suitable for what has been described as 'the new house of the oldest Athena'. The surviving Erechtheum inscriptions establish that at least eight artists or craftsmen were employed. It is worth noting that in the accounts no names are given to the figures listed and described. The existing remains are too damaged for the detection of individual contributions, though there are visible differences of skill. Some of the drapery is well preserved, and a similarity of style has been detected with the Caryatids. The epigraphical evidence fixes the date of the sculpture in the last decade of the fifth century, despite the fact that some of its characteristics might suggest a much earlier date.

THE FREE-STANDING SCULPTURE

The Acropolis displayed much else in the sphere of the graphic arts, pre-eminently in sculpture. This is clear from the ancient guide-books and commentaries. There is preserved from Antiquity the work of Pausanias, of the second century AD, 'A Tour (or Description) of Greece', which includes a visit to the Acropolis. It has already been seen that his treatment of the site is incomplete, and his route obscure; elements of his narrative are also of very little immediate relevance. In his case (and no doubt the same was true of other ancient writers had their works survived), a strong impression is given of confusion of dates and artists, arising from ill-read inscriptions, confusion of personalities of the same name, and the tales of ignorant guides. In this last respect the Acropolis has not changed much from ancient times.

It is as well, therefore, that we possess a selection of Archaic sculpture, buried in Antiquity and disinterred in the nineteenth century. There is not only the architectural sculpture, already discussed, but also free-standing dedications, supplemented by a wealth of inscriptions from statue bases. And although for the Classical and later periods down to the time of Pausanias, the sculpture has disappeared, inscribed bases again, in many instances, survive to supplement his narrative.

Some of the works mentioned by Pausanias were major manifestations of Greek art: some in bronze, and possibly one or two in gold and ivory. But among the mass of statues which must have made of the Acropolis a close-packed, largely open-air museum of art, piety and history, three were outstanding, and one the very focus of the glory of Athena and Athens, even if the 'ancient statue' held the prime place in sanctity and cult.

THE ATHENA PARTHENOS

This foremost work of art was the great gold and ivory statue of Athena, the work of Pheidias, which matched the statue of Zeus at Olympia, which he executed after his departure from Athens. Pausanias,

Fragmentary free-standing sphinx, found on the Acropolis and now in the Acropolis Museum.

Athenian four-drachma coin
with the Athena Parthenos as symbol.

who so neglected the sculptural decoration of the Parthenon, gives a full description of the Parthenos:

> 'The statue itself is made of gold and ivory. On the middle of the helmet rests the figure of a sphinx, and on either side of the helmet griffins are represented. The image of Athena stands erect, and wears a tunic reaching to the feet. On its breast is represented in ivory the head of Medusa, and a Victory about four cubits in height stands on one of her hands, while in the other she holds a spear, and close to the shield is a serpent, which no doubt represents Erichthonios; on the base of the statue the Birth of Pandora is wrought in relief.'[4]

Ancient writers, of various periods, give further details. Pliny the Elder records its height as twenty-six cubits, and mentions the Battle of the Greeks and Amazons on the convex face of Athena's shield, (in which it was said Pericles and Pheidias were represented), and that of the Gods and Giants on the other, while the battle of the Lapiths and Centaurs were represented on the sandals of the goddess. Here was a link with the Parthenon metopes. Pliny adds: 'the Victory is especially marvellous'. A contemporary, Thucydides, gives the weight of the gold used as forty talents, and a well-known story was that, on the advice of Pericles, Pheidias made it detachable, so that when he was charged with embezzlement it could be weighed and his honesty vindicated. Not that this availed him anything in the spate of attacks on the friends of Pericles, which must have started in 439 BC.

Naturally much attention has been paid to this work, which vanished in the Late Roman or Byzantine period. Modern scholars have demonstrated with assurance certain facts about it: that the figure and its base, 26 cubits (11·544 m. high) stood under a ceiling 13·106 m. high, spanned by beams of cypress wood ·648 m. square in section and 10·998 m. long. A great vertical timber ·756 m. by ·451 m. in section rose from a socket in the base to form the main support or armature of the statue. The Victory carried by Athena was 4 cubits (1·797 m.) high. It would have been possible to support the arm by means of an iron armature (there would have been a nice problem of forging it) attached to the vertical beam, but there would always have been a danger of gradual distortion. Hence the much debated possibility of a pillar under Athena's right hand, which appears in the Varvakeion statuette. There are two other suggestions: the fact that a fourth-century BC relief shows a pillar apparently inserted later as an addition to the original relief might suggest that the arm was unsupported at first. On the other hand, a coin of the Imperial Roman period would suggest that there was an olive tree and an owl in place of the pillar. Indeed it might have been possible by some device to balance the Victory on one side by the shield and serpent on the other.

The mode of its construction has given rise to a great deal of debate, and some suggestions seem far too ingenious. A model, it has been suggested, was followed by a carefully finished life-size statue which, in turn, was enlarged by mechanical means. It may indeed be that one of these models was preserved to later periods. The observations of Gorham Phillips Stevens may be quoted on the final figure:

> 'The outside portion of the core was built up of wooden blocks. ... The blocks were bonded together like the blocks of a marble wall and tied to a "backbone" with struts. Thus the core was really a statue in wood, which the sculptor could bring to the highest degree of finish. ... The gold plates, which were a respectable three-quarters of a millimetre thick and extremely malleable, were then pressed into the irregularities of the wooden statue, and held in place by screws with gilt heads. If the gold plates were removed, the statue would be revealed as a carefully finished wooden statue.'[5]

The ivory portions of the statue could be glued or tenoned into place. Alternatively the gold could be attached to grooves in the wood, or in bronze strip, or there could have been an underlying bronze plating over the whole surface to be covered with gold. Some such technique may have been used for the gold-covered Victories dedicated on the Acropolis and forming part of the gold reserve of the state. On the other hand, the clay moulds for gold drapery found at Olympia and probably used for the figure of Zeus by Pheidias might suggest that the problem of the attachment of the gold was less simple.

It is difficult to decide on the effect the statue would produce, as is also the case for the Zeus. In Antiquity the majestic divinity of the latter was commented on. Modern taste might feel the elaborate decoration would produce a garish impression, but the large scale would in some measure reduce this, as would the gloom of the temple. Gorham Phillips Stevens has expressed his view of the Athena thus:

'Suppose that you, reader, are an ancient Greek taking part in the famous Panathenaic procession. All the way from the Dipylon to the Parthenon you are walking in the open air, with the statues, monuments and buildings on either side bathed in the fantastically brilliant summer light (the

The Varvakeion statuette of Athena, based on the statue of Athena Parthenos.

The Lenormant statuette of Athena, showing on the base a relief of the Birth of Pandora.

procession took place in August) until you enter the Parthenon. What an overwhelming impression the Athena makes on you, due not alone to the marvellous beauty and masterful technique of the statue, but also to the unexpected features you encounter – the large size of the statue, the lavish use of gold and ivory, the mystic subdued light inside the temple contrasted with the broad sunlight outside the temple!'[5]

Like the Zeus at Olympia, the Athena at Athens had to have special treatment. So Pausanias mentions when writing of the Zeus:

'The floor in front of the image is flagged, not with white but with black stone. Round about the black pavement runs a raised edge of Parian marble to keep in the olive oil which is poured out. For oil is good for the image at Olympia, and it is this that keeps the ivory from suffering through the marshy situation of the Altis. But on the Acropolis at Athens it is not oil, but water, that is good for the ivory in the image of the Virgin. For the Acropolis being dry, by reason of its great height, the ivory image needs water and moisture.'[6]

Traces of an enclosed space have in fact been found in front of the area on which the pedestal of the statue was placed.

It is a nice problem whether Pausanias was in fact contemplating the original statue. Certainly in 296–5 BC the Athenian tyrant Lachares, to pay his mercenaries, stripped off the gold plate, 'leaving the goddess nude'. It has been suggested that later the gold plate was replaced by gold leaf. Again, the cypress wood ceiling of the temple and the internal structure of the statue itself must have presented a fire risk of the first order. The temple, as traces show in the *cella, pronaos* and east doorway, did suffer a disastrous fire, probably in Roman times to judge from the character of the restoration which followed. It is hard to believe the statue survived the fire. It could be restored from the model, and the water basin appears to have been adjusted. The suggestion has been made that the statue which perished in the fire was itself a restoration, in which an olive tree or tree trunk supporting the right hand and its Victory was replaced by a column.

The subsequent history of the statue is obscure. It has been thought that it remained in the Parthenon until the fifth century AD, and was then taken to Constantinople, where it was in the tenth century.

What happened to it thereafter is unknown. It may have perished, like the Bronze Athena, in a riot, or in the sack of AD 1204.

The statue naturally attracted the admiration and interest of Antiquity, and inspired the Varvakeion statuette, a copy 1·041 m. high with its base. It was found in an Athenian house, where it was clearly a treasured object, and may be of Hadrianic date. The unfinished Lenormant statuette, impressive for all its small size (·419 m.), was also found in Athens on the Pnyx. Its date is not easy to determine, but may be in the first or second centuries AD. Both have been much discussed in connection with details of the original. The helmeted head of Athena clearly attracted attention in Antiquity for the elaboration of its detail. Thus it appears on a well-known gem, on an elaborate gold earring from a Scythian burial at Kul-Oba in South Russia, and on other plaques recently found in Thessaly. A fine head inspired, perhaps, by the dignity of the Parthenos rather than by its elaboration, is on the obverse of a 'New Style' Athenian four-drachma

Head of Athena on an Athenian four-drachma coin, possibly inspired by the Athena Parthenos of Pheidias.

piece. Later Athenian bronze coins, of the Imperial Roman period, which so often in their types refer to the festivals, buildings and antiquities of the Acropolis, also show the Parthenos, and other works of art; thus a fine type from this period may, at some distance, be inspired by the central portion of the western pediment.

The story that Pheidias, who decorated the exterior of Athena's shield with the Battle of the Greeks and Amazons and the interior with the Battle of the Gods

The Strangford Shield (now in the British Museum)
which copies the exterior decoration
of the shield of Athena Parthenos of Pheidias.

and Giants, placed likenesses of himself and Pericles among the Greeks, naturally attracted interest. Thence perhaps came the copying of the shield, which produced the Strangford Shield. It was in any case a notable work, which may be reflected in reliefs found in the mud of the Piraeus.

THE BRONZE ATHENA

A famous landmark of the Acropolis was another work of Pheidias, in this case a statue in the open air. It is commonly called Athena Promachos, 'Athena the Defender', and it stood some 40 m. east of the

Propylaia and just about on its axis. In some restorations it is made to back on a supposed Mycenaean wall, part of a three-sided enclosure around the 'ancient temple' of Athena. The statue stood on a podium (of which fragments and indications of its setting still survive), which supported trophies (or these may have been separate). It bore an inscription: 'The Athenians set this up from the spoils of the Medes.' The accounts relating to its construction survive; these indicate that 'the Bronze Athena', as it was called officially, was started c. 465 BC and completed in the period 458–455 BC, when incidentally the Athenians were engaged in less successful hostilities with the Persians in Egypt. The statue is thus described by Pausanias (as one of two offerings from spoils taken in war):

'. . . one is a large bronze image of Athena from the spoils of the Persians who landed at Marathon, the work of Pheidias; the Battle of the Lapiths and Centaurs on the shield, and the other reliefs are said to be the work of the engraver Mys but designed by Parrhasios. ... The point of the spear and crest of the helmet of this Athena are visible even to mariners as they approach from the side of Sounion.'[7]

The Athenians were inordinately proud of the victory they gained unaided (except for the Plataians) at Marathon in 490 BC. It happens, however, that Demosthenes states the Bronze Athena was set up as a monument to Athenian valour from money contributed by the rest of the Greeks. If so, it may be said the significance of this gesture was lost on the later Athenians who were pre-eminently inspired by their own particular victory. If Demosthenes is correct, it is more likely to have been a memorial of the events of both 490 BC and 480–479 BC. The work in relief on the shield (with the ever-recurring theme of victory over barbarism) and elsewhere was by an artist-craftsman well known for his technique of metal relief and engraving, and associated in other works with Parrhasios as designer. If Pausanias is right in his information, they must have been very young when given this important commission.

For seamen coming from the direction of Sounion, after rounding Cape Zoster, the statue was visible to the left of the Parthenon over the stoa of Artemis Brauronia. It is not to be thought that it overtopped the temple, in which case it would have to be twenty or more metres high. We are, in fact, ignorant of its size, though it has been estimated (on no very good grounds) to be somewhere around seven and a half to nine metres in height. Similarly there is no accurate information on the placing of the spear and shield. The shield may have been at her side (as in the Parthenos), or ready for defence on her arm. Some late bronze coins of Athens show the statue alone; others show it (or a version of the Parthenos) in a view of the west end of the Acropolis, complete with Roman stepped ascent. The ancient sources do not all agree that it was the work of Pheidias. One held it to be by the Elder Praxiteles. A modern scholar of a past generation conjectured it commemorated the so-called

Opposite: The Bronze Athena (Athena Promachos)
represented on an Athenian bronze coin of the
Imperial Roman period, now in the British Museum.
Below (left): Composite Athena statue on an Athenian
bronze coin of the Imperial Roman period. It has the
spear of the Promachos and the Victory of the Parthenos.
Below (right): Athenian bronze coin of the Roman
Imperial period showing a view of the Acropolis from the
north west, with the Erechtheum, the Bronze Athena
and the Roman staircase ascent.

Peace of Kallias with Persia, but the dating of the
accounts must prove this wrong.

From the welter of confusion and misinformation
afforded by Byzantine writers it seems to emerge as
likely that the bronze Athena, like so many other
statues, was taken to Constantinople to embellish
Constantine's New Rome. It seems to have been
placed in the Market-place, and it may have perished
in AD 1203, as a Byzantine historian, Niketas Choniatos relates:

'But the more drunken among the crowd also
dashed in pieces the image of Athena which stood
on a column in the Forum of Constantine. In

stature it rose to the height of about thirty feet and
was clothed in garments of the same material as the
whole statue, namely of bronze.'[8]

THE LEMNIAN ATHENA

To these large and awe-inspiring figures of the warrior
goddess is to be added a third, set up as a dedication
on the Acropolis, and given some prominence since
'Pheidias deigned to sign his name on it'. The three
are coupled together by the Roman rhetorician
Aristides as 'the ivory Athena at Athens, the bronze
Athena, and the Lemnian Athena'. The charm of this

Above: Marble head possibly copying the Lemnian Athena of Pheidias.
Opposite: Head found on the Acropolis. It has been explained as a portrait of a Neoplatonist and dated about 400 BC. It could, however, be the head of a barbarian, and of a late fourth or early third century date.

latter seems particularly to have impressed Antiquity among the works of Pheidias. As Pausanias puts it: 'An image of Athena, surnamed the Lemnian, after the people who dedicated it. This image of Athena is the best worth seeing of the works of Pheidias.' The emphasis is on maidenly beauty, and when Lucian engaged in confecting an ideal of feminine beauty by selecting characteristics from well-known Greek works of art, he wrote:

> 'Pheidias and the Lemnian goddess shall bestow on her the likeness of her countenance, her delicate cheeks and finely proportioned nose.'

This bronze statue, not necessarily of large size, was a dedication of a work of Pheidias by the Athenian colonists sent to the island of Lemnos in the Northern Aegean between 451 and 448 BC. Copies of it have been seen in a statue at Dresden, and in a charming head in Bologna. The Dresden statue indicates that she held a spear, and a gem which seems to reflect the same statue shows her carrying her helmet. This youthful Athena, therefore, was created by Pheidias before he set to work on the Parthenos. It probably stood inside the northern side of the Propylaia.

OTHER WORKS OF ART

It has already been pointed out that the Acropolis and its buildings, colonnades and precincts, were crammed with dedications and commemorative statues. As all the great Greek religious centres were, it was much like a museum, especially for a visitor like Pausanias in the second century AD, when the greatness of Greece was an admired memory, and its material remains an object of cultural appreciation and envy.

The Persian sacking of Athens and the Acropolis meant that when the Athenians returned in 479 BC to their ruined city they piously collected and buried earlier dedications. This clear break meant that much was preserved (along with the colour used to enhance it) which would otherwise have disappeared through the gradual attrition of the passage of centuries. Thus we have preserved for us the 'dedication of Rhombos', the so-called Calf-bearer, the charming Peplos Kore, and a whole series of female statues, and some male, to bridge the gap between the primitive figures of the seventh century and the accomplished sculpture of the post-Persian War period. Some pieces are made even more significant by skilfully detected joins in recent

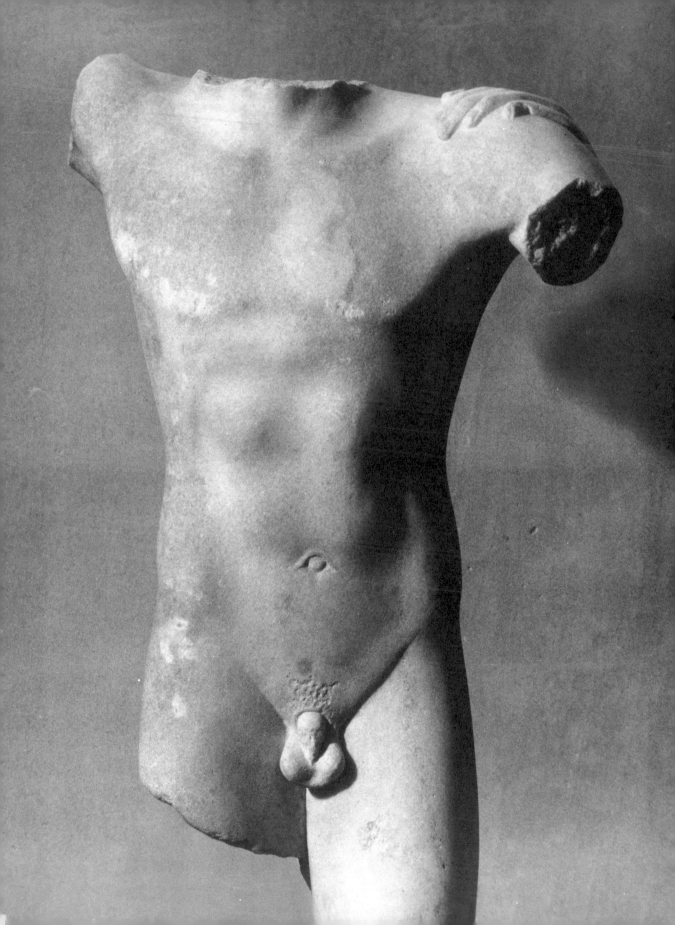

Opposite: Marble torso of a young man, found on the Acropolis.

Below: Archaic marble head, found on the Acropolis.

Opposite: Fragmentary relief in marble of a potter.
Below: Archaic marble horseman found on the Acropolis.
A composite of a cast of the Rampin Head
(in the Louvre) and the torso and fragments of the horse.

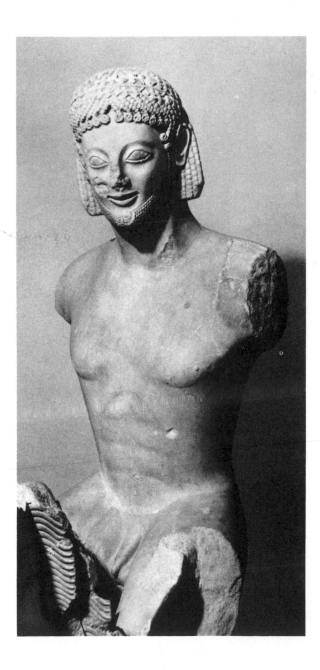

Below: A seated Athena found on the north slope of the Acropolis. Possibly by Endoios.
Opposite: The calf-bearer (*Moschophoros*).
Overleaf: The western Propylaia and the temple of Athena Nike.

times, as the Rampin Horseman, the head of which is in the Louvre, and the rider's body and fragments of the horse in Athens. Or again the Lyons Kore, the upper portion of which is in France and the lower portion in Athens, thus demonstrating the way in which archaic fragments can be scattered in the modern world. Horse fragments and riders arrayed in painted costume in the Thracian manner show the ancient Athenian preoccupation with horses, and, indeed with dogs, as one splendid creation shows. As well as free-standing three-dimensional figures there are relief sculptures, some readily recognisable dedications, such as the relief dedicated by a potter, shown with his favourite cup. There are the infinitely intriguing 'Acropolis bases' with their pictures of games and pastimes, such as ball games, hockey and cat-and-dog fights. These actual sculptured bases and dedications are supplemented by a great mass of earlier inscriptions, which give among others the names of several known artists; thus the dedication of a tithe (*dekate*) by a well-known potter, Nearchos, and the dedication made by Antenor, son of Eumares, sculptor of the group of the Tyrannicides carried away by Xerxes from Athens. Other well-known potters appear, such as Andokides and Onesimos. There are, in addition, the dedications of all manner of persons, such as craftsmen from the industrial quarter of Kollytos and Melite, fishermen (as the one who made his offering to Poseidon 'of the Golden Trident'), fullers and even whores.

A powerful impression of a mixture of works of art and antiquarian bric-à-brac is given by Pausanias in his peregrination of the Acropolis. It may be noted he had forerunners who found ample material for major works: Polemon, who composed four books on votive offerings, and Heliodoros (of the second century BC) who devoted no less than fifteen books to a description of the Acropolis. Pausanias is able to list famous names whose dedicatory inscriptions frequently survive: the Aphrodite of Kalamis; the Perseus and Athena and Marsyas of Myron; the Brauronian Artemis (perhaps in gold and ivory) of Praxiteles; the Diitrephes and the statue of Pericles by Kresilas, and the Apollo of the Locusts of Pheidias. It is possible that names and dates have been confused, and one wonders if the group of Hermes and the Graces at the entrance to the Acropolis (where there was a sanctuary of the Graces), could really have been a work of Socrates the philosopher and suitable to his dates, as Pausanias puts it, 'which is said to have been

Opposite: The eastern façade of the Propylaia.
Above: Painted terracotta slab, with running warrior,
found on the north side of the Acropolis.

made by Socrates son of Sophroniskos'. Sometimes Pausanias does not mention the artist; sometimes, as in the so-called 'Sons of Xenophon' at the entrance to the Acropolis, he shows little sense of chronology or capacity to read inscriptions accurately. A great mass of athletes, historical figures (such as Pericles, Timotheos and his son Conon the famous Athenian admiral) and mythological figures was mixed with the spoils of victories such as Plataia, and memorials such as 'the bronze chariot made out of a tithe of spoils taken from the Boeotians and Chalkidians of Euboea', which was a memorial of a famous victory of the infant democracy of Athens in 506 BC. Pausanias also mentions a supreme oddity, referred to by Aristophanes: 'There is also set up a bronze figure of the so-called Wooden Horse.... Menestheus and Teucer are peeping out of it, and so are the sons of Theseus.' The theme was well suited to the naïvety of very early Greek art, as its rendering on a primitive relief-decorated jar shows. The choice of the peeping heroes is very suitable for Athens, but it is hard to see how Stronglion, the fifth-century artist whose name appears on the surviving inscription, rendered the creature and its lurking inmates. On rare occasions not only do we have the reference of Pausanias, but probably also the figure itself, as for example the seated Athena of Endoios dedicated by Kallias, who was either the Athenian mentioned by Herodotus whose disreputable conduct at Marathon, so it was said, won him a great fortune, or a Kallias of an earlier generation.

It must not be forgotten that the Acropolis also housed paintings. The presumed panel paintings in the Erechtheum relating to the ancient family of the Boutadai have already been mentioned. Of manifest importance were those in the *Pinakotheke*, the 'Picture Gallery', in the north wing of the Propylaia. It contained what were probably moveable panel paintings, since some were by the great painter Polygnotos, who 'flourished' between 480 and 457 BC. They must, therefore, have been painted well before the construction of the Propylaia. There were epic scenes relating to Troy and the Home-coming of the Heroes. Of later date, among others, was a picture of Alkibiades, that specimen of the ultra-jeunesse dorée of Athens with whom the Athenians had an extraordinary love-hate relationship. He had himself employed a wall painter to decorate his own house, but even more 'tyrannical and illegal', as it was put, was his pictured appearance in the Pinakotheke.

Head of a late archaic horse found on the Acropolis.

6. Epilogue

What has gone before, in terms of cult, buildings and the graphic arts, relates to an independent city-state undistinguished at first and then, in the sixth century, burgeoning into a leader in Greek culture and politics and finally, after the crisis of the Persian invasion, emerging as one of the two great states of Greece – the other being Sparta. In inter-state politics and in culture and ideas, these two represented a polarisation of Greek civilisation. On the one hand, in Sparta, was discipline and subordination of the individual to the community; on the other, in Athens, freedom of thought and action (at any rate in theory, though practice at various times might be different), and a so-called democracy. It must be supposed that the Athenians would have been as puzzled as ourselves to define it with precision. In the last quarter of the fifth century the two ideologies clashed in war, ending in a Spartan victory. Thereafter, in terms of political and social ideas, both sides must have experienced many preoccupations: in Sparta as much as in Athens. In Athens the idea of democracy triumphed again, with a considerable element of sweet reasonableness between opposed factions. A period of self-questioning followed and backward-looking nostalgia for a democracy which, in some respects, had never been. The triumph against the Persians, and particularly the victory at Marathon, was a living inspiration, as were also the great buildings on the Acropolis. Such inspiration was badly needed in the crucial period when Athens, like other Greek city-states, found herself overshadowed and out-classed in diplomatic and military terms by Macedonia under Philip II and his son Alexander the Great.

In effect the turning point for Athens and the Acropolis was reached at the end of the fifth century. At that point the dynamic and actual relevance of Athens ended – coincident with the virtual completion of the Acropolis buildings – and it might be said that the seventy or so years to 323 BC saw the appearance of outstanding personalities indeed, but principally the power of a marginal member of the Greek world. Alexander's conquest of the Persian Empire, and the emergence of his successors, brought about the appearance of great kingdoms such as Pergamon, Macedonia, Egypt and the vast realm of the Seleucids. Public and inter-state affairs, and indeed Greek culture and ideas, became oecumenical. The inevitable result was that, politically at any rate, the Greek city-states became parochial. And when Rome emerged from the latter part of the third century BC as the master of the Eastern Mediterranean and successor to the Hellenistic kingdoms, the process was accelerated by internal strife in Greece, and external dominance by Rome – though Athens escaped the destruction which befell Corinth. It was an increasingly inglorious period for the Greeks, and in many respects for Athens herself. If, in 407 BC, the Athenians had been forced to melt down the temple treasures (including the gold-covered Victories), at any rate it had been the decision of an independent state, and Athena herself had been spared, and her great statue preserved inviolate. In 296–5 BC the tyrant Lachares stripped the gold off the statue to pay his mercenaries, and he was in effect but the creature of a Hellenistic war-lord Kassandros. The Acropolis had seen foreign intruders before, but nothing demonstrating so much humiliation and abasement as the lodging of another war-lord, Demetrios the Besieger, in the Opisthodomos of the Parthenon as guest of the maiden Athena, who earlier, by a lucky accident, had escaped the indignity of receiving a robe embroidered with the likeness of Demetrios and his father.

On the other hand the great past of Athens, her cultural significance (though there were new rivals such as Alexandria), her literature and schools of philosophy, gave her a special place in the minds of Hellenistic rulers and cultured Romans. It also made her, when the Romans were firmly established as

The Propylaia. Looking from the south-west wing to the north-west wing (Pinakotheke) and the Monument of Agrippa.

masters, a city to be plundered of works of art, though in general Athens suffered less from war, strife and plunder than other Greek cities or Greek areas such as Sicily. Athens on occasion benefited from the generosity of Hellenistic rulers such as the Pergamene kings, who gave to the city the stoa under the south side of the Acropolis, the Stoa of Eumenes as it is called, and the great stoa on the eastern side of the Market-place – the Stoa of Attalos – now restored to serve as a museum [14]. On the Acropolis itself Pergamene respect and generosity set up yet more sculpture. Pausanias records:

'At the south wall are figures about two cubits high, dedicated by Attalos. They represent the legendary war of the Giants who once dwelt about Thrace and the Isthmus of Pallene, the fight of the Athenians with the Amazons, the battle with the Medes at Marathon, and the destruction of the Gauls in Mysia.'[1]

The recurrence, in fact, of themes already existing in the Parthenon and elsewhere in Athens: the triumph of order and civilisation over brute force and barbarism, for which, in the eyes of the ancient world, Athena and Athens stood as symbols.

The Athenians of the Classical period flattered themselves that a special good fortune was theirs. Even if their judgement and policy decisions were ill-advised, none the less *Dysboulia* (Ill Counsel) turned to *Euboulia* (Good Counsel). It might certainly be said they came off better, on occasions, than they deserved: even when the city, under the leadership of a tyrant, in the second decade of the first century BC, abandoned her allegiance to Rome and took the side of the Pontic King Mithridates VI in his war against Rome. The tyrant made his last stand in the Acropolis, and Athens suffered siege and ferocious slaughter when Lucius Cornelius Sulla attacked and reduced her. The philosophic groves were cut down to make siege engines, though the latter were far less destructive than gunpowder. On the other hand, we gather that the city ran with blood; Athena's lamp on the Acropolis was extinguished, and Athenian pride and morale wholly gone. The Athenians were finally delivered, for, as Sulla put it, he spared 'the Many for the sake of the Few, the Living for the sake of the Dead', making, as Plutarch adds, 'some honourable mention of the ancient Athenians'.

Thereafter, once the Roman Civil Wars were ended, and the Principate established, Athens must have been a pleasant place to live in: a centre of culture and education, and certainly of tourism. There are two important monuments. One is the monument of Agrippa on the west slope of the Acropolis, close to the entry of the Propylaia and the descent to the Klepsydra Fountain, and the other is the temple of Rome and Augustus immediately to the east of the Parthenon. The high base of the former monument still stands. In Antiquity it was surmounted by a quadriga in honour of the man who did more than anyone else to promote the cause of Caius Julius Caesar Octavianus (who in 27 BC was entitled Augustus), and then to establish the Principate and bring peace to the faction-torn Roman world. The temple of Rome and Augustus, on the Acropolis as in the rest of the Roman Empire, marked the union of the concept of Rome, in cult, with that of its ruler, conceived as greater than human. It was not quite the open admission of deity, but well on the way to it. '*Praesens deus habebitur*', said the poet Horace, and the Emperor must have seemed much more present and effective to bless and protect than Athena – though as we know from St Paul's observation, the Athenians were still much preoccupied with unseen powers, even those they could not identify.

Leaving aside the extravagances of Nero, it is clear that in the Empire for a long while Athenian culture and philosophy, and the classical tradition in art, attracted the attention of the Romans, above all of the Emperor Hadrian. The embellishment and amenity of the lower city owed a very great deal to him (he completed the temple of Olympian Zeus), and he took a close interest in its public life and religion. So did Herodes Atticus, the millionaire rhetorician friend of Marcus Aurelius, whose wealth caused the Panathenaic festival to be celebrated with particular splendour, and who built the stadium (restored by a modern benefactor of Athens) and the theatre named after him.

Athens and the Acropolis thus entered the third century as a material city and cultural centre of the first order, even if politically negligible. Soon, however, the growing crisis of the Roman world, internal strife and the conflict of pretenders to the imperial position, set up and overthrown by the armies, combined with economic difficulties and barbarian attack to affect Greece and Athens like other areas of what seemed to be a disintegrating empire. The vulnerability of Athens was strikingly demonstrated in AD 267 by an event which has been called 'one of

The eastern façade of the Parthenon, and an inscribed
fragment of the Temple of Rome and Augustus.

the most significant turning points in the history of
Athens'. Already in AD 253 a barbarian incursion
penetrated to Thessalonike, so that the Emperor
Valerian took measures to fortify the Greek cities,
and among them Athens, whose walls had been
neglected since the sack by Sulla in 86 BC. But these
repaired walls were inadequate to save Athens from
a raid of the Gothic Herulians in AD 267, which
devastated the lower city with fire and slaughter. In
the sequel the defences of Athens were again strengthened, using the debris of the sack. The Acropolis and
an area to the north of it were fortified as an essential
defensible circuit which could be garrisoned, as the
wider circuit of the Classical period could not. The
defence wall ran from the west end of the Acropolis,
which was entered by the Beulé Gate (so named after

the archaeologist who disinterred it from later
fortifications), down the North Slope to join the dis-
membered Stoa of Attalos, then south-east between
the Roman Market and the Library of Hadrian, then
south again to join the north-east corner of the
Acropolis.

The incorporation of every sort of stone fragment
in the wall indicates the same urgency as the construction of the walls of Athens after the Persian
sack of 480–479 BC, but with a difference. It has been
well put by Homer Thompson, American excavator of
the Athenian Market-place:

'One wonders to what extent the Athenians of that
day were conscious of the historical significance of
what they were doing. Like their ancestors who

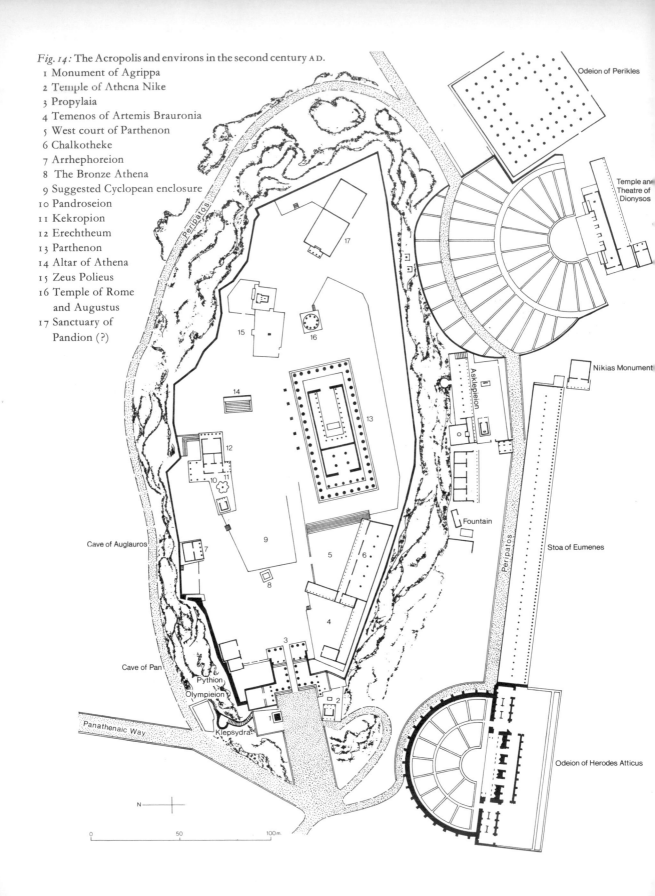

Fig. 14: The Acropolis and environs in the second century A.D.

1 Monument of Agrippa
2 Temple of Athena Nike
3 Propylaia
4 Temenos of Artemis Brauronia
5 West court of Parthenon
6 Chalkotheke
7 Arrhephoreion
8 The Bronze Athena
9 Suggested Cyclopean enclosure
10 Pandroseion
11 Kekropion
12 Erechtheum
13 Parthenon
14 Altar of Athena
15 Zeus Polieus
16 Temple of Rome
   and Augustus
17 Sanctuary of
   Pandion (?)

Odeion of Perikles

Temple and Theatre of Dionysos

Nikias Monument

Asklepieion

Fountain

Stoa of Eumenes

Peripatos

Cave of Auglauros

Cave of Pan

Pythion

Olympieion

Klepsydra

Panathenaic Way

Peripatos

Odeion of Herodes Atticus

N

0   50   100 m.

Hübsch print, 1819. The Acropolis from the west,
showing fortifications linking
the Propylaia to the Theatre of Herodes Atticus.

had fought the Persians, they were sacrificing a rich inheritance in the interests of security; but whereas that earlier occasion had marked the end of the beginning of Athenian greatness the event with which we are immediately concerned was to mark the beginning of its end.'[2]

But it may also be added that it was a beginning for the Acropolis once more as a fortress, a function it was to perform for roughly another sixteen hundred years. So its great buildings were saved, and the Acropolis fortifications and the area surrounded by the Herulian wall remained the core of Athens. The ravaged area outside appears to have lain in ruins until the beginning of the fifth century, when the outer circuit was made defensible and a wider area of the city rebuilt. It is to be noted that the fortified inner circuit blocked the traditional Panathenaic processional way, so that the festival procession was either abandoned or followed some other route. Yet later an inscription of the earlier fifth century AD records that a citizen named Plutarch three times paid for the sacred ship to be conveyed to the Acropolis, which must surely mean to the Beulé Gate and no further.

The centre of lower Athens remained for long in a sorry state, and exposed to attack, as in AD 396 by Alaric the Goth, who was reduced, tradition said, to a less hostile frame of mind by Athena Promachos and Achilles. Rebuilding within the outer circuit of walls took place in the early fifth century AD, but this has been explained as a contraction from without the walls, and so not evidence of renewed prosperity, but the reverse. None the less, Athens still had the advantage of her schools of philosophy, and attracted the interest of exalted members of imperial official-dom and the emperors who promoted both the schools and the material ambience of the city. How-ever, a series of historical events was ultimately to prove fatal: the foundation and embellishment of New Rome by Constantine in AD 330; the division of the Empire between Honorius and Arcadius in AD 395; the foundation in AD 425 by Theodosius II of the university of New Rome; and, finally, the closure of the philosophical schools by Justinian and the expulsion of scholars in AD 527. Where education

Above: Wall of the Parthenon *cella* showing traces of
Christian painted decoration.
Opposite: View of the south wall of the Acropolis over
the Theatre of Dionysos.

failed, technology did not last much longer. The
water-mill in the Market-place ground into silence
in the last quarter of the sixth century. Although the
Acropolis might be safe, the great danger of the age,
namely barbarian attack, was shown by widespread
devastation at the same time.

Visitors had long since commented on the decline
of Athens. In AD 429 Proklos had had a vision of
Athena, displaced from the Acropolis, seeking refuge
in his humble dwelling. And at some later date the
Parthenon was converted into the Church of the Holy
Wisdom. The entrance was placed at the west,
windows were opened in the side walls, it was decorated with a mosaic and frescoes, and a bishop's
throne was brought from the Theatre of Dionysos.
In similar fashion the Erechtheum was made into a
church dedicated to the Mother of God. It was
entered from a porch at the west, and the floor level
was reduced to that of the western and central
divisions. The creation of a nave and aisles and an
eastern apse did considerable damage to the interior
and to the eastern entrance wall, but not to the eastern
porch. Moveable pagan images and works of art were
already gone; some Christian defacement of archi-

tectural sculpture probably took place, but things
might have been worse. The great buildings of the
Acropolis were in a large measure protected under the
mantle of Orthodox Christianity and Byzantine
power, exercised, latterly, in a very feeble manner
from Constantinople.

The glory of ancient Athens and her unique
position in the Ancient World were still recognised
by Byzantine rulers and learned men. The same was
true after the capture of Constantinople by the Fourth
Crusade in AD 1204. Beginning with the establishment
of the Franks in Greece and the Aegean, with dukes
at Athens, the city, and the Acropolis as its fortified
centre, became inextricably involved in the events of
the mediaeval Mediterranean: the rise and fall of the
Franks; the manoeuvres of the Catalan Grand
Company, the Aragonese of Naples, the Navarese,
and finally the Acciaiuoli of Florentine origins, and
the Venetians. The story is one of fantastic complexity, in which the Acropolis was the centre of government and defence. Its fortifications were strengthened
by uniting the Acropolis walls in a great *enceinte* with
the Theatre of Herodes Atticus. The tall 'Frankish'
tower was erected, which figures in early views of

Above: The Acropolis in 1670, under Turkish occupation; before the Morosini siege and destruction.
Opposite: The Acropolis after the explosion. View from the south-west by Captain Verneda.

Athens. It was demolished only in the last quarter of the nineteenth century. With the disappearance of the Byzantine Orthodox rulers, the Parthenon became the Catholic Church of Notre Dame, and under the protection of St Peter. One is tempted to think of Athena and Poseidon! Athens herself became Settines, and under the Catalans the Parthenon was Seu de Santa Maria de Cetinas. Under the Acciaiuoli it returned to Orthodoxy.

The year 1388, when Nerio, second of the Acciaiuoli, entered the Acropolis and laid claim to the Duchy of Athens, saw the penetration of the Turks to the Balkans, and the year 1389 the Battle of Kossovo. The end of this period came with the capture of Athens by a general of Mohammed the Conqueror in 1456, three years after the fall of Constantinople.

During this period, despite the many changes of regime, Athens appears to have benefitted from her links with Europe, both culturally and materially. The great past was remembered, even if in a vague and muddled manner, which included confusing Pheidias and Praxiteles with Christian saints. Peter IV of Aragon, who became suzerain of the Catalans of Athens in 1377, shows this vaguely conceived sense of the importance of the past when he speaks of the Acropolis as 'the greatest jewel of the world and of such worth that all the Kings of Christendom could not make its like'. And even the conversion of the Propylaia into a ruler's residence did no great harm. Scholars could travel to Athens and see the Acropolis even if other ancient remains were overwhelmed. Thus Cyriacus of Ancona came to Athens in the first half of the fifteenth century to see what he called 'the noble temple of the goddess Pallas', and admired the figures of men and horses in the pediments. Furthermore the Franks and their successors came eventually to know the Greeks and to regard them as equals. In other words the land and the people were not detached from the glorious past.

However, all this was to end for a long while through the Turkish conquest. It mattered relatively little that the Parthenon was converted into a Turkish mosque with the addition of a minaret at the western end. On the other hand, the east end of the Erechtheum was allowed to fall into ruins and the western portion converted into a house complete with harem. At this time, or more probably earlier, the inter-columniations of the Propylaia were walled up. The dislike or, at best, the indifference of the Muslims to art portraying the human figure constituted a threat to the sculptures of the Acropolis buildings. Still worse, the Acropolis became an important fortress at a time when the use of artillery was greatly developed. In 1683 the Turks were repulsed from before Vienna by John Sobieski. As a sequel the Venetians embarked on a policy of conquest in Greece, which in 1687 led to the siege of the Acropolis by Count Koenigsmark, lieutenant of Morosini. In preparation for such an attack the Turks had turned the site of the temple of Athena Nike into an artillery battery, using the ancient stones as part of the fortification. They stored their gunpowder within the Parthenon. The Venetians appear to have known this and directed their mortars on the temple-mosque. The gunpowder was detonated and the Parthenon ruined, especially the north and south colonnades. It was not the first explosion on the Acropolis: somewhere around 1656 gunpowder in the Propylaia had been detonated by lightning. How sincere were Count Koenigsmark's

regrets it is difficult to say. One effect of the explosion was to bring much of the structure and its decoration to the ground, so that there is every likelihood that pieces were taken away as souvenirs. The Venetians were much given to the practice of 'souvenir hunting' for reasons of culture or prestige. The most famous example is the supposed body of St Mark; others, the lion outside the Arsenal at Venice, the bronze horses of St Mark's Cathedral, and objects in the Treasury. As a token of his victory, Morosini sought to remove the horses from the western pediment. The tackle broke and the sculptures were smashed to pieces.

The supreme irony was that those who shattered the Parthenon were themselves influenced by a renewed interest in Athens and the Acropolis which had arisen in the seventeenth century when relations between the Turks and the west were less hostile. This was due initially to Jesuits and Franciscans who settled in Athens, and was encouraged by the ambassador of Louis XIV to the Sublime Porte. The Marquis de Nointel obtained permission for drawings to be made (probably after 1674) of the Parthenon sculptures.

N

0   50   100 m.

Fig. 15: The Acropolis at the time of the rising against the Turks. (Shading indicates blocks of occupied or ruined buildings, divided by lanes.)

1 Outer gate
2 Theatre of Herodes Atticus
   incorporated in outer fortifications
3 Erechtheum
4 Parthenon with Christian and Turkish modifications
5 Post-explosion Turkish mosque
6 Propylaia incorporated into inner fortifications
7 Frankish tower
8 Descent to ancient fountain
9 Former Pinakotheke
10 Church of the Panayia Speliotissa
11 Outer Turkish fortifications

Above: The Erechtheum from the south-west in 1750, by James Stuart (1713–1788).

These drawings, or some of them, are preserved in the Bibliothèque Nationale in Paris, and a reference on the flyleaf to a painter Jacques Carrey has led to them being called the 'Carrey drawings'. Whatever the problem of authorship, they give priceless information, especially for the western pediment before the depredations of Morosini. The same ambassador promoted the journey to Athens of Jacob Spon and George Wheler (1675), whose names are associated with an account of travels in Greece, including visits to the Acropolis, which was known to the entourage of Morosini. They were the first of a long series of travellers and observers who had to overcome the obsession of the Turks with the dangers of spying: from Dalton (1749), Pars (1765), to Dodwell, Gell and Smirke in the early nineteenth century.

Below: Houses on the Acropolis east of the Parthenon, and the small mosque within it.
Opposite: The clearing of the Propylaia. About 1838.

It must be wondered at times what they made of it all, and of the contemporary Greeks, if they recognised the latter at all as related to the famous people of antiquity. It is indeed easy to see that even the Franks were aware of the great gulf fixed between the Greeks of antiquity and the mixture of Slavs, Albanians and others who formed the population of the Greece of their day. The alienation of the present from the past was made even more profound by two centuries in which Greece had become difficult of access. This was less so in the seventeenth century, but another difficulty was the ignorance of Greek art, and the difficulty of distinguishing Greek from Roman art after so long a period of Roman domination. The problem is illustrated by Spon's belief that the sculpture of the Parthenon belonged to the age of Hadrian, an idea repeated on the flyleaf of the Carrey drawings, and repeated yet again by that apparent doyen of artistic appreciation, Payne-Knight, at the time of the Elgin controversy. The ultimate effect

both of the conquests of Alexander and of the patronage of Rome had been to confuse the issue of what was Greek. When the renewal of contact and enlivening of interest took place in the seventeenth century, it was an impulse which had started in the Romanised West in the Renaissance, when the rediscovery of Greek literary culture was accompanied by the recovery of ancient works of art from the earth. In Italy they were largely the former prized possessions of the Romans: sometimes (but rarely) Greek originals, and more often copies. Thus the marbles from Italy on which Thomas Howard (b. 1585) spent a great fortune, are described by Michaelis: 'If we measure these aspirations [that is, the expenditure and the effort] by the results, certainly most of the sculptures of Roman origin ... seem rather insignificant. For there are only a few specimens which rise above the level of mediocrity'.[3]

Those who went further afield to Greece and beyond – as William Petty did on behalf of Thomas Howard – brought back sometimes better spoils, destined to form a 'Classical' taste in sculpture, as their drawings were to do in architecture, though it was generally Hellenistic or Roman, and hardly ever true Greek. A further point to be noted is that the architect, the prospector for artistic spoils, and the gentleman traveller found little that was attractive in the wretched and shifty inhabitants of Greece sitting amid the ruins of past greatness and – supreme irony – more often than not the ruins of Roman greatness. In Britain and elsewhere, Classical Greek was studied, but as a living influence the products of Greek genius were difficult to distinguish from those of Rome, while the opinions of Imperial Rome strongly influenced the view of the contemporary Greeks. The toast of the Society of Dilettanti was 'Grecian taste and Roman spirit'. But what, in effect, was Grecian taste? Rome, as the vehicle of Greek culture, was clearly more influential in art, architecture and Classicism in literature, whatever the ultimate origins

of the ideas involved. And the statesman and the soldier saw themselves clad in the toga or the cuirass of the Romans. It is a striking phenomenon. In 1697, and so after the renewal of Western knowledge of the Acropolis, John Evelyn published his *Discourse of Medals Ancient and Modern and of the Use to be derived from Them*, in which he spoke thus of the wretched Greeks: [once] 'great Legislators and Assertors of Liberty; by accidental and barbarous Revolutions and Mixtures become at present the most ignorant, rustic, abject, false and universally degenerous' – 'Camel-keepers', as Evelyn points out in another place. In Art, models and examples were required, but they were not Greek. The Romans held the field. The same is true of Joseph Addison's *Dialogues upon the Usefulness of Ancient Medals*, first published in 1721. The 'Ancient Medals' are almost exclusively Roman coins, though Greek were available for study. The quotations which illustrate them are Latin. The purpose of collecting them Addison gives thus: 'The first and most obvious one ... is showing us the faces of all the great persons of Antiquity'. So, too, Alexander Pope, in his verses on the work, writes in reference to what he calls the dim brood of 'Pale Antiquaries' and coin collectors:

'Theirs is the vanity, the Learning Thine.
Touch'd by thy hand, again Rome's glories shine:
Her Gods and godlike Heroes rise to view,
And all her faded garlands bloom anew.'

It was at this point, or about a generation later, that the renewed contact with Greece began to register. The effects of these renewed contacts came, in terms of a renaissance of ideas, in the later eighteenth century, and the Acropolis played a pre-eminent part in the process. The foundations of this renaissance were laid by the enquiring travellers and wide-ranging collectors characteristic of the period, such as Sir Richard Worsley (1751–1805), who travelled in the East Mediterranean with his draughtsman Willey Reveley, and went to Troy in 1786. He also met Goethe in South Italy. There was the new stimulus of what might be called digging archaeology: the discovery of Pompeii and of Herculaneum and its bronzes. Above all, there was the influence of Winckelmann through his *History of Ancient Art* (1764), though in fact Greek art could hardly be known properly or widely yet.

Goethe saw the drawings of the Parthenon sculptures which Sir Richard Worsley had brought from Greece. They produced an immense impression on him, and he lived long enough to experience the artistic impact of the Elgin Marbles when they were brought to Europe. This event, and the revolt of the Greeks against their Turkish masters – both centred in the Acropolis – represent a crucial stage in the rediscovery of Greece, which led through Gladstone, Grote, Schliemann, Sir Arthur Evans and many others to Greek history and archaeology as we know them today.

This is not the place to examine in detail the controversy on Elgin's removal of the Pheidian sculpture of the Parthenon, its 'rape' as Lord Byron sought to represent it. In fact Elgin did little more than Count Choiseul-Gouffier and the French antiquarian Fauvel would dearly have liked to do. Some sculptures had already been dislodged from their original positions, even before the great explosion, and many after. Whatever the terms of the *firman* Elgin received from the Sublime Porte, whether 'to excavate and take away' or to 'take away and excavate', there can be no doubt of the reasonableness of his alarm at the jeopardy in which the sculptures stood. If architectural elements were indeed overthrown in the process of removing the sculptures, this was a lesser evil than the threat of the lime-kiln or use as building material, as in the case of the temple of Athena Nike. If at first sight it seems vandalism that Elgin removed a Caryatid, a column of the eastern porch of the Erechtheum, and pieces of its architectural decoration, it is well to reflect that the eastern end of the Erechtheum was a ruin, as is clear from more or less contemporary drawings. The Maiden Porch of the Caryatids had already been literally ransomed from destruction. The North Porch was in use as a powder magazine, and Elgin and his agents knew what had happened to the Propylaia and the Parthenon when in similar use. The sculptures remaining *in situ*, and their architectural framework, have continued to suffer ever since, and whatever may be felt on the present retention of the marbles outside Greece, Lord Elgin deserved gratitude rather than the abuse he in fact received. Had they not been brought to London they would assuredly have arrived in Paris.

The misjudgement of Payne-Knight, who believed the marbles to be Hadrianic, now seems ridiculous. None the less, in pointing out the impossibility of all this great mass of sculpture being from the hand of Pheidias, he served as a useful corrective to the over-enthusiastic, such as Benjamin Haydon, who must,

Upper picture: The walled-up North Porch of the
Erechtheum. William Gell.
Lower picture: The excavations to the north and
west of the Erechtheum, the site of the discovery
of archaic sculpture in 1886.

however, be given credit for his championship of the marbles and of Elgin. The marbles came to England in 1812 and languished in 'a dirty penthouse' and elsewhere until 1817, when they were purchased by the state amid a storm of controversy. Against the ill-conditioned and uncomprehending attitude of Byron is to be set the admiration the sculptures inspired in Keats, who was taken to see them first in March 1817. He felt in contemplating them like 'a sick eagle looking at the sky'. Joseph Severn tells us: 'He went again and again to see the Elgin Marbles and would sit for an hour or more at a time beside them rapt in revery'.

The Greek War of Independence did more than produce a romantic respect for the Greeks, linking them once again with their heroic ancestors, the 'men of Marathon'. Equally it freed the Acropolis from the presence of the Turk and permitted restoration and excavation, and the final stage in the long history of the *polis*: its preservation as an archaeological monument. It was thus possible to excavate the hill to bed-rock, a process which revealed the mass of archaic sculpture buried before and after the Persian sack. This comprised both free-standing and architectural sculpture, with which was found also a wealth of pottery and small works of art such as terracottas. These discoveries laid the foundation for the modern knowledge and appreciation of Archaic Greek art. The perspective lengthened by the Elgin marbles was extended still further in this advance. Again, it became possible to study the earlier building developments on the Acropolis outlined in this book. The rock-surface, when it had been cleared of all the soil, gave evidence of the emplacement of walls and statue bases. The clearance of the top of the rock has been followed by an extensive exploration of its sides: the Panathenaic Way; the North Slope with its various traces of shrines, Mycenaean houses, and the Mycenaean underground cistern; the South Slope with its theatres, Stoa of Eumenes, Asklepieion, and more recently the uncovering of industrial establishments and houses which show how close to the rock the densely packed area of work and habitation came.

The Acropolis is a palimpsest of history. It is a battered remnant compared to its original state, but in view of the many vicissitudes of fortune it is surprising so much remains, surviving so many perils, and still facing two more, the feet of tourists and atmospheric pollution.

Opposite: Athena receiving worshippers: a family going to sacrifice.
Overleaf: Looking east towards the Asklepieion and the Theatre of Dionysos beneath the south face of the Acropolis.

Notes on the Text

CHAPTER 2

1. *Iliad* [ii, 546–56]
2. Euripides, *Ion* [24–6]
3. *Odyssey* [vii, 78–81]
4. Ibid. [xi, 301–5]
5. Euripides, *Iphigenia at Aulis* [247ff.]
6. Thucydides, *The History of the Peloponnesian War* [i, 12], author's translation
7. Thucydides, *The History of the Peloponnesian War* [i, 9], translated by Richard Crawley, Everyman Library, London, 1957
8. Emily Vermeule, *Greece in the Bronze Age* [pp. 282–3], University of Chicago Press, Chicago and London, 1964
9. Pausanias, *Description of Greece* [i, 26], translated by Margaret Verrall in *Mythology and Monuments of Ancient Athens*, 1890
10. Pausanias, *Description of Greece* [i, 24, 4], translated by J. G. Frazer, London, 1898
11. Theophrastus, in Porphyry, *De Abstinentia* [ii, 29], translated by Jane E. Harrison in *Mythology and Monuments of Ancient Athens*, 1890
12. Aristophanes, *Lysistrata* [640–7], translated by B. B. Rogers, Loeb Classical Library, London, 1924
13. Pausanias, *Description of Greece* [i, 27, 4], author's translation
14. Euripides, *Ion* [10–13], translated by Angus Hulton
15. Ibid. [285], translated by Angus Hulton
16. Ibid. [20ff.], translated by Angus Hulton
17. Euripides, *Ion* [492ff.], translated by A. W. Verrall, 1890
18. Pausanias, *Description of Greece* [i, 23, 7], translated by Margaret Verrall in *Mythology and Monuments of Ancient Athens*, 1890
19. Aristophanes, *Lysistrata* [645]
20. Hesiod, *Theogony* [886–900], translated by H. G. Evelyn-White, Loeb Classical Library, London, 1914
21. Ibid. [924–9]
22. Ibid. [886–900], alternative version
23. *Homeric Hymns* [xxviii, 1–16], translated by H. G. Evelyn-White, Loeb Classical Library, London, 1914
24. Pindar, *Olympian Ode* [vii, 38], author's translation
25. Euripides, *Ion* [452], translated by Angus Hulton
26. Pausanias [i, 22, 4]
27. Thucydides, *The History of the Peloponnesian War* [ii, 43], translated by Richard Crawley, Everyman Library, London, 1957
28. Demosthenes [xxxii, 13], author's translation

29. *Iliad* [vi, 303]
30. Euripides, *Heraclidae* [777–83], translated by Angus Hulton
31. Plutarch, *Lives* [*Life of Demosthenes*], translated by Dryden and revised by A. H. Clough, Everyman Library, 1957
32. Philostratus the Sophist, *Lives of the Sophists* [550], translated by W. C. Wright, Loeb Classical Library, London, 1922
33. Aristophanes, *The Knights* [551–94], translated by B. B. Rogers, Loeb Classical Library, London, 1924

CHAPTER 3

1. Herodotus, *History* [vii, 51], translated by G. Rawlinson, Everyman Library, London, 1952
2. Thucydides, *The History of the Peloponnesian War* [i, 89], translated by Richard Crawley, Everyman Library, London, 1957
3. Plutarch, *Lives* [*Life of Pericles*], translated by Dryden and revised by A. H. Clough, Everyman Library, 1957
4. Ibid.
5. Demosthenes, *Scholia* to xxii, 13–14 (*Anonymus Argentinensis*, ed. Meritt, Wade-Gery and Macgregor in *Athenian Tribute Lists* [i, T9; ii, D13]), author's translation

CHAPTER 4

1. Herodotus, *History* [viii, 53–8]
2. Herodotus, *History*, translated by G. Rawlinson, Everyman Library, London, 1952
3. Demosthenes [xxiv, 136]
4. A. W. Lawrence, *Greek Architecture* [pp. 110–1], Penguin Books, Harmondsworth, 1957
5. Ibid. [p. 111]
6. D. S. Robertson, *Handbook of Greek and Roman Architecture* [pp. 118–22], Cambridge, 1945

CHAPTER 5

1. Pausanias, *Description of Greece* [i, 24, 5], author's translation
2. Herodotus [viii, 55].
3. P. E. Corbett, *The Sculpture of the Parthenon* [p. 21], Penguin Books, Harmondsworth, 1959
4. Pausanias, *Description of Greece* [i, 24, 5], translated by H. Stuart Jones in *Select Passages from Ancient Writers illustrative of the History of Greek Sculpture*, 1895
5. Gorham Phillips Stevens, in *Hesperia XXIV* [p. 243],

6. Pausanias, *Description of Greece* [v, 11, 5], translated by J. G. Frazer, London, 1898
7. Pausanias, *Description of Greece* [i, 28, 2], author's translation
8. Niketas Choniatos, translated by H. Stuart Jones in *Select Passages from Ancient Writers illustrative of the History of Greek Sculpture*, 1895

CHAPTER 6

1. Pausanias, *Description of Greece* [i, 25, 2], translated by J. G. Frazer, London, 1898
2. Homer Thompson, in *Journal of Roman Studies* [pp. 64–5], 1959
3. A. Michaelis, *Ancient Marbles in Great Britain*, Cambridge, 1882

Notes on the Illustrations

Page 21 The Klepsydra Fountain. The Classical well-house, constructed 475–450 BC to replace a group of wells, is buried beneath the floor of the Roman well-house. The well-head in the photograph gives access to the ancient cistern.

24 The belief that Philippides, the long distance runner sent as a messenger from Athens to Sparta at the time of the battle of Marathon, encountered Pan who asked why the Athenians did him no honour despite his good will to them, led to the establishment of a cult of Pan in this region of the Acropolis.

Note the two reliefs (pages 54 and 55).

27 In the foreground are two herms (pillars surmounted by a head of Hermes) of the type set up at road junctions. One bears a reference to the Council of the Areiopagos.

29 The photograph was taken at the time of the North Slope excavations, before the area was landscaped.

32 Paris, Louvre F 204. Attic red-figured amphora by the Andokides painter. The bringing up of the monstrous canine guardian of the gate of the Underworld was one of the Labours imposed on Herakles by Eurystheus. The date of the vase, c. 520 BC.

34 Berlin 2537. Fifth-century Attic red-figured cup by the Codrus Painter.

35 A hydria (water-jar), Naples 2422, by the Kleophrades Painter (Epiktetos II). It has been suggested that the woman is Helen, and the man Menelaos, her husband, rather than Ajax and Cassandra. The Palladion was so named as a statue of Pallas Athene; Pallas, a name of uncertain meaning, has been explained as meaning 'brandisher of the spear' or 'virgin'.

37 Red-figured cup in the British Museum (E 48), showing the exploits of Theseus against Skiron and Kerkyon. By Douris, c. 480 BC.

50 Between the sanctuary of Eros and Aphrodite and the approach to the Mycenaean postern through the North Wall have been discovered a spear point and arrow heads, probably evidences of the Persian attack in 480 BC. The same may be true of the skeleton of a soldier (?).

53 Attic red-figured *pelike*, E372, in the British Museum.

54 National Museum, Athens 6233.

59 Attic red-figured *pelike*, E 410, in the British Museum.

60 Attic black-figured amphora, 1555, in Munich. Belonging to the Group of the Antimenes Painter, c. 520 BC.

61 (left) Attic black figured olpe, M.538, in the Villa Giulia, Rome, belonging to the Leagros Group.

61 (right) Attic black-figured amphora, Berlin 1686, by the Painter of Berlin 1686. Date c. mid-sixth century BC. 'The best of the best'. Probable representation of a sacrifice to Athena Nike at an open-air altar, such as that on the site of the temple of Athena Nike.

64 Attic red-figured cup, G 104, in the Louvre. By the Panaitios Painter, c. 490 BC.

66 Attic red-figured jug, Berlin 2415, belonging to the Group of Berlin 2415. Date c. 460–450 BC. Note the tools hanging on the wall. The picture is a link between Athena Hippia and Poseidon Hippios, and between Athena Ergane and Hephaistos.

71 In the Acropolis Museum. British Museum, *Parthenon* pl. xl; B.M. cast, slab II of the north side of the frieze. Found in 1833 beneath its original position on the Parthenon.

72 In the Acropolis Museum. British Museum, *Parthenon* pl. xlii. Cast in the British Museum. From the north side of the frieze.

113 See Payne and Young (Bibliography 21), 47–48 and plate 127. Acropolis Museum 1342. Two pieces were found (a) in 1833 near the Klepsydra Fountain; (b) in 1859–60 on the east side of the Acropolis. Its style described as Ionian or Attic-Ionian, and its height (1.205 m.) fit the fragment on page 143 below. Some authorities feel the style is too late for these two fragments to belong to a frieze on the Archaic Temple, possibly showing, like the Parthenon, the Panathenaic procession.

119 Length 3·40 m. Found in 1888 to the east and south-east of the Parthenon. The applied colours can be seen in Wiegand (Bibliography 20) plate IV.

142 The photograph here reproduced of the reconstruction in the Acropolis Museum shows the horizontal *sima* and waterspouts lacking in Wiegand (Bibliography 20) fig. 135. See Wiegand for the colour. See *ibid.* 148–155.

143 See Payne and Young (Bibliography 21), 47–48 and plate 127. Acropolis Museum 1343. Found in 1859 near the Propylaia by the south wall of the Acropolis. Ht. 0·44 m.

The style and block dimensions are identical with page 113 above. See the comments there.

146 Found in 1882 to the south-east of the Parthenon. See Wiegand (Bibliography 20) plate VIII and 192–95.

148 (upper picture) Found in 1888 to the east and south-east of the Parthenon. For the applied colours, see Wiegand 214 ff., and fig. 230.

148 (lower picture) Payne and Young (Bibliography 21) 51 and plate 131. Acropolis Museum 143. It seems to have been one of a pair. It has variously been taken to have something in common with the Giants of the Archaic Temple, Payne and Young (Bibliography 21) pls. 36 and 37, or with the lion's head waterspout (page 149).

149 Payne and Young (Bibliography 21) 51 and plate 132. Acropolis Museum 69. Ht. 0·32 m. Marble. Date about 520 BC. For a restoration of the *sima* in colour, see Wiegand (Bibliography 20), plate X.

159 Note that, apart from the central figures, the torso of Selene or Nyx is already displaced.

164 (above) From the Hermitage Museum, Leningrad M 1872.130.

165 Note that the figures 2 and 3 from the corner still survived in the Dodwell drawing of 1821.

168 Acropolis Museum 727. The right arm is raised at a slant. The head is from the centaur on metope VII of the south side, which represents a Lapith gripping a Centaur by the throat and thrusting him back. The rest of the metope is in the British Museum.

172–3 Acropolis Museum 856. Found in 1836 below the east end of the Parthenon. In the British Museum it is replaced by a cast as Slab VI of the eastern frieze. If the female figure is Demeter she may have held an ear of corn (in bronze) in her right hand.

175 Acropolis Museum 670. Payne and Young (Bibliography 21), 35 and pls 65–66. She wears a tunic (*chiton*) only. Date *c*. 520 BC.

176 Acropolis Museum 674. Ht. 0·92. Payne and Young (Bibliography 21) 34–35 and plate 75. Date *c*. 500. She has been described as 'shy, reserved and self-contained', and her sculptor as 'a discoverer of what is essentially feminine in the structure of the female body'.

177 Acropolis Museum 698. Payne and Young (Bibliography 21), 44–45, and plates 109–112. Date *c*. 480 BC. The so-called 'Kritian Boy', since it is thought to reflect the style of Kritios and Nesiotes in their group of the 'Tyrant-slayers'. The weight rests on one leg with consequent modification of the anatomy rendering. The head may be an ancient replacement of the original.

179 If the object in the upper left-hand corner is rightly identified as a bird cage, then it is reasonably suggested that the young man is releasing his pet birds for the last time. On his right is his small slave boy registering the melancholy which does not ever appear in the serene countenances of the dead on Classical gravestones. Behind the slave is a gravestone surmounted by a feline.

180 The drapery has been condemned as 'affected', in contrast to the greater achievement of the relief shown on page 181 (right).

182 Acropolis Museum 1073 and 1074. 1073: two male figures in *himatia*, from the first block on the south side (?). There is a standing figure leaning on a stick, and a seated figure of a youth, who may be engaged in writing down an oracle.

183 Acropolis Museum 632. Payne and Young (Bibliography 21) 10 and plates 5–6. Marble. Found (1882–83) east of the Parthenon. Dated in the first half of the sixth century.

190 From the Museo Civico, Bologna.

191 Acropolis Museum 1313.

192 Acropolis Museum 145. Payne and Young (Bibliography 21) 43 and plates 105–106. Date 520–510. Possibly a figure of Theseus grappling with one of his opponents (indicated by the fingers on his shoulder). Another Acropolis fragment may represent his hand on his opponent's throat. The pose is twisted but still symmetrical, and therefore less advanced than that on page 177.

193 Acropolis Museum 643. Payne and Young (Bibliography 21) 37–38, and plate 71. 'One of the great works of Attic sculpture' (Payne). Dated to the latter part of the decade 520–510.

194 Acropolis Museum 1332. Payne and Young (Bibliography 21) 48 and plate 129. The shape of the cups held by the seated potter would seem to indicate a date around 530 BC, though the relief is sometimes dated later. Part of a dedicatory inscription on the left hand border.

195 Acropolis Museum 590. Payne and Young (Bibliography 21) 4 and plates 11 a–c. Date *c*. 560 BC. The oak wreath the horseman is wearing may indicate that he was a victor in the Pythian (Delphic) Games.

196 Acropolis Museum 625. Payne and Young (Bibliography 21) 46 and plate 116. Described as 'a work of great power'. Pausanias mentions the dedication of a seated Athena, the work of Endoios, by a Kallias. One of this name might have made such a dedication in the period around 490 BC; another a generation or more earlier. The date of Endoios is uncertain. Both Payne and Dickins (in his *Catalogue of the Acropolis Museum* I) date the statue to a period before the Persian sack of Athens, to 530 BC or before. Some have felt that its weathering precludes its being buried only fifty years after its creation. It was in fact found on the North Slope below the Erechtheum and it may have survived the sack as some statues seem to have done.

201 Casson, *Catalogue of the Acropolis Museum* ii, 306, 67. A terracotta slab, Ht. 0·655 m., with a cream-coloured slip. The subject, a warrior running to the left is rendered in black, dark red, yellow-brown, carmine and white. The obliterated name at the top left-hand corner is an indication of the political manoeuvres of the early decades of the fifth century BC and those going back into the sixth century, involving the great family of the Alkmeonidai. Found in 1885 on the north side of the Acropolis.

203 Acropolis Museum 697. Payne and Young (Bibliography 21) 52 and plate 139. Forepart of a horse in marble. It has been described as the 'latest of the Acropolis horses'. To be dated to the end of the sixth century.

207 The temple of Rome and Augustus, founded after 27 BC. A round temple on a square base.

211 In the foreground, in the front row of the Theatre of Dionysos, is the inscribed ornamental chair of the priest of Dionysos of Eleutherai. Such a chair as this was used as the bishop's throne in the Parthenon when it was converted to a Christian church. For the view see also the bronze coin on page 189 (right).

216 Houses on the Acropolis east of the Parthenon. From Stuart and Revett, *Antiquities of Athens* (1751–1753).

217 The clearing of the Propylaia. Painting by Sir Charles Fellowes dated about 1838.

221 Acropolis Museum 581. Payne and Young (Bibliography 21) 48–49, plate 126. Ht. 0·665. Found on east side of the Parthenon in 1883. Athena wears a helmet with a crest painted on it. The worshippers offer a pig, which might connect with what is known of fertility rites.

Acknowledgements

Sources of Illustrations

In addition to the photographs by Werner Forman the author and publishers have made use of the following sources of illustration, whose help and permission they gratefully acknowledge: Alison Frantz, 47; The American School of Classical Studies, Athens (Travlos Collection) 91; The Benaki Museum, Athens 217; The British Museum 37, 174, 219 (upper picture); John Freeman Ltd 159, 164, 165, 209, 212, 213, 216; Gabinetto Fotografico Nazionale, Rome 61; The German Archaeological Institute, Athens 29, 55, 56, 58, 141, 147, 185 (left), 185 (right), 219 (lower picture); The Hermitage Museum, Leningrad 164 (above); Hirmer Verlag, Munich 32, 35, 64, 179; Museo Civico Archaeologico, Bologna 190; The Royal Institute of British Architects 215; Staatliche Antikensammlung, Munich 60; Staatliche Museen, Antikenabteilung, East Berlin 34, 66; Staatliche Museen zu Berlin, West Berlin 61; Philipp von Zabern, Mainz 160.

Literary Sources

The author and publishers wish to thank the following for their permission to quote from the publications listed below:

American School of Classical Studies, Athens: *Hesperia*, 1955; Cambridge University Press: *Handbook of Greek and Roman Architecture*, D. S. Robertson, 1945; J. M. Dent and Sons, Ltd (Everyman Library): *The History of Herodotus*, transl. G. Rawlinson, 1952, *Plutarch, Lives*, transl. A. H. Clough, 1957, *Thucydides, The History of the Peloponnesian War*, transl. Richard Crawley, 1957; William Heinemann Ltd (Loeb Classical Library): *Aristophanes*, transl. B. B. Rogers, 1924, *Philostratos and Eunapius, The Lives of the Sophists*, transl. W. C. Wright, 1922, *Hesiod, Theogony*, transl. H. G. Evelyn-White, 1914, *Homeric Hymns*, transl. H. G. Evelyn-White, 1914; Penguin Books Ltd: *The Sculpture of the Parthenon*, P. E. Corbett, 1959, *Greek Architecture*, A. W. Lawrence, 1957; Society for the Promotion of Roman Studies: *Journal of Roman Studies*, 1959; University of Chicago Press: *Greece in the Bronze Age*, Emily Vermeule, 1964.

Chronological Table

Of the dates given below none prior to 600 BC is established in any true sense. They have, with many variations of opinion, been established *relatively* by the sequence of material remains, and, in some cases (but only broadly) in an *absolute* manner by the contacts existing with Egypt and the Near East, where dates are better established through the existence of written material, and converted through Oriental, Hellenic, Hellenistic and Roman systems to our own BC/AD system, which depends particularly on the Hebraic-Christian genealogy from Abraham to Christ. Greek dating systems depended on lists and on calculations involving generations varying in length. Hence the considerable variation in the dates given to notable events.

c. 2500 BC	The end of the Neolithic culture in the more advanced parts of Greece.
c. 1900	The generally accepted date for the beginning of the Middle Bronze Age.
c. 1570	The beginning of the Late Bronze–Mycenaean culture. The Shaft Graves of Mycenae.
c. 1500	The eruption of the volcano of Thera.
c. 1450	'Greeks' at Knossos.
c. 1375	The Destruction of Knossos, and pre-eminence passing to the Mainland.
c. 1270	The date for the destruction of Troy suggested by Blegen, its second excavator.
c. 1240	A more likely archaeological date for the destruction of Troy. Note that this is closely tied up with the following.
c. 1200	A convenient round figure for the destruction of Mycenaean Palace structures. This is bound up with the division between the cultural periods Late Helladic III B and Late Helladic III C, which varies from 1230 BC to 1180 BC
1193–83	*Eratosthenes'* dates for the siege and destruction of Troy. Note that there was a wide spectrum of alternative dates advanced in Antiquity, from 1334 to 1135 BC.
c. 1075–850	The Sub-Mycenaean and Protogeometric cultural periods, commonly called the 'Dark Age of Greece'.
c. 850–700	The Geometric period, so-called from the prevailing mode of pottery decoration.
c. 750–594	The period of aristocratic rule in Athens.
c. 632	The attempted tyranny of Kylon at Athens.
594	The archonship of Solon.
c. 547–510	The Peisistratid tyranny in Athens.
546	The defeat of Lydia by the Persians, followed by the Persian advance to the Aegean.
507	The establishment of the Cleisthenic democracy.
506	The defeat by Athens of the Thebans and Chalcidians.
499–493	The Ionian Revolt.
490	The First Persian Invasion of Greece. The battle of Marathon.
483	The building of the Themistoclean fleet.
480	The Second Persian Invasion. The first sack of Athens. The battle of Salamis.
479	The second sack of Athens. The battles of Plataia and Mykale.
477	The founding of the Delian League.
477–462	The extension of the League under the leadership of Kimon.
469	The victory won by Kimon over the Persians at the River Eurymedon.
462	The exile of Kimon, followed by the establishment of the Radical Democracy.
458–445	The First Peloponnesian War.
454	The transfer of the League Treasury to Athens.
450/449	The transfer of 5000 talents to the Treasury of Athens to finance the Building programme.
449	? The Peace of Kallias with Persia.
448	? The proposed Panhellenic Conference.
447/6	The first Parthenon building account.
438/7	The dedication of the Parthenos.
438	? The exile of Pheidias.
437/6	The first Propylaia building account.
433/2	The last building accounts for the Parthenon and the Propylaia.
431–421	(The Great Peloponnesian War) The Archidamian War, ended by the Peace of Nikias.
415–413	The despatch and defeat of the Athenian Expedition against Syracuse.
413–405	(The Great Peloponnesian War) The Ionian War.
411	The Oligarchy of the Four Hundred.
410	The restoration of the democracy.

405	The defeat of Athens at Aigospotamoi.
404	The Thirty Tyrants. The Acropolis garrisoned by the Spartans.
403	The restoration of the democracy.
359	Philip II becomes ruler of Macedonia.
356	The birth of Alexander (III, the Great).
338	The battle of Chaironeia.
336	Philip II assassinated. Alexander becomes king of Macedonia.
336–330	The conquest of the Persian Empire.
323	The death of Alexander the Great.
323–31	The foundation, rise and decline of the Hellenistic monarchies.
296/5	Lachares strips the Parthenos of her gold.
215–205	The First Macedonian War between Philip v and Rome.
200–196	The Second Macedonian War. Philip decisively defeated by the Romans, now essentially committed to Greece.
196	Quinctius Flamininus declares Greece 'free' at the Isthmian Games.
171–168	The Third Macedonian War. The battle of Pydna and the end of Macedonian independence.
146	The Roman destruction of Corinth and the end of Greek 'Liberty'.
88	Mithridates VI of Pontus overruns Asia Minor.
88	Athens joins Mithridates.
87–86	The siege and capture of Athens by Cornelius Sulla.
31	The battle of Actium and the end of the Civil Wars.
27	Caius Julius Caesar Octavianus receives the title Augustus.
AD 112–113	The Emperor Hadrian in Athens, and serves as archon.
	The Emperor Marcus Aurelius (AD 161–180) founds the University of Athens.
267	The Herulian sack of Athens.
330	The foundation by Constantine the Great of New Rome.
395	The division of the Empire between East and West.
396	Attack on Athens by Alaric.
425	The foundation of the University of New Rome by Theodosius II
527	The closure of the University of Athens by Justinian.
	Greece under the Byzantines until AD 1204.
1204	The capture of Constantinople by the Fourth Crusade.
1204	Otho de la Roche invested as Lord of Athens.
1225	Guy de la Roche succeeds.
1260	Guy de la Roche becomes Duke of Athens.
1311	Walter of Brienne (the last Frankish ruler) killed at the battle of the Cephissus in Boeotia.
1311–1388	The Catalan-Aragonese dominance in Athens.
1374	Nerio Acciaiuoli, Florentine Lord of Corinth, seizes Megara.
1379	Invasion of Catalan territory by the Navarese Company.
1388	Nerio captures the Acropolis.
1389	The victory of Kossovo for the Turks in Serbia.
1395	The Venetians formally take over Athens.
1397	The lower town temporarily occupied by the Turks.
1453	The capture of Constantinople by the Turks.
1456	Athens taken over by the Turks.
1683	The Turks repulsed from Vienna.
1687	The siege of Athens by the Venetians and their allies. The explosion in the Parthenon.
1764	Winckelmann publishes his *History of Art*.
1809–11, 1823–24	Lord Byron in Greece.
1811	Beethoven composes *The Ruins of Athens*.
1812	The Elgin Marbles are brought to London.
1821	The Greeks beseige the Acropolis for the first time.
1827	The Turks retake the Acropolis.
1827	The Battle of Navarino, a victory for Britain, France and Russia, the future 'guarantors' of Greece.
1833	The Acropolis recovered.
1834	Athens the capital of the free Greek kingdom.

Bibliography

The following brief Bibliography avoids for the most part specialised works and articles, and those in foreign languages, with two exceptions (20, 28). Those works marked * will provide sufficient information for further reading both in books and periodical literature.

A. GENERAL HISTORICAL BACKGROUND

(1) J. B. Bury, *History of Greece* (Macmillan), ed. 3 (1951).

*(2) R. M. Cook, *The Greeks till Alexander* (Thames & Hudson. 1961).

(3) C. G. Starr, *The Origins of Greek Civilisation* (Cape, 1962).

(4) N. G. L. Hammond, *A History of Greece* (Oxford), ed. 2 (1967).

(5) A. Andrewes, *The Greeks* (Hutchinson, 1967).

*(6) Victor Ehrenberg, *From Solon to Socrates* (Methuen, 1968).

B. MYTH, CULT AND RELIGION

*(7) W. K. C. Guthrie, *The Greeks and their Gods* (Methuen, 1950).

(8) H. J. Rose, *A Handbook of Greek Mythology* (Methuen), ed. 6 (1958).

C. MYCENAEAN CIVILISATION IN GREECE

*(9) E. Vermeule, *Greece in the Bronze Age* (Chicago, 1961)

D. GREEK SCULPTURE

(10) A. W. Lawrence. *Classical Sculpture* (Cape, 1929)

(11) G. M. A. Richter, *Archaic Greek Art* (New York, 1949).

(12) R. Lullies and M. Hirmer, *Greek Sculpture* (Thames and Hudson, 1957).

*(13) G. M. A. Richter, *The Sculpture and Sculptors of the Greeks* (Yale), ed. 3 (1950).

E. GREEK VASE PAINTING

(14) Martin Robertson, *Greek Painting* (Skira, (1959).

*(15) R. M. Cook, *Greek Painted Pottery* (Methuen, 1960).

F. GREEK ARCHITECTURE

(16) D. S. Robertson, *Greek and Roman Architecture* (Cambridge), ed. 2 (1945).

(17) A. W. Lawrence, *Greek Architecture* (Penguin Books), ed. 2 (1967).

G. THE ACROPOLIS

(18) J. E. Harrison and M. de. G. Verrall, *Mythology and Monuments of Ancient Athens* (Macmillan, 1890).

*(19) I. T. Hill, *The Ancient City of Athens* (Methuen, 1953).

H. ACROPOLIS SCULPTURE

(20) Theodor Wiegand, *Die archaische Poros-Architektur der Akropolis zu Athen* (Cassel, 1904). For applied colour in particular.

(21) H. Payne and G. Young, *Archaic Marble Sculpture from the Acropolis* (London, Cresset Press, n.d.).

I. THE PARTHENON

(22) A. H. Smith, *The Sculptures of the Parthenon* (London, 1910).

(23) B. Ashmole, *A Short Guide to the Sculpture of the Parthenon* (London, 1950).

(24) C. J. Herington, *Athena Parthenos and Athena Polias* (Manchester, 1955).

(25) P. E. Corbett, *The Sculptures of the Parthenon* (Harmondsworth, 1959).

(26) D. E. L. Haynes, *An Historical Guide to the Sculptures of the Parthenon* (London, 1962).

(27) *Greece and Rome*, Supplement, 1963, *The Acropolis*, Ed. G. Hooker.

J. THE POST-ANTIQUE PERIOD

A useful introduction concerning the Acropolis:

(28) J. Baelen, *La chronique du Parthénon* (Paris, 1956).

On the Franks:

(29) W. Miller, *The Latins in the Levant* (London, 1908).

On the historical background to the whole period, in great but enthralling detail:

*(30) *The Cambridge Medieval History*, ed. 2, volume IV, 1 (Cambridge, 1966), especially pp. 279–330 and 389–430.

Glossary

Abacus: a low square block, the topmost element of a Doric column.

acropolis: the fortified hill-centre of a Greek polis, or city state.

adyton: the most sacred inner sanctuary of a temple.

agalma: an object of splendour, and so the image of a diety.

agora: the market-place of a Greek polis.

aigis: the goatskin combined with the Gorgon-mask to form the particular badge of Athena.

akroterion: decorative sculpture placed above the three angles of a pediment.

Anatolia: Asia Minor, especially the central plateau and the eastern mountains.

anta: a rectangular pilaster, surmounted by a moulding, terminating the side walls of porches, etc.

antefix: a vertical ornament attached to the lowest range of covering tiles (over the joints of the flat rain tiles) above the cornice of a building.

Anthesterion: Attic month, the equivalent of the latter half of February and the first half of March.

apobates: heavily-armed infantry-man, manoeuvring from a moving chariot.

apotropaic: averting the evil eye.

apse: the curvilinear end of archaic houses and other structures, or of the basilical type of building.

architrave: the stone beam resting on the columns of a peristyle or colonnade.

archon: 'ruler'; the term for a principal magistrate.

archon basileus: 'the king-archon', retaining the residual (religious) functions of the ancient king (basileus).

Areios Pagos: 'Hill of Ares' (if, in effect Areios refers to Ares), adjacent to the Acropolis, more commonly called Mars Hill.

Arrhephoroi: the child bearers of sacred objects from the Acropolis via the Cave of Aglauros to the sanctuary of Eros and Aphrodite. It is clear from finds in the latter area that the objects were snakes and phalloi, like the skira (q.v.).

Arrhephoreion: the building on the Acropolis where the Arrhephoroi lived.

Arrhetophoroi: an alternative form of Arrhephoroi, the bearers of unmentionable (secret) objects.

asty: the lower town as opposed to the polis or citadel rock.

Attic foot: Athenian unit of measurement (as distinct from those in use elsewhere), generally given as 29.57 cm.

Baldacchino: a canopy supported on pillars.

basileus: the Greek term for an hereditary king.

bastion: a projecting element in a defensive system of fortifications.

Boedromion: Athenian month, the equivalent of the second half of September and the first half of October.

Boukoleion: the 'ox-steading.'

Boutadai: the clan claiming descent from the 'ox-tender.'

Bouzygai: the clan of the 'ox-yokers.'

Caryatid: the female supporting figure (said to be named from the statuesque females of Karyai in Laconia) used in the south porch of the Erechtheum, and elsewhere at an earlier date.

cella: the central walled portion of a Greek temple.

Chalkeia: a festival of Hephaistos, the Smith God, the patron of bronze-workers.

cist graves: burials lined with slabs to form a rough box.

Cleisthenic constitution: the moderate democratic constitution of Athens ascribed to the late-sixth-century legislator Cleisthenes.

coffered (ceiling): ceiling with a system of recessed panels between beams.

colonnade: a range of columns as in a portico or peristyle.

column drum: the separate elements composing a column shaft.

console: S-shaped bracket supporting a horizontal cornice over a door, or some other decorative element.

cornice: the uppermost element of a temple entablature, or a projecting moulding, as above doors.

cubit: an ancient unit of measurement, from elbow to the tip of the middle finger. Naturally variable, but commonly given as 45-55 cm.

cuirass: a breastplate.

Doric (column): type of column with abacus, torus, fluted shafts (the flutes meeting at a sharp edge (arris)), and *no* base.

Dorian: one of the traditional divisions of the Hellenic race (particularly associated with Sparta), from Doria, their supposed motherland.

dado: slabs placed vertically at a wall base.

dekate: a tithe or one tenth as an offering.

Delian League: the league largely of Ionian states formed in 477 BC against the Persians, with its centre at Delos.

Diipolia: the festival of Zeus Polieus.

Dipylon Gate: the double gate (hence the name), otherwise the Thriasian Gate, between the Outer and Inner Kerameikos; the starting point of the Panathenaic procession (at the Pompeion).

drachme: a standard silver coin, the equivalent of six obols *(oboloi),* through the similar word for spits *(obeloi),* and the similar word *dragma* (a handful) thought of as the silver replacement of a handful of iron rods used previously as currency.

Elaphebolion: the Attic month, the equivalent of the second half of March and the first half of April.

Eleusinian Goddesses: Demeter the corn goddess, and her daughter Kore or Persephone; the latter carried off by Hades and subsequently spending six months on earth and six in the Underworld, the symbol of the sown corn coming again to life.

Eleusinian stone: grey-black stone from Eleusis.

emery: abrasive stone (corundum) from the island of Naxos.

Enneapylon: The Ninefold Gate; the suggested name for a possible element of the early Acropolis walls.

entablature: the architectural elements above the columns in a Doric, Ionic or Corinthian temple.

entasis: the subtle swelling of a column (particularly a corner column) to compensate for the effects of light otherwise producing an illusion of concavity.

epheboi: the youth of Athens at the time of their organisation for military training.

Erechtheid: adjective relating to the following.

Erechtheidai: the aristocratic Athenian clan claiming descent from Erechtheus.

Erechtheum: the composite temple given to the worship of Athena, Poseidon – Erechtheus and Boutes, on the north side of the Acropolis.

Ergane: title of Athena as patroness of arts and crafts.

fascia: a flat band between mouldings; the division of the Ionic architrave.

figurine: a small three-dimensional figure, generally of clay, used as a votive offering or as a toy.

firman: a document issued by the Turkish Sultans, directed to regional governors, with a view to facilitating concessions of various kinds.

gable-base: the floor of the triangular pediment of a building, on which rested the pedimental sculpture.

Gamelion: the Attic month, the equivalent of the second half of January and the first half of February.

Gaieochos: a title of Poseidon as 'Earth-Sustainer.'

Gegenes: 'Earth-born.'

(Ge) Karpophoros: 'The Fruit-bearer', a title given to the goddess Earth.

Ge-Themis: a combination, in a cult title, of two goddesses with related functions.

Hedos: word for a statue, implying a seated type.

Hekatombaion: the Attic month, the equivalent of the latter part of July and the first half of August.

Hekatompedon: the supposed 'One Hundred-foot Temple'.

Hephaisteion: the temple of Hephaistos and Athena (formerly called the Theseum) on the west of the Marketplace.

Herakleidai: the 'Children of Herakles', the traditional leaders of the 'Return' and of the 'Dorian Invasion.'

Herulian Wall: built in Athens as a defence after the sack of AD 267 by the Heruli, a tribe of the Goths.

Hesperids: 'the daughters of Evening', guardians of the Golden Apples in the Far West.

hexastyle: (Doric façade): with six columns.

hieropoioi: Athenian state officials concerned with religious ceremonial.

hieron/hiron: a sacred place, temple or temenos.

hipped (roof): roof form of which the rear element slopes backwards and downwards instead of forming a vertical gable.

hoplite: a heavily-armed infantry soldier.

Horai: the goddesses of the Seasons, attendants on the greater gods and goddesses.

Indo-European: descriptive of a group or groups of related languages, originally evolving in the area north of the Black Sea and dispersed from India to Ireland at various dates. Proto-Greek belonged to this group.

Ionian: One of the three traditional divisions of the Greek race, the supposed descendants of Ion, including particularly the Athenians and the Asia Minor Greeks of Ionia.

Ionic (order): the architectural style distinct from Doric and Corinthian, characterised by the ram's horn column capital, and a column with flutes separated by a ribbon (tainia) and with a moulded base.

isodomic (masonry): arranged in regular courses of blocks, uniform in thickness and length, with joints centred on the block below.

Kallynteria: the festival at which the ancient statue of Athena was decked and arrayed.

kanoun (*plur.* kana): a reed basket carried in the Panathenaic procession by the maiden Kanephoroi, or Basket-bearers.

Kekropion: the sanctuary or tomb of Kekrops.

Kerameikos: the 'Potters' Quarter': the cemetery area of Athens outside the Dipylon Gate.

kerkope: the cicada.

Klepsydra: the name (= 'Water-thief') of a well on the north-west of the Acropolis.

Kodridai: the descendants of the traditional last king of Attica, Kodros.

kore: a maiden; thence the name for architectural or dedicatory maiden statues. Kore, daughter of Demeter, was the maiden par excellence.

Kourotrophos: 'Nurturer of Youth'; cult epithet of Demeter.

labrys: the Carian term for the double axe.

lintel: the beam over a doorway.

Maimakterion: the Attic equivalent of the second half of November and the first half of December.

Medontidai: the supposed 'royal' family of Athens, the descendants of Medon 'the Ruler'.

megaron: the 'great hall' of the Mycenaean and epic palace.

Meilichios: 'the kindly, gentle', cult epithet of Zeus.

Metageitnion: the Attic month, equivalent of the second half of August and the first half of September.

metope: the space between the triglyphs (q.v.) in a Doric frieze, filled by a slab generally decorated with painting or sculpture.

Moiragetes: 'ruler of the Fates'; an epithet of Zeus.

Moirai: the Fates.

Mounychion: the Attic month, equivalent of the second half of April and the first half of May.

mutule: a rectangular slab decorated with guttae (resembling round stone pegs) on the projecting underside (corona) of the cornice in the Doric order.

narthex: the portico or vestibule of an Early Christian or Byzantine church.

Neleidai: The descendants of Neleus, king of Pylos, father of Nestor; through Melanthos associated with Athens and Ionia.

Nike: Victory.

Obsidian: volcanic glass found on Melos and elsewhere.

oikema: a room or treasury.

opisthodomos: the rear section of a temple cella.

Oschophoria: the festival of the carrying of vine shoots with grapes.

palimpsest: a manuscript with its original text erased and replaced by another.

Palladion: the archaic Trojan statue of Pallas Athene.

Palmette: stylised fan-shaped (from palm-leaf) leaf complex used as decoration in architecture, vase-painting etc.

Panathenaia: the great festival of Athena at Athens.

Panathenaic (amphora): the container of the olive oil given as a prize at this festival.

Pandia: the festival of the 'all-embracing god' (Pandion).

Pandroseion: the sanctuary of Pandrosos on the Acropolis.

pannychis: a night festival.

Parthenon: the place of the virgins or Virgin.

parthenos: a virgin.

Peisistratid, Peisistratidai: the family of Peisistratos, the sixth-century tyrant of Athens.

Pelargikon: the area on the north-west of the Acropolis, 'the place of the storks.'

Pelasgikon: the alternative name for the same area, as associated with the ancient people of Attica, the Pelasgoi.

Pelopids: the descendants of Pelops.

Pentelic (quarries): the main source of Attic marble, on Mount Pentelikon bordering the plain of Athens.

peplos: a heavy, sleeveless, woollen garment, worn folded and fastened with brooches at the shoulders.

peripatos: the path around the Acropolis.

peristyle: the colonnades surrounding a building such as the cella of a temple.

Perseids: the descendants of Perseus.

pilaster: an engaged pillar, used to terminate a wall.

Plynteria: the festival of the cleansing of the archaic statue of Athena.

podium: a platform (with steps) supporting a building or statue.

Polias: epithet of Athena, as Guardian of the City.

polis: the Greek city state.

polites: a citizen of the polis.

Pompeion: a building outside the Dipylon Gate, from which the Panathenaic procession was organised.

poros: coarse limestone used in archaic architecture and sculpture.

portico: a building with side and rear walls, and an open columned front. Alternatively called a stoa.

Posideion: the Attic month, equivalent to the second half of December and the first half of January.

Praxiergidai: a guild (?) concerned with the care of the ancient statue of Athena.

Procharisteria: ceremonial relating to the germination of the sown corn.

prodomos: the outermost element (vestibule) leading to the cella proper of a temple.

pronaos: as above, s.v. prodomos.

propylaia: the complex of structures on either side of an entrance gate to a walled area.

prostomiaion: some (uncertain) element in the western section of the Erechtheum.

Protocorinthian (pottery): the seventh-century orientalising type produced at Corinth; the forerunner of the Corinthian orientalising and black-figure.

Protogeometric (pottery): the earliest stage (after Subgeometric) of development of linear decoration and of improved profiles in pottery leading to the Geometric style of the ninth and eighth centuries BC.

Prytaneion: the public building containing the hearth and centre of public life of Athens.

Pyanopsion: the Attic month, the equivalent of the second half of October and the first half of November.

Pythion: the shrine or cult area of Apollo Pythios (Apollo of Delphi or Pytho).

quadriga: a four-horse chariot group.

regula: a stone band, equalling the triglyph placed below it, below the upper fillet of the architrave: with six stone pegs or guttae.

return: a continuation in a different direction of a wall or moulding.

rhapsode: a 'stringer together' or reciter of epic lays.

Rhusipolis: 'Saviour of the City'.

shaft grave: a rectangular burial chamber cut in the stereo, lined with stone-work and roofed with beams, brushwood and earth.

sherds: fragments of pottery.

sima: a continuous decorated band (above the horizontal cornice), as an alternative to antefixes, formed by up-turned rain-tiles acting as a gutter. Provided with water-spouts.

skira: offerings in the shape of snakes and phalloi made to Athena at the Skirophoria.

Skirophorion: the Attic month, the equivalent of the second half of June and the first half of July.

Spartan: a full citizen of the city state of Sparta.

stele: an inscribed slab or sculptured grave stone.

stoa: a pillared portico.

Stoa Poikile: the Painted Stoa, so named from its frescoes.

stomion: possibly a well mouth in the western section of the Erechtheum.

stylobate: the platform surface on which the columns of a peristyle stand.

synoecism: a uniting of smaller elements to form a city state, such as Attica.

Synoikia: the festival celebrating the above event.

Talent: the major unit of weight, or the monetary equivalent of 6000 drachmai.

temenos: a sacred precinct.

Thallophoroi: 'branch-bearers'; participants in the Panathenaic procession.

Thargelion: the Attic month, the equivalent of the second half of May and the first half of June.

torus: the cushion-type element of a Doric capital.

traditio: an account (of temple treasures) handed on from one annual body of commissioners to another.

triglyph: in the frieze of the Doric order, blocks of which the height exceeds the width, decorated with two full and two half vertical grooves. Sometimes interpreted as the beam-ends of the original wooden structure.

tympanum: the back wall of a pediment.

Index